ROSEMARY LOW

FEMALE HEROES
OF BIRD CONSERVATION

INSIGNIS
PUBLICATIONS

Copyright © Rosemary Low 2021

ISBN 978-1-7399130-0-7 (Pbk)
ISBN 978-1-7399130-1-4 (Hbk)

All rights reserved. No part of this publication may be reproduced, stored in any retrieval system, or transmitted in any form or by any means, electronic, mechanical, recording or otherwise, without the prior permission of the author.

Published in the UK by
INSiGNIS PUBLICATIONS,
Mansfield, NG20 9PR.
www.rosemarylow.co.uk

Printed in the UK by Biddles of King's Lynn
Graphic design by Airton de Almeida Cruz (São Paulo, SP, Brazil)
Cover design: Rosemary Low

I DEDICATE THIS BOOK TO TWO GREAT SCIENTISTS working in Brazil, one past, one present, one female, one male.

Emílie Snethlage (1868-1929) was not only an extraordinarily brave explorer, working alone in the most dangerous parts of Brazil, but her descriptions of Brazilian birds and taxonomic assessments formed the base for ornithological studies for more than 70 years.

Carrying on that work today is **Prof Dr Luís Fábio Silveira,** Scientific Director of the Museum of Zoology of the University of São Paulo (MZUSP), also Curator of Birds. The bird collection is the most complete of Brazilian birds. His work is focused on the systematics, taxonomy and conservation of Neotropical birds, including some Critically Endangered endemic Brazilian species. During the last 17 years he has travelled to all Brazilian biomes during collecting trips, publishing more than 160 scientific articles, 17 books and 81 book chapters. He has also described 15 species of birds new to science. Luís works on national councils related to animal welfare and in the development of public policies for conservation of natural resources in Brazil.

Not only is he a great mentor to his students, but his help and enthusiasm when I was writing this book were extremely important to me.

Acknowledgements

I am deeply grateful to the subjects of my chapters who responded so willingly with information and photographs. My thanks to Mike Toms of the BTO for making available scans of Emma Turner's photographs and to Library and Archives Canada for the use of the photograph of Louise and Gleb de Kiriline. Lars Lepperhoff kindly accessed and contributed the photograph of Monika Meyer-Holzapfel.

I would also like to thank my valued friend Alena Winner for her help. Her enormous contribution to the world of parrots in publishing the *Papousci* and *AWI* magazines must also be mentioned.

Contents

Introduction 1
1. **To be a Woman:** Advantage or Discrimination? 3
2. **Women in Zoos** – and the Role Model, Katharina Heinroth 12

Female Heroes of the Past 24
3. **Althea Rosina Sherman,** USA 1853-1943
   Pioneer Ornithologist, Author and Artist 25
4. **Etta Lemon (neé Smith),** UK 1860-1953
   Harriet Hemenway (née Lawrence) USA 1858-1960 31
5. **Emma Turner,** 1867-1940
   Photographer, Author and Passionate Bird Observer 41
6. **Emílie Snethlage,** Germany/Brazil 1868-1929
   World-renowned Ornithologist and Explorer 50
7. **Magdalena Heinroth, née Wiebe,** Germany 1882-1932
   Researcher, Author and Photographer: recorded development of young
   of 1,000 European Birds 57
8. **Margaret Morse Nice,** USA 1883-1974
   Innovator in Field Ornithology and Ethology 62
9. **Len Howard,** UK 1894-1973
   Ground-breaking Books on Bird Observations 70
10. **Louise de Kiriline Lawrence, (née Flach),** Sweden/Canada 1894-1992
    Self-taught Ornithologist and Conservationist 75
11. **Phyllis Barclay-Smith,** UK 1902-1980
    Of world renown in Ornithological Circles 82
12. **Rachel Carson,** USA 1907-1964
    Author of *Silent Spring* – started Environmental Movement 88
13. **Anne LaBastille,** USA 1933-2011
    Documented Extinction of the Giant Grebe 95
14. **The Amazing Female Authors** 105

Present-day Female Heroes 113
15. **Careers, Marriage and Families** 114

I

16. **Françoise Delord,** France 1940-
   Founder, ZooParc de Beauval 118
17. **Bernadette Coutain Plair,** USA 1943-
   Reintroduced Blue and Yellow Macaw to Trinidad 122
18. **Anna Croukamp,** Brazil 1946-
   Bird Park founder and Atlantic Forest conservation 129
19. **Lorin Lindner,** USA 1955-
   Unites traumatised War Veterans and mistreated Parrots 137
20. **LoraKim Joyner,** USA 1957-
   Parrot Conservation in Central America 142
21. **Neiva Guedes,** Brazil 1962-
   Saviour of the Pantanal Hyacinth Macaws 151
22. **Colleen Downs,** South Africa 1963-
   Scientist and Teacher 159
23. **Nicola Crockford,** UK 1964-
   World renowned for Shorebird Habitat Protection 165
24. **Elisabeth Schlumpf,** Switzerland 1966-
   Wild Bird Rescue and Education 173
25. **Gláucia Seixas,** Brazil 1966-
   Intensely dedicated to the Blue-fronted Amazon Parrot 178
26. **Caroline Blanvillain,** France/Polynesia 1966-
   Saving Critically Endangered Polynesian Species 184
27. **Andrea Angel,** Chile 1968-
   Albatross Specialist 191
28. **Silvana Davino,** Brazil 1968-
   Wild Bird Rescue and Environmental Education 198
29. **Kilma Manso,** Brazil 1971-
   Fights Illegal Wildlife Trade; Lear's Macaw Conservation 204
30. **Sarah Otterstrom,** USA/Central America 1972-
   Working to support Wildlife and Impoverished People 213
31. **Jennifer Smart,** UK 1972-
   RSPB Scientist and Wading Bird Specialist 218
32. **Sara Inés Lara,** Colombia 1973-
   Founder of Women for Conservation 222
33. **Alicia Manolas,** Australia 1982-
   Biomonitor Assistance Animal Trainer 228
34. **Sarah Comer,** Western Australia
   Fieldwork with Critically Endangered Species 232
35. **Memorable Moments** 237
36. **The Future for Women in Conservation** 242

Index, People 247
Index, Bird Species 251
Index, Conservation and Rescue Organizations 254

Introduction

I have nothing but disdain for the obsession with objects of financial and fashion values and electronic gadgetry. For my heroines, beauty lies in nature not in designer handbags. They do not amass shoe collections worth thousands of pounds or dollars; they treasure the natural world and devote (or devoted) their lives to its protection and biodiversity.

I am told that the word 'heroine' will soon be obsolete which is why I chose *Female Heroes* for the title of this book. Whichever term is used, it applies to all my subjects here – and to many more whose inspiring work I do not yet know about. Inevitably many readers will exclaim: 'Why did she not include X?' Two reasons: my ignorance of their work; in some countries there are no organisations to promote the work of women who would surely qualify. And a desire to keep the book to a certain length to make it affordable.

How did I come to write this book? As a journalist and author, for just over 50 years, I have specialised in writing about parrots and conservation – my two passions in life. I started as an aviculturist and after a few years I realised that there was a disconnect between people who keep parrots and those who strive to conserve and observe them in their natural habitats. It would be mutually beneficial if they came together. Parrot keepers could raise funds for parrot conservation if I wrote about the endangered plight of parrots in avicultural magazines, and they could also learn about parrot diets, feeding and breeding habits from papers of which they were unaware, published by scientists. In some cases parrot keepers and zoos could inform the field workers of breeding data (incubation and fledging periods) which are very difficult to acquire in their field studies, because many parrots nest in inaccessible places.

Anyway, in 2018 I started to write a series of articles entitled 'People Helping Parrots' for the popular monthly UK magazine *Parrots*. I soon realised that nearly all my subjects were female. There is a book here, waiting to be written, I thought! As I started to write outside my usual sphere and researched women of the past, I became filled with amazement, awe and admiration. These women gripped me! I was totally hooked on the theme. The author of 30 or so published books, I can say that never had I enjoyed writing a book so much! The research led me into different fields and to read books written by these fascinating women, some of whose names were new to me. Especially in the 19th century, I was in a different world! And I needed also to write about social aspects of the 19th and 20th centuries to ensure my readers understood how difficult was the work my heroines were carrying out. What I love about them is that they seemed never to doubt themselves. They just got on with what they were good at. They were truly remarkable women who combined their fieldwork and research, and published very significant papers, in an era when everything was more difficult for women.

And not only that! Some travelled in extremely dangerous unknown territories where white *men* had feared to tread! In her long skirts, Emília Snethlage, courageous and self-reliant, travelled in Brazil, amputated her infected finger when a piranha had eaten the tip and, after contracting malaria, walked for miles in inhospitable forest, shaking with fever. In the 1930s, the amazing Lucy Cheesman travelled repeatedly in the Pacific islands. In the New Hebrides she stayed with a tribe of cannibals who had rarely been approached by Westerners before.

In researching some of the amazing women of the 19th and early 20th centuries I was extremely impressed by their commitment to a particular species or topic. In some cases the longevity of their studies was extraordinary. For example, Margaret Morse Nice produced a 247-page treatise on the Song Sparrow, the result of hours and days, months and years of observation and work. In fact, she started when she was nine years old and published 45 years later!

Everyone knows about Gilbert White's *Selbourne* and yet the writings of Emma Turner, Margaret Nice and Len Howard, for example, with such tender detail in their observations, far surpass White or today's male nature writers – in my opinion. I think they have a special feminine perspective, and combined with being talented writers, their works are actually masterpieces.

Today's heroines are exceptional in other ways. I hope that their stories in this book will inspire girls and women to pursue their dreams and aspirations, even in the difficult conditions of the underdeveloped countries. It will not be easy – but their achievements will inspire yet more women to join their ranks and to receive the recognition they deserve, proving over and over again that women who are given the opportunity are the equals – and often the superiors – of men.

1. To be a Woman: Advantage or Discrimination?

When she was in her 20s, Jeanne Baret, born in 1740, became the housekeeper and then the mistress, of Philibert Commerson. He was invited to join an expedition aboard the store ship *Étoile* in 1765. The appointment allowed him a paid servant. As women were not allowed on French navy ships, she boarded separately, disguised as a man. The couple visited many countries and Jeanne proved to be an excellent botanist, who catalogued Commerson's plants and notes. Her gender was discovered and when the ship reached Mauritius they made their home there.

That story is the epitome of discrimination against a highly capable woman. But it was nearly three centuries ago and occurred in a male-dominated society, so it does not surprise us. Another injustice against women is lack of recognition for work achieved, which might even have been credited to a man. A classic example is the case of Elizabeth Gould (1804-1841). She was the wife of John Gould, the renowned ornithologist whose classic books made history for their artwork. His sketches and notes formed the blueprints for nearly 4,000 illustrations by the best bird artists of the era. Many of these illustrations were signed 'John Gould' or his name appeared next to that of the main artist. In fact many of the paintings were made by Elizabeth – at least 650. She once commented that the only recognition she had received was the letter 'E' when her husband condescended to allow the discreet signature E. Gould or J. and E. Gould. He never drew attention to her contributions. When she sat for a portrait in 1841 the artist suggested that he should depict her holding a palette and brushes. Her husband did not allow this. In their place a Cockatiel sat on her hand!

In the USA, Hildegarde Howard (1901-1998) was the first scientist to specialise in studying fossil birds and bird evolution. In her 69-year publishing career she authored over 150 articles and described over 50 species, including the first toothed bird from North America. Because she was female, she was prohibited from joining class field trips as a student. This did not deter her; she went on to become a world authority on avian palaeontology and spent a decade as chief scientist at the Los Angeles Natural History Museum.

In the same era (1912-2008) and in the same country, Barbara Blanchard DeWolfe's lifelong work on the White-crowned Sparrow (*Zonotrichia leucophrys*) was among the first to demonstrate important natural history differences between races of a given species. Previously, biological variation was identified through analysis of stuffed birds or skins. Barbara DeWolfe studied living populations in California and Alaska and documented key differences in their breeding behaviour, gonads and song structure. Discrimination during her academic career was all too frequent. Her PhD supervisor had suggested that, as a woman, she might prefer a less taxing project on worms! She refused. She went on to become a successful academic at UC Santa Barbara.

In 1924 when Emma Turner penned *Broadland Birds* and papers that she submitted to important ornithological magazines, she wrote under the name of E. L. Turner. In the 1930s Rachel Carson, who went on to achieve world-wide fame with *Silent Spring*, was writing articles for the *Baltimore Sun*, describing the pollution by industrial runoff of oyster beds in Chesapeake Bay. She urged changes in oyster seeding and dredging practices and political regulation of the effluents. She signed her articles 'R. L. Carson'. Both these talented women disguised their gender in the hope she would be taken more seriously than with a feminine name. Gwendolen Howard (Chapter 9) published her books in the 1950s under the name of Len Howard. She too feared that a female author would not be credible.

Experiences in Brazil

Unfortunately, today gender discrimination still occurs. Natalia Luchetti is a taxonomist. Her first fieldwork was with the tapeworms of stingrays. She soon met an unjustified attitude from fishermen. They believed that having a woman on the boat brought bad luck. Evidently, not enough has changed since Jeanne Baret's day. As a helminthologist, in 2012 Natalia started to study a certain group of parasitic worms and their coevolution with the host in Amazonia. There are very few researchers on bird cestodes in the world and no one focuses on Neotropical birds. She looks for new genera and species and what influences their distribution. There were no tapeworms described for antbirds[1] (Thamnophilidae) and she found about 80 new cestode taxa, inhabiting 81 species and subspecies.

'The existing protocols did not work in Neotropical rainforest, as the identification keys do not include our unknown fauna. So this is what inspires me: to uncover the parasite biodiversity in Neotropical birds. When I

---

[1] A varied group of birds, named after the habit of some species of following ant swarms, which disturb and make available insects on which they feed.

started people thought that I was not able to work in the forest. I am thin, with very pale skin and long hair, and I wear glasses – a typical "urban girl". More than once I had to "prove" that I could be there with no problems and that I could carry my heavy backpack. Strangely enough, the worst comments about my presence in the field came from two women!' She has made 20 field trips, some lasting more than one month. She told me:

Maria Fernanda Gondim.
Photograph: L. F. Silveira.

'On my first trip with the ornithological team from the Zoology Museum of the University of São Paulo (MZ-USP), the field coordinator took me and three guys to the airport. She was clearly bothered about something. About a week later, my professor, Luís Fábio Silveira, told me that she complained a lot to him when I arrived, asking him why he sent that "Barbie doll" to the field. He told her to wait; after some days, she called him and apologised, saying she was wrong and that I worked very well.'

The advisor of Natalia's Master's project also disliked taking girls into the field. On the other hand, he liked female assistants in the laboratory because he thought they were more careful with tiny specimens. Some cestodes are only 0.5mm in length.

Conservation has always been the inspiration for Brazilian veterinarian Maria Fernanda Gondim. She has worked with a conservation project in the wild for the Brazilian tapir (*Tapirus terrestris*) and has been employed in institutions that provided captive-bred animals for reintroduction. She currently works in a private zoo which is dedicated to conservation and reintroduction projects, such as that for the Brazilian Merganser (*Mergus octosetaceus*). Outside the zoo, she does some consultancy in the field.

When working on fauna rescue in the north of the country, in a remote location, she suffered different types of harassment from men. She said: 'There were calls from the engineers there almost daily. Once, a security technician approached me shamelessly, to ask me out.' An engineer attended and made arrangements for the relocation of that employee. 'Another time, I was called to rescue an anaconda that was trapped in a manhole. Dozens of men gathered around the manhole to accompany the rescue and were laughing and joking about the situation. I almost doubted my ability.' Although many women suffer work place harassment from men, when you are the only woman and in a remote outdoor situation, it feels more threatening.

Once, during an interview to work in a zoo, her future boss mentioned that all the keepers were men, and he was unsure whether they would respect her orders. Later a man was hired to take on the responsibility of coordinating these employees. 'At the same time, the fact of being a woman, makes some colleagues protect us in some situations, such as in riskier handling or where it is necessary to carry heavy weights', she said.

Working with females might be advantageous in an unexpected way, especially where identification is concerned. Police constable Tony Barnes has interviewed more than 2,000 witnesses over 11 years to make computer-aided images of suspects' faces. He said that women tended to have better visual recollections of criminals. 'In my experience ladies are better e-fit witnesses than men. They seem to pay more attention to faces,' said Scotland Yard's only e-fit officer. 'They are therefore more helpful than men at catching crooks.' (*Sunday Times,* January 25 2021).

Ana Beatriz Navarro has a Master of Science degree (MZ-USP). She experienced situations in the field that left her at a disadvantage for just being a woman. 'I feel that we are constantly afraid and worried about risky situations in the field, which leads me to never go alone to my study areas. However, even if accompanied, I have experienced embarrassing situations of harassment by men who were not members of the work team' she said. 'Situations like these made me feel objectified and devalued, when my recognition should be for the effort and success of my work.'

Although she had not experienced any gender discrimination when applying for a job, she believed that it was more difficult to get her articles published than those of male colleagues who work on the same topic; however, this is not easy for any researcher.

Attitudes of some male colleagues

Letícia Soares Marques de Oliveira is 23 years old and studying a group of birds called leaftossers, also at Sao Paulo's zoology museum. She told me:

'I overheard comments from an older colleague who said that women cannot work in conservation, because it means going to the field and that work is too heavy. It might be necessary to collect birds by shooting them, and tolerating bad conditions, and women can't take it. I confess that this comment made me doubt my ability.'

'However, I have just returned from my first field trip and I could not be happier. I believe that I worked

*Leticia with a Great Antshrike (*Taraba major*), a forest species.*
Photograph: Leticia Soares Marques de Oliveira.

very well, I collected using different methods, I processed the material and I worked hard. My conclusion was that nobody should tell me how far I can reach or what I can do. Only I can answer these questions and I determine what I can handle. I am very happy to have had that first field experience and I am already looking forward to the next ones.'

Also in Brazil, Marina Somenzari described her natural passion for Nature, evident since childhood. She spent three years in São Paulo Zoo as a graduate student. As a biologist, she worked as an assistant curator of ornitholog-ical collections at São Paulo's Zoology Museum for almost ten years. She has carried out ornithological surveys, for research and in connection with licensing processes for dams, roads and energy transmission lines all over Brazil. In conservation biology, she has been involved since 2009, at the start of the Brazilian National Action Plan for Endangered Parrots of the Atlantic Rainforest. Since 2015 she has worked for the Brazilian National Centre for Research and Conservation of Birds (CEMAVE) of the Brazilian Ministry of the Environment, with one year out to work at a zoo. Her work is now mainly related to conservation planning and biodiversity data management.

Has she experienced gender discrimination I asked her? 'Unfortunately, yes – and repeatedly', was her reply. 'In almost all the fieldwork I have ever done, especially away from big cities. The first discrimination related to the fact that I was driving. The experience was even worse if I was driving a pick-up truck, which I normally was. Sometimes in gas stations, the men around commented – among themselves or out loud – how surprised they were to watch a woman show "enough" driving ability. Sometimes they even congratulated me as if it was really exceptional to see a woman driving well.'

On several occasions she was asked by men, and sometimes by women, how she could risk traveling alone in remote areas. 'Often, the next question was if I had a husband and how could he let me do that. After hearing that I

Female Heroes of Bird Conservation

Marina Somenzari.
Photograph: Marina Somenzari.

was single, they would say they believed that if I was married or had any kind of romantic commitment, I would not be there. And, even worse, that my partner would never agree with that kind of work. How offensive!'

For some years Marina has worked on parrot surveys, including local community interviews which provided valuable interchange of knowledge. She was in very close contact with different people and communities. She found that that the approaches needed for effective conservation outcomes are broader than is generally believed and, especially, that people are central to it.

I asked: have you experienced gender discrimination when applying for a job? 'Sadly, my answer is again, yes. I have experienced it and have witnessed other female colleagues experiencing the same awful situation. I had to hear loud and clear that really incredible scientific expedition opportunities that came by were absolutely forbidden for us women. The explanation presented was that we would put all the team at risk because the expedition would be in very remote locations (normally in the Brazilian Amazon) and our presence would provoke local people to try to assault us. The men of the team would not put their scientific opportunities at risk. At the end of the conversation, they were always trying to convince us that actually, they were "taking care" of us, and that we should be grateful.'

Barbara Tomotani, also from Brazil, studies how climate change affects the daily and seasonal lives of birds. She has never experienced any obvious form of gender discrimination and neither has she experienced it as an advantage, except for a few grants and job openings that favour female researchers specifically, and counts as an advantage. This good situation seems to be more common in European countries. She works in the Netherlands and feels that she needs to work much harder than her male colleagues to have a chance of getting jobs.

In the 1990s few women were carrying out field research. In Brazil, one of them, Zilca Campos, was studying the caiman (a type of crocodile) and helped Neiva Guedes (Chapter 21) a lot when she was working with the Hyacinth Macaw in the Pantanal. When I asked Neiva what it was like to be a woman in the

Barbara in the Hoge Veluwe National Park, the Netherlands, on her way to monitor nest-boxes.
Photograph: Erik Kleyheeg.

field in the 1990s, she told me: 'I never suffered harassment or discrimination in the countryside. But I had difficulties in opening heavy gates, unloading the car and carrying heavy equipment. However, the women in the Pantanal were very sympathetic and they were my great partners.'

Europe and Africa

In Europe and Africa, BirdLife International partners are proud of employing women. Cape Verde is an archipelago in the Central African Ocean, consisting of ten volcanic islands. Patrícia Rendall Rocha is the Communications Manager for the NGO Biosfera. She says: '… women can do everything as men do. There are no privileges when you're in the field monitoring turtle nests at 4am. Sometimes I take things to heart, like when people think they are superior because I am younger, I am a woman, or because I'm black – or all three. It is a daily struggle but I continue to join the body of women who break the barriers, one brick at a time!' (Abiadh, 2019).

In Macedonia, Aleksandra Bujaroska said: 'My biggest achievement is using environmental law to demonstrate a change in Macedonian society – from apathy to bringing environmental policies onto decision makers' radar. There is even greater apathy and underestimation that you can achieve change in society if you are a woman… It was a challenge to make my conservative male colleagues take me seriously. In the conservation field women are harder workers but are not seen as leaders. To overcome these challenges, I needed to demonstrate that I deserved the trust of everyone. This involved changing my behaviour and clothes for a more serious appearance…'

Asunción Ruiz is the Executive Director of SEO BirdLife, one of the largest Spanish environmental NGOs in terms of technical and financial scope. She said she would tell women that 'nothing and no one should ever cut their wings and that, in times of difficulty, they should join forces and flock together. All of us are needed for science to fly high and live up to its potential. It is completely inconceivable that in the 21st century society we think that we can progress without girls and women having access to equal participation and progress. A society can only advance if all people have the same opportunities' (Abiadh, 2019).

If you are a woman of colour, you might encounter discrimination on two accounts. One young lady from the Caribbean told me:

'If I don't speak about it, I am condoning it. I was employed on a conservation project which I agreed to because I believed I could practise my academic training. Instead I was constantly schooled on international conservation NGO best practices even though some were completely irrelevant in the local context. Soon enough the project became a stepping stone for the one leading person who had to approve everything: email drafts, letters and phone conversations had to be scripted and approved. The job should have been a stepping stone to working with local government and larger organisations, from which I was left out. I noticed that the more comfortable the manager became in certain circles, the more cocky he became. He felt that it was okay to belittle me and also to criticise or laugh at my culture. When I finally got the courage to make him aware of his behaviour and pointless ideas, he reported me to the project advisors. But I had good relationships with them and I had been updating them with respect to what had been happening. Eventually I left because I felt that I had no real purpose on the project and his behaviour could blacklist me in the local conservation groups.'

'People think discrimination is in the killing of people of colour – but that's just part of it. Discrimination is in the small acts; the way someone speaks to you, offering below minimum wage because you don't have the post graduate experiences that students from wealthier countries have, intentionally leaving you out of meetings that directly affect the work you are doing, and questioning the way you make decisions.'

It is very disappointing that certain people, who believe they are superior, are not giving support and encouragement to their colleagues in conservation.

In male-dominated countries and groups

In some countries the traditional subservient role of women makes it difficult for them to participate as leaders in conservation fieldwork. Writing of this problem, Awatef Abiadh said: 'In Libya, for example, a woman cannot go into the field alone. She must have a "mahram" to accompany her

– even her little brother is enough to give trust to all who see her. In Tunisia field trips have caused me many disagreements with my family, because "a girl who walks alone in the mountains with boys will have less chance of getting married." From a young age women are intended to become good wives, which limits their field of action. Rare are women who act differently and rare are men who support this progression' (Abiadh, 2019).

Also in Libya, Thoraya Ouhiba wrote: 'As I cannot go alone to the field, I support partnerships and collaborations so we can go as a group.' She established the Oxygen Society to focus on training and awareness of women, and to promote equitable gender representation in environmental work, especially in fieldwork. 'I imagine Oxygen as the lungs for women to breathe.'

Women: you are female!

You might think there were no advantages to being a woman in a man's world in the early years of the 20th century – but not so. Some women used their charms, often unconsciously, to influence their male counterparts. The writing and photographs of Emma Turner (Chapter 5) about the Norfolk Broads, won her wide acclaim. Her close friend was local gamekeeper Jim Vincent, who punted her across the marshes. She once said to him: 'If only I had been a man' and he stopped punting and replied 'Law, Miss, do you think I'd have slaved away night and day as I did in the old days, if you'd been a man – not me!'

Of course, it helps to have a captivating personality, which must have been true in Emma's case. She wrote about the people of the Norfolk Broads: 'From both landowners and marshmen I have always received kindness and help. At first the native population looked on me as a harmless lunatic.' They spoke of her as the mad naturalist. (Parry and Greenwood, 2020).

In 1970s Anne La Bastille (Chapter 13) went to Guatemala City to meet the Minister of Agriculture. She explained to him her idea for Operation Protection of the *Poc* (grebe): enforcement, habitat management, education and appreciation, and finally a reserve. He was enthusiastic. Anne wrote: 'I was becoming aware of two things: being a blond female scientist from a foreign country helped more than it hindered. I was not considered a threat, whereas a male professional from abroad, unless most diplomatic, might have aroused feelings of competition or inadequacy on the part of less educated or experienced colleagues.'

References

Abiadh, A., 2019, Meet the women inspiring change in the Mediterranean, *BirdLife Magazine,* April-June, 42-45.

Parry, J. and J. Greenwood, 2020, *Emma Turner A life looking at Birds,* Norfolk and Norwich Naturalists' Society.

2. Women in Zoos
– and the Role Model, Katharina Heinroth

Women naturally take the role of carers, which is why there are far more female nurses than men. So why has this not been the case with zoo keepers? Presumably, the reason is tradition. The number of large and dangerous animals in zoos resulted in men being hired. Women were employed only in the children's part of a zoo which contained mainly domesticated animals. In Oklahoma, Tulsa Zoo opened in 1927 but it was not until 1964 that the first female keeper was employed. By 1980 there were nine male and nine female keepers. These figures were representative of other zoos in the USA.

Franklin Park and Stone zoos, which make up Zoo New England, employ 54 zookeepers, 37 of whom are women. Three of the five curators and most of the veterinarians are female. The women do the full range of jobs once performed exclusively by men, including lifting hay bales and building fences. They are trained to use rifles to tranquilise animals.

According to a workplace survey conducted in 2000 by the American Association of Zoo Keepers, 75% of zookeepers in the USA were female. Women with advanced science degrees were working as curators, nutritionists, researchers and veterinarians. Seventy percent of graduates of veterinary schools each year were women, according to the American Veterinary Medical Association. In the UK the Royal College of Veterinary Surgeons held a survey in 2019. One question related to gender. Of those who selected female or male, 58% were female and 42% male. This suggested that the 'feminisation' of the veterinary profession has continued since the last survey in 2014, when female respondents outnumbered males for the first time.

But back to the USA. Probably the most famous woman in an American zoo was Belle Benchley, employed for two weeks in 1925 while the book-keeper was on holiday. She became the executive secretary of San Diego Zoo in California from 1927 to 1953 but, unfairly, she did not receive the title of Director until just before she retired.

Since that time perhaps only one woman has been appointed as a zoo director of a mainstream zoo, not including those in zoos that they founded. There have been female zoo curators in bird departments – but the number is small compared with that of their male counterparts. Europe seems to be falling behind the rest of the world in this respect.

How does one qualify to become a curator? One way would seem to be to acquire years of hands-on, practical experience, perhaps as a valued keeper, as was the case with Jo Gregson at Paignton Zoo in Devon. In the same era Laura Gardner became Curator of Birds at London Zoo in 2016, having formerly acted as a consultant for one year and as bird collection manager for three years. She had lost her job at the iconic moated Leeds Castle in Kent when its outstanding small bird park closed due to financial reasons. Laura started to work with birds in 1987, at Birdworld – one of the best bird parks in the UK. She was the curator at Leeds Castle from 1997 to 2012 and was especially successful in the breeding of toucans and small hornbills. She lacked a science-based degree; her rapport with birds was a more relevant attribute. Laura grew up in Jersey, knowing the famous zoo there and deciding that she wanted to be a zoo keeper. Summer holidays were spent 'helping' the keepers. She said: 'I vividly remember meeting Gerald Durrell who shook my hand – I didn't wash my hands for a week after that!'

The other route to becoming a bird curator, usually only in specialist collections, applies to aviculturists who have acquired expertise with a certain group of birds. They have a depth of knowledge that would be lacking in a curator with a wider remit or a curator who had worked only in the veterinary profession. A few excellent vets have actually bred birds in their own aviaries – but most have not.

In the UK, Janet Kear was a scientist and the curator of a superb collection of waterfowl. The great waterfowl expert and artist Sir Peter Scott founded the world-famous collection at Slimbridge, Gloucestershire, and the other centres of the Wildfowl and Wetlands Trust (WWT). When Janet Kear completed her PhD at Cambridge he recruited her in 1959 – and she never left. She was the Trust's avicultural co-ordinator from 1974 to 1977, curator of WWT's Martin Mere Wetlands Centre in Lancashire from 1977 to 1991, then director of all its centres from 1991 to 1993. In that year she was made an OBE.

Janet Kear became the first woman President of the British Ornithologists' Union. She served on numerous committees. Her name was strongly associated with the captive breeding of the Hawaiian Goose, or Nene (*Branta sandvicensis*) which narrowly escaped extinction when, by 1949, only 30 were known to survive. Breeding at Slimbridge saved it and she co-authored *The Hawaiian Goose,* published in 1980, the definitive monograph. She also co-authored *Flamingos* (papers from a symposium, plus captive care) and wrote *The Mute Swan* (1988), *Man and Wildfowl* (1990) and *Ducks of the World* (1991). *Ducks, Geese and Swans,* which she edited. It was in press when she died and remains as a lasting memorial to her work.

In the 21st century it seems that preference is often given to those who apply for a curator's position if they hold a degree. In my opinion, practical knowledge and the way someone relates to the animals in his or her care is much more important. An excellent example of this is the Brazilian Marcia Weinzettl, curator at Loro Parque, Tenerife which holds the largest collection of parrots in the world. The majority of the birds are located in an off-site breeding centre belonging to Loro Parque Fundación. Marcia was appointed curator in 2016. Previously she supervised a number of parrot breeding facilities in Brazil. She worked with many rare and difficult species, including the threatened Golden Conure or Parrot (*Guaruba guarouba*). At one time she was working with 160 pairs of these iconic, appealing birds, in addition to many other species. This is real, hands-on experience, without which a degree counts for almost nothing. Her aim when taking the position was to rapidly increase the percentage of parent-reared young – which she achieved. Previously there had been emphasis on hand-rearing, which is rarely beneficial for the individual bird or for the species. It was soon apparent that she applied rigorous protocols, especially to diet and environmental enrichment.

One hundred years earlier the term 'environmental enrichment' relating to animal welfare was unknown. Few curators had relevant degrees but those responsible for making appointments at London Zoo knew that passion for the subject from childhood and practical experience were more important than scientific knowledge. The zoo employed two female curators.

Lucy Evelyn Cheesman (1881-1969)

This versatile collector, curator and author was born in Kent, UK. Her mother encouraged her, at a very early age, to collect flowers, moss and glow worms. Evelyn, as she was known, had set her mind on becoming a veterinary surgeon, but in 1906 the Royal College for this profession did not admit women. The law changed in 1919 to allow women to train as veterinarians, lawyers and civil servants but by then she was (since 1917) the Assistant Curator of Insects at London Zoo. In 1920 she

Evelyn Cheesman in the field.
Source: Natural History Museum Library.

was made the first female Insect House Curator. When she took over the house it was almost empty. She collected insects herself, invited children to do the same and acquired exotic species from Covent Garden fruiterers who sometimes found spiders lurking in their bananas!

In 1923 Evelyn went on her first expedition, to the Galápagos Islands. Aboard ship she acquired important skills, including skinning and preserving lizards and birds. From the Galápagos she went on to collect in the South Pacific, in the Marquesas Islands and Tuamotu Atolls in 1924 and to the Society Islands in 1925. In her lifetime she led eight expeditions there. She became the first woman to undergo a solo trip around this region – a journey even men refused to undertake on their own. She was not the first courageous and fearless female of this era to explore a region which men had considered too dangerous – Emilia Snethlage had done the same in the Brazilian Amazon. And both women were in their early forties at the time!

Evelyn left the zoo in 1926 to collect privately and later, at age 48, to collect insects and small animals for the British Museum (Natural History). When she officially left the zoo, she made further expeditions in the New Hebrides (now Vanuatu) and South West Pacific including New Guinea and New Caledonia. These collections were extremely important, revealing much information about species dispersal, extinction, climate change and the biogeography and the evolutionary history. Her final expedition was to Vanuatu in 1953, at the age of 73 after a hip replacement! What a remarkable woman! She had fostered good relations with the indigenous people she encountered. Their knowledge of local wildlife, trails and hazards was invaluable both to her work and safety.

Her meagre income had been supplemented by writing 16 popular books chronicling her adventures and discoveries (see Chapter 14). In 1955 Evelyn Cheesman was awarded an OBE and a Civil List pension for her contributions to entomology, finally giving her some financial security. She continued to work at the Museum, writing and classifying specimens, until her death in 1969.

Joan Procter 1897-1931

Joan Procter was born in London on August 5 1897. Her father was a stockbroker, and her mother was an artist. Her grandfather, William Brockbank, was an amateur botanist and geologist. Very unusually for a girl, she had a passion for reptiles from an early age. Her special pet, a Dalmatian wall lizard, sat on the table beside her at mealtimes (with long-suffering parents!) and travelled everywhere with her. During her visits to the British Museum (Natural History) she met George Boulenger, Keeper of Reptiles and Fishes. When she left school, Boulenger invited her to work under his direction. In 1916

Female Heroes of Bird Conservation

Joan Procter – a snake and a tortoise were named after her.
Photograph: Vaughan.

she became his assistant, working in a voluntary capacity. In this way she also became an academic and, at the age of nineteen, she presented her first scientific paper to the Zoological Society of London (ZSL). The subject was Central and South American pit vipers.

In August 1917 Joan was elected as a Fellow of the Zoological Society (FZS). This was an extraordinary honour for a 20-year-old – and a female! When Boulenger retired in 1920, she took charge of reptiles at the museum. Through her publications and correspondence she became internationally recognised as a leading herpetologist. The University of Chicago awarded her an honorary Doctor of Science (DSc), in 1931. She was elected as a Fellow (FLS) of the prestigious Linnean Society of London, in recognition of the high quality of her taxonomic work.

In 1923 Joan became Curator of Reptiles at London Zoo. Before she left her employment at the museum, she was building scale models of the new aquarium tanks for the Reptile House, the first of its kind in the world. This talented woman was also a modeller and she designed with artistic skill the rock work and backgrounds of the exhibits. In the following two years, she also designed the rockwork for outdoor enclosures for antelopes and other animals.

Joan became an expert in handling large pythons and crocodilians. The first two Komodo dragons to arrive in Europe were exhibited in the Reptile House when it opened in 1927. This species had a reputation as a dangerous animal that could (and had) killed humans but she established an extraordinary rapport with them. Her good care, feeding and routine handling resulted in dragons described 'as tame as dogs.' One dragon named Sumbawa became her particular pet and accompanied her when she walked around the Zoo.

All her life she was ill with intestinal problems and in constant pain – and that makes her accomplishments all the more remarkable. She died at her home in London on September 20, 1931, aged only 34. She had achieved so much in her short life and surely had so much more to give. Her death was a great loss to the world of herpetology and to zoos.

In 2018 the beautifully illustrated book (40 pages) entitled *Joan Procter, Dragon Doctor*, was published for children. Sadly, there is no biography.

Monika Meyer-Holzapfel 1907-1995

In Switzerland, Monika was the director of Tierpark Dählhoelzi in Bern, more often known as Bern Zoo, from May 1943 to December 1969. She was born on April 14 1907 in Lausanne. Her father was from Austria but she took Swiss nationality. She studied zoology, botany, geology and mineralogy in Bern and Munich, Germany. From 1933 she was assisting Prof. Fritz Baltzer in lecturing at the zoological institute of Bern University and in 1943 she became a lecturer there. From 1954 to 1973 she held the honorary title of professor in animal psychology, behavioural research and biology. Then she followed Prof. Dr. Heini Hediger as director of Bern Zoo, living there in a house by the river Aare. A bird dealer came regularly with a van full of exotic birds and Monika would make purchases, especially for the tropical house, and she bought animals and added aviaries for pheasants.

A prolific writer, she published many scientific papers and popular books about animals, such as *Tiere, meine täglichen Gefährten* (*Animals, my Daily Companions*) (Benteli-Verlag, 1966). In the way that she wrote about the birds, it was obvious that for her an animal was an individual with needs and a will. In 1944 she became the first woman in Europe to run a zoo, preceding Katharina Heinroth by a few months. She must have been a very tough lady because when she took

Monika Meyer-Holzapfel.
Photograph: Burgerbibliothek Bern.

over at Tierpark Dählhölzli, which belongs to the city of Bern, she was sent as keepers rough men who were of no use in other departments of the city. At that time zoo-keeping was not regarded as a proper job with a lot of responsibilities. She married Gilbert Victor Meyer in 1940 and had two daughters.

Elsewhere, the lack of women in zoo positions continued despite the fact that there were some outstandingly successful role models – usually as keepers, and much more rarely as directors or curators of important mainstream zoos. The role of curator has undergone a natural change over the decades and tends to be more hands-on today. A very well-known male bird curator at a famous zoo was renowned for rarely being seen outside his office! The best curator is one who has a good relationship with his staff and with the birds. The best curator will be seen walking around the collection every day and observing with care every feathered creature, large or small, common or rare.

Katharina Bertha Charlotte Berger Heinroth 1897-1989

The best curators care deeply about the welfare of individual birds, as did Magdalena and Oskar Heinroth, whose story is related in Chapter 7. Magdalena died in 1932. In that year Oskar employed Katharina Berger as his secretary, to help him type manuscripts. She was born in Breslau, near the Polish border, in 1897. Zoology was her interest from an early age, when she kept frogs and other animals. At the age of 22 she enrolled in PhD courses in zoology, botany, paleontology (fossils), geography and geology. Spirited and confident, she is said to have received four marriage proposals before graduation. Graduating in 1923 with work on the hearing of reptiles, she was the first woman to receive a doctorate at the zoological institute of Breslau University. She spent her nights conducting research on bees and springtails (tiny invertebrates) and during the day she worked as a secretary, librarian or administrative assistant (Mohnhaupt, 2019). Katharina and Oskar married in 1933. It was her second marriage; the first had ended in divorce.

As related in Chapter 7, Oskar had become assistant curator at Berlin Zoo in 1904. A brief explanation is needed here for the sake of clarity. There are

Katharina Heinroth.
Photographer: unknown.

two zoos in Berlin; the other, in the former eastern sector, founded in 1955, is known as Tierpark (animal park) Berlin. The 160ha (395 acre) site in Friedrichsfelde became very important in the breeding of rare animals. This site was prepared by countless volunteers, including schoolchildren, who also helped to raise funds.

The Heinroths lived in the Aquarium at the Berlin Zoo. On their rooftop terrace they kept carrier pigeons and, together, they carried out research on the pigeons' sense of direction. This famous building still stands today, after being rebuilt. Then it contained 8,300 fishes, reptiles and amphibians. At the start of the Second World War, in 1939, the Berlin Zoo (in what was to become West Berlin) was considered to be the most important in the world, with 4,000 mammals and birds of 1,400 species. In November 1943 and January 1944 much of the zoo, in the vulnerable city centre, was destroyed. The Americans bombed Berlin during the day and the British took over when dark fell. On one dreadful night 753 British bombers

The Aquarium at Berlin Zoo.
Photograph: author.

dropped 2,500 tons of explosives and seven hundred of the 2,000 animals died.

The unspeakable atrocities of humans upon humans are hard enough to contemplate but the terror, bewilderment, pain and death of defenceless caged animals is worse, in my opinion. Twenty one major fires raged through the zoo which Katharina helped to extinguish. A crocodile was found lying in the street at the entrance to the Aquarium. The force of the explosions had ejected it out of the tropical hall and the cold had killed it. In the following days the famished zoo staff feasted on crocodile tail soup.

Tragically, in April 1945, just before the war ended, Berlin Zoo became a battleground for enemy action, with Soviet tanks blasting through its walls. The Heinroths were devastated by the destruction of this valuable collection and by the deaths of so many animals that they knew so well. To have kept the zoo alive through those terrible years was heroic – but for nothing. At the end of the war only 91 animals were still alive – including a Shoebill, a male elephant and a young hippo. Some animals were killed and eaten by starving Berliners. The Shoebill was kept in one of the few undamaged bathrooms. The Shoebill (*Balaeniceps rex*) is an intriguing giant stork-like bird (See Chapter 36). Its beak is enormous, up to 20cm (8in) wide. How did they get food for him, I wondered?

At the time of Oskar's death in 1945, the director of Berlin Zoo was Nazi sympathiser Lutz Heck. Heck was a close friend of Hermann Göring, one of the most powerful figures in the Nazi party. Through his contacts, German zoos could feed their animals. When, in May that year, Germany lost the war, Heck, who had been the director since 1931, fled into southern Germany. He had had the foresight to evacuate 750 animals of 250 species to zoos in other cities (Mohnhaupt, 2019). However, only one (a giraffe) was returned after the war. In 1945, Berlin was split into two, with West Berlin isolated and controlled by the Allies and East Berlin under Soviet control.

Katharina was tending injured local people in the zoo's enormous air-raid shelter. She must have been very strong to endure so much, including being raped by Russian soldiers. By then Oskar, 74 years old, was recovering from pneumonia, and was given an injection by a nurse that hit a nerve and paralysed his right leg. Katharina nursed him. The Aquarium was almost totally destroyed. The staff had fled or been conscripted into the German army. Katharina wanted to get her and Oskar out but he could no longer walk. He asked her to get the 'poison pills' (probably fearing that he would be shot) but they were in the demolished apartment. They stayed in the air raid shelter until the following morning when soldiers ordered them out. The Heinroths tried to survive in the cellar of the apartment until Oskar was too ill to stand. She took him out in a wheelbarrow, continually moving to overcrowded cellars. When the Soviet troops left the zoo Katharina returned to the apartment and with the help of two zookeepers, made one room habitable. But Oskar died on May 3. His death was a tragedy – but he was a fortunate man in having married two remarkable women who totally complemented his work and were truly devoted to him.

In 1945 Katharina's steely determination saved what was left of the zoo. The keepers and the animals which survived were given a new life. In August she and her assistant Werner Schröder were appointed interim head and deputy head. In September she became the permanent director. Katharina then faced the seemingly impossible task of rebuilding a zoo without electricity or a functioning sewer system, and in a city occupied by four different foreign military forces. Her nickname was 'Katharina die Einzige' ('the one and only Katharina'). She had every skill needed to run a zoo – and more: a deep knowledge of animal behaviour, extensive hands-on experience of rearing animals, and the strength and fortitude that propelled her to rebuild a zoo that had been razed to the ground. At the same time, she faced competition and unfair criticism from the new Tierpark Berlin. Of course its director strongly promoted his zoo, to the degree that before the Berlin Wall was built, West Berliners travelled to the Tierpark in hordes to see the new attraction.

Katharina had great determination. In 1948 the blockade of Berlin, which lasted one year, resulted in its two million residents becoming desperately short of food. A new British commander told her she must get rid of all the animals, cut down some of the 400-year-old oak trees, plant spinach and keep chickens. She absolutely refused. She filed a complaint to the British forces and the Berlin bureau for open space planning – but she was threatened with legal action. She stood her ground and the commander finally relented. What a brave, indefatigable woman!

She revived the zoo with limited financial resources. She travelled widely to acquire new animals and to raise private donations. In October 1949 Schröder's idea of staging an Oktoberfest in the zoo was wildly successful. Four million visitors arrived during the four week period. This became an annual fund-raiser.

As only the second woman zoo director in Europe, she had the additional challenge of working in a society strongly dominated by men. Worse still, there were misogynists waiting to oust her. In the late 1940s, when she was recovering after a period in hospital, several board members stated that running a zoo was too strenuous for a woman, although she was highly regarded in professional zoo circles. In 1950 she was one of the first four German zoo directors readmitted to the International Union of Directors of Zoological Gardens.

In 1954 in *Der Tagesspiegel* newspaper, Lutz Heck, now living in Wiesbaden, made derogatory remarks about the management of the zoo. Soon after, Otto Radke, spokesman for the zoo shareholders, declared that the zoo should be run by a man with an international reputation. This was the beginning of the end for Katharina, even although by 1955 the zoo exhibited nearly 2,000 animals and she had expanded it to 28ha (70 acres). She ran a zoology lecture course at the Berlin Technical University and she made a weekly radio broadcast about animals. But she was exhausted, working 16-hour days. Other zoos offered her positions but she was too devoted to her own zoo to leave. Then she was told the zoo's Board wanted her to resign. She was allowed to name her successor and to train him for six months. She was forced out with a monthly pension of 900 marks in December 1956. Her health was no longer good.

Katharina was to live for a further 33 years. The fourth volume of the major work on the birds of central Europe, *Mitteleuropäische Vögel* (1962), which had been started by Oskar, was written by Katharina and J. Steinbacher. Apart from numerous scientific and popular articles, she wrote a biography of Oskar (Heinroth, 1971) and her autobiography in 1979, which was sub-titled (in German) *My life with Animals in Breslau, Munich and Berlin* (Heinroth, 1979). Katharina Heinroth died on October 20, 1989, just before the fall of the Berlin Wall. As requested in her will, she was buried in the grounds of the zoo, next to her husband. Thanks to her Berlin Zoo had become great again. She had proved that women had an extremely important role to play in zoos, that they were the equal of men in every respect. During her working life she had a constant battle against misogyny.

Today women are accepted in every role in the zoo but remain under-represented in the position of curator. Women excel in hand-rearing; their patience and more gentle touch make them particularly suited to this role. But do not take my word only! I asked Louise Peat, who worked in several UK zoos. She responded:

> 'First of all I believe we should change the name from keepers to carers as ultimately that should be a keeper's role. In my experience of zoos, the word 'carer' has become quite lost on some people who call themselves professionals. The majority of females have an innate nurturing quality; they see the small details and pay attention to them. Many men tend to be quite heavy handed; this may be beneficial when working with larger mammals, but it rarely has positive rewards when working with birds.'

> 'All the females I have worked with, who I admire and have learnt from, had unending patience, compassion and a hunger to do the absolute best for the individuals in their care. When they failed they would take it personally, scrutinise everything and then plan for success at the next opportunity. When given the chance, females who can carry the caring attitude into higher positions in zoos are able to greatly influence the standard of care, quality of life and health of the animals, and ultimately improve success rates. In the UK, Jo Gregson and Laura Gardner and in the Netherlands, Cathy King, have all achieved this. However, I do sense that it was hard work and they had to fight for it.'

> 'In my opinion, there are only a few men in high positions who share the same attitude; the majority appear to be more business-minded. I know a zoo has to be run as a business, but anyone knows that quality work will achieve more results long-term than shoddy work! I think zoos would be more productive and better places if there were more women in higher places. By women, I mean people who started as keepers, not those who got their positions through degrees and have no practical experience.'

Founders of the Suffragette movement in 1911 would have been proud of Louise's words! They started International Women's Day (IWD), celebrated every year in early March. It continues to drive action and change for gender parity whilst celebrating the achievements of women.

Mark Habben of Wildwood in Kent sent an appreciative letter to his colleagues on IWD in 2021. He asked:

> 'Are we doing enough individually to ensure that we have an inclusive

work place where we treat men and women the same? Where we recognise gender bias and act against it? Our industry has improved significantly in recent years. We have made immeasurable improvements in animal care and welfare, we take a scientific, evidence-based approach to husbandry and behaviour, we look at the ethical implications of what we do, we breed critically endangered species and actively engage with *in situ* field programmes – some of which see zoo-bred animals returned to the wild. Many of these achievements and progressive steps have had women driving them forward – occasionally to considerable opposition.'

'When I was at university studying Biology, my dissertation was on the importation of North American Colubrid snakes. I reached out to the then Curator of reptiles and aquarium at London Zoo, Dr Heather Koldeway – who had then achieved a fantastic position as the only female curator and only female senior animal manager at London Zoo. She helped me with a lot of information, despite being incredibly busy. I was asked a few years ago to present at International Women's Day and to talk about a woman who has inspired me. I spoke about Heather. She is now Professor Heather Koldeway and has spent the past few years as Head of Marine and Freshwater Conservation for ZSL, establishing protected marine reserves in critically important coral habitats around the world. She exemplifies to me what a strong leader should be. She is collaborative, driven, supportive and inspiring.'

I hope that her story, and those of the other subjects of this chapter, will motivate women in zoos to strive for more influence, especially in ways to improve animal welfare and enrichment.

References

Heinroth, K., 1971, *Oskar Heinroth – Vater der Verhaltensforschung*. Wissenschaftliche Verlagsgesellschaft, Stuttgart.
Heinroth, K., 1979, *Mit Faltern begann's,* Kindler, Münich. Mohnhaupt, J. W., 2019, *The Zookeepers' War,* Simon and Schuster.

Female Heroes of Bird Conservation

Female Heroes of the Past

Etta Lemon

Evelyn Cheesman

Joan Procter

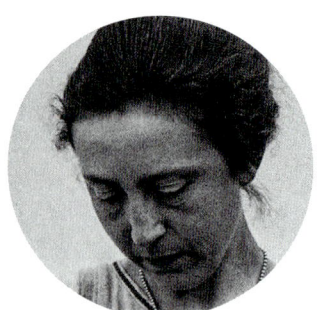
Magdalena Heinroth

Emma Turner

Phyllis Barclay-Smith

Rachel Carson

3. Althea Rosina Sherman
USA 1853-1943
Pioneer Ornithologist, Author and Artist

During the period 1850 to 1880 several women who became notable figures in bird conservation were born in the USA, Germany and England. This was in an era before the word conservation had ever been applied to the natural world. They were pioneers. They were so far ahead of their time.

Althea Sherman could trace her ancestry to Suffolk, England and, through William Bradford, to a Mayflower descendant. She was born in Clayton County, north-east Iowa, on October 10 1853, to Mark Bachelor and Melissa Sherman, the fourth of six children; there was a sister who died in early childhood. In 1865, her father sold his farm and the family spent a year in Fayette, Iowa, before moving, in 1866, to National, Iowa, to a newly built house on Main Street.

At that time only a post office and a blacksmith's shop existed in National; it grew to a population of 200 people. In her early teens Althea attended Upper Iowa University at La Fayette; she went on to Oberlin College. More than 40 years later she attributed her success as a scientist partly to the training in Latin and Greek she received in the classical course there. She graduated with a Bachelor of Arts degree in 1875. In 1882 she received her Master's degree.

For four years she taught in schools. By then drawing was no longer just an ornamental branch of education. The mechanical, practical aspects of drawing as a craft and as a tool to facilitate other kinds of work, were recognised. It was usually as a teacher of drawing, not painting or art, that Althea Sherman found employment. Far more skilled in the use of the pencil than the brush, she used this skill in her own research on birds, in finished studies and in sketches in her notebooks of visual details. The margins of her early journals often featured thumbnail drawings of new birds observed near her home, with notations about colours and arrows to point out identifying features (Wood, 1989).

A former pupil remembered her fondly from 40 years previously, saying she had never known another teacher like her. Miss Sherman took the pupils into the woods and showed them flowers, ripening seeds, how leaves were constructed and how to identify trees by their bark.

Female Heroes of Bird Conservation

Althea Sherman in 1907.
Photograph: State Historical Society of Iowa.

She then studied at the Arts Institute in Chicago and at the Art Students' League in New York City. From 1882 to 1887 she was a drawing instructor at Carleton College in Minnesota. In 1892 she moved to Tacoma, Washington where she was employed in the same way in the city schools. Art was not only her profession – it was also her joy. With pencil and brush and an enormous amount of talent, she put her love of the natural world on paper and canvas.

In 1895 her life changed suddenly. She had to return to her parents' home. With her medical doctor sister Amelia, she took care of her parents. Her mother was ill and died in the following year. In 1902 her father passed away. He had been a highly successful farmer and had given her the best education money could buy.

It so often happens that events which initially bring dismay or disruption, in Althea's case giving up teaching, are the first steps to a much more advantageous or fulfilling life. Previously she lived a busy urban existence with little time to study nature. All she needed was the time and the place to set her on a new career. She now had the time and her parents' property, alive with nesting birds, was the perfect place. On her father's death he left enough funds to support her and her research for the rest of her days. Now 49, she could devote all her time to the study and painting of birds and other wildlife.

She had plenty of subjects in her garden and orchard, and in the surrounding pasture and swamp. Her beautiful painting of an American Goldfinch inspired the Iowa legislature to adopt it as the state bird. At the 1922 convention of the American Ornithologists' Union (AOU) in Chicago she exhibited three paintings. Her birds were charmingly accurate, with a soft and delicate touch, and her love for them was evident. One of them caused Luis Agassiz Fuertes to exclaim in admiration: 'That Brown Thrasher has more life and personality than any bird I ever painted!' He was one of the world's finest bird painters, also a renowned ornithologist and traveller, and even today his paintings fetch astronomical sums.

Althea Sherman was not just a bird observer: she became a scientist who corresponded with the leading researchers of her time. She joined 15 scientific societies and subscribed to 26 scientific and ornithological journals, which published 70 0f her articles. Her papers on the breeding ecology of Screech Owls and Kestrels brought her national acclaim. Arthur Cleveland Bent used her work in several of the books in the series *Life Histories of North American Birds*.

As an indication of the esteem in which she was held, in 1912 she was one of only four women elected as a member of the AOU – and membership was limited to one hundred people. Important publications such as *Who's Who of the Women of the Nation* and, remarkably, even *American Men of Science*, made entries under her name.

Her work on the Northern Flicker (a small woodpecker), which took 15 years to complete, was achieved after experimenting with nest-box designs that suited her and the flickers. Made from soap crates, they were nailed up inside her famous red barn to coincide with holes that the flickers had drilled. Each box had a peephole in the top and a door near the bottom that enabled her to examine the eggs and nestlings, to weigh them and to determine the incubation period (Sherman, 1910). She illustrated the article with three of her drawings.

In November 1913 this independent woman was at last able to travel, spending ten months visiting 20 countries and covering 3,300 miles. She wrote about her findings in Europe, the Middle East and Asia in three issues of the *Wilson Bulletin* and in her book *Birds by the Wayside*.

Althea Sherman contributed important scientific articles on birds to such publications as the *Auk* and on bats to the *Journal of Mammology* (vol. 10, 319-326, 1929). She amazed experts with the depth of her knowledge. Many of her papers were the result of long-term studies. In 1926 she wrote in a letter: 'I count 20 years all too short for a thorough acquaintance with the birds of my own dooryard, where 31 species have been pleased to nest.'

Catbirds, Brown Thrashers, Flickers and American Robins were her subjects for 33 years, Phoebes for 31 years and Red-winged Blackbirds for 29 years. Her research uncovered previously unknown facts, not published until she had the scientific proof she needed. She studied Screech Owls for 26 years and actually paid people to kill them, because of the heavy toll they took on the local bird life. This might seem shocking, but only someone who follows the life histories of the birds on their patch can understand how much damage can be done by one predatory species whose numbers are excessive.

Her most famous work related to the Chimney Swift – and it seems unlikely that many other people have gone to such lengths to study the nesting habits of one bird species. In 1915 she built a big tower. This solid structure was 9m (30ft) high and 2.7m (9ft) square, with a 60cm (2ft) square chimney running down the centre – complete with observation holes – and a staircase winding around it. What an extraordinary and unique initiative! People came from far and wide to see 20 or more Swifts clinging to its walls. In one exceptional week she had 56 visitors. Her cleverly designed observation windows consisted of two panes of glass meeting in a wide V that jutted into the chimney. She could put her head into this opening and look up or down without unduly frightening the birds. By shading one of the openings with paper and placing a lamp there, she made nocturnal observations. Her journals devoted to this species covered 18 years and more than 400 pages. That it was an extraordinary achievement needs to be emphasised. Sadly, her plan to publish these records never materialised. What a loss to science!

'Her work was independent and thorough in a laboratory that had no duplicate. Her alluring and original style made her work interesting beyond the circle of the strictly scientific', wrote Mrs H. Taylor in 1943. 'She was the busiest woman I ever knew and she accomplished the most. Her method of work, her ever-widening interests, her eagerness to give the world the results of her studies kept her life full and made her interesting and inspiring to others.'

Her paper on Experiments in Feeding Humming Birds during Seven Summers was read at the 31st annual congress of the AOU in New York and published in the *Wilson Bulletin* (vol. 25 (4), December 1913) and reprinted in *The Avicultural Magazine* (Third Series, vol. VI (11): 328-332 and (12): 381-389, 1915). Althea Sherman's carefully observed and recorded observations of the Ruby-throated Hummingbirds in her garden made it a delight to read. Big beds of colourful tiger-lilies and phlox, and bottles filled with sugar water, attracted the tiny nectar feeders.

The extraordinary Swift tower.
Photograph: Special Collections and University Archives, Iowa State.

'More or less fighting ensues as soon as another bird comes on the scene, and the tumult of battle increases with each new arrival until the presence of six or seven of these tiny belligerents makes the front yard appear like the staging of a ballet. With clashing sounds and continuous squeaking cries they chase each other about, often swinging back and forth in an arc of a circle with a sort of pendulum like motion. Sometimes they clinch and fall to the earth, where the struggle is continued for many seconds.'

Interestingly, throughout the seven years of the experiments on food intake and preferences, only female hummingbirds were seen to drink from the bottles of sugar water.

When she entered her hide to spend the day observing a pair of Mourning Doves, she took her knitting with her, to better tolerate the monotony of this task. However, Sharon Wood made a valid point, suggesting that domestic jobs intruded on her time in ways unknown to a male ornithologist. Sometimes she could not maintain a perfect watch on her bird tower because she had to make supper. She was conscious of discrimination against women in the professional societies to which she belonged; but in the 'laboratory' that she had created, she had to be neither admitted nor hired, she had only to work and to write (Wood, 1989).

Mrs Taylor had written: 'Hers was not a buoyant personality radiating sunshine and joyousness. It was a rugged personality shaped with reality, strength, vision; ready ever to face and endure the weather of human experience. She radiated mental and physical health, power, understanding.'

Due to arthritis in her hands she ceased to publish her work after 1933. This was a loss to ornithology, especially as many of her projects were unfinished. In later years she used a typewriter for her correspondence. By then she was saddened to notice that birds were not as plentiful as in her youth.

Sharon Wood's comments on this observation unfortunately resonate today even more strongly: '… woven through these cycles are her poignant observations of the long-term changes that occurred during a lifetime of nearly ninety years: the native plant and animal species that disappeared under the pressures of agricultural development; the new species that arrived to replace them; the changing weather patterns that affected not only crops but also the birds and animals that shared the land with farmers' (Wood, 1989).

She left 70 journals and 250 pieces of art (Althea Sherman Collection Special Archives) to the State Historical Society of Iowa in Des Moines. Her 60 closely written notebooks were left with a wish that someone should shape her writings into a book. A friend obliged, and *Birds of an Iowa Dooryard* was published in 1952 by the University of Iowa Press. It was an 18-chapter tribute to Althea's nearly 40 years of absorbed, painstakingly accurate work. But perhaps her greatest legacy was that of a female trail blazer in ornithology and, furthermore, a woman who was self-taught and worked completely on her own. She was unique not only of her time but surely remains unique to this day.

When she died on April 16 1943 she was laid to rest in the National (Farmersburg) Cemetery close to her home. A replica of the Swift Tower now stands in the old church yard; many bird generations after Althea erected her tower, the Chimney Swifts are rearing their young close by.

Rosalie Barrow Edge 1877-1962

In New York City, on November 3 1877, Mabel Rosalie Barrow was born to wealthy parents. After a number of years in high society she became a passionate birder. Unlike Althea Sherman, raptors were to become the focus of her conservation work. In 1929 she received a pamphlet written by Willard Van Name called 'A Crisis in Conservation.' The pamphlet attacked the National Association of Audubon Societies (NAAS) for allowing hunting on its land in Louisiana. As a life member of that organisation, Rosalie was incensed. In 1932 she saw pictures taken of hawks dying in the Kittatinny Mountains of eastern Pennsylvania. She attempted to get the Audubon Society to buy what later became known as Hawk Mountain, but she failed. She then began a year-long campaign to raise the $3,500 necessary to purchase the site. She was successful and on New Year's Eve 1932, she successfully founded the Hawk Mountain Sanctuary near Kempton, Pennsylvania. This determined and influential woman died thirty years later, in November 1962. The non-profit association she founded still runs the Sanctuary today, saving birds, conducting research and running educational programmes.

References

Sherman, A. R. 1910, At the sign of the Northern Flicker, *Wilson Bulletin*, 22, 135-171.

Taylor, H. J., 1943, Iowa's Woman Ornithologist Althea Rosina Sherman, The Althea R. Sherman Memorial Issue, *Iowa Birdlife*, XIII (June): 19-35.

Wood, S. E., 1989, Althea Sherman and the Birds of Prairie and Dooryard: a scientist's witness to change, *The Palimpsest*, 70 (4): 164-185.

4. Etta Lemon
(neé Smith) UK 1860-1953
Harriet Hemenway
(née Lawrence) USA 1858-1960

Two remarkable women were separated by the Atlantic Ocean, but not separated in time. Almost all their years overlapped, with the American campaigner living seven years longer. In the UK Etta Smith's passion for birds was so strong that when she was only 18 she started to use her powerful intellect to stir up indignation at the hideous trade in bird plumage which arose from the vanity of women. That was in 1878. In that year Harriet Hemenway was 20 and no doubt enjoying a full social life that befitted a young lady from an affluent family. It was not until she was 38 years old that she took the same path as Etta.

Harriet

Harriet Lawrence was born in Massachusetts, USA, in 1858, into an influential Boston family. Her father campaigned to abolish the slave trade and to facilitate the emigration of freed African Americans. He was important enough for a Kansas town, Lawrence, to be named after him. Harriet loved nature and perhaps unusually for a woman in that era, she was a keen bird-watcher. In 1881 she married Augustus Hemenway, from another local socialite family.

Margaretta (Etta)

In 1860, two years after Harriet's birth, Margaretta Smith was born on November 22 on the Kent coast, not far from Dover. Always known as Etta, she was the oldest of three, with a brother Edward and a sister Woltera Mercy. Their father, Captain William Elisha Smith, was a born-again Christian who organised preaching events. Their mother, Louisa, was a Barclay of Blackheath, a family renowned for their philanthropy and Evangelical zeal.

In March 1867, when Etta was seven years old, her mother died in childbirth, together with the baby. Nine months later her father married again. But instead of being in a loving family, eight-year-old Etta and seven-year-old Mercy were sent to a boarding school in Suffolk. This seems to have been a common method of dealing with probably unwanted step-children. There were 30 pupils. The woman in charge,

31

Mrs Umphelby (a name that could have come from a Dickens' novel) was chosen for her religious beliefs; she was a Revivalist Evangelist.

Missionary work was the unspoken subtext of her education. Etta spent eight years in that school and was then sent to a finishing school in Switzerland – another custom of that era applied to girls from well-off families. On their return further education was never considered and they were expected to occupy themselves with charitable work until they found a husband.

Etta had other ideas. She did not conform to the fashions and the rituals of the Victorian lady. In a way she did conform because she would soon be campaigning – not for human rights but for those of the birds she loved. Meanwhile she worked for her father, promoting the Evangelization Society. It was unusual in having several women speakers. Etta watched them in action and in doing so she learned how to speak in public. She assisted with the society's publications, writing tracts, poems and children's literature.

Etta's father commuted to his office in the West End of London, the Society's headquarters just off The Strand, taking the train from Blackheath station to Charing Cross. Etta went with him. Any commuter know that you tend to see the same people on the station platform, and often strike up an acquaintance, as Etta and her father did with William Lemon and his son Frank. William told Etta about the Fur, Fin and Feather clubs being formed across the country and that he was campaigning to open a local branch of the RSPCA. Frank had recently graduated from Cambridge University and had followed his father to practice law.

Etta was 18 years old when she started writing letters to women in the congregation of the church she belonged to, in Blackheath – then in Kent, now in south-east London. Her purpose was to admonish the offending women who wore hats decorated with the skins and plumes of birds (Boase, 2018). As the congregation filed down the aisle she opened her notebook and began to write: Peacock, Asian pheasant, eagle, grebe, heron, hummingbird, swallow, robin, blue tit and chaffinch. That season whole owls' heads with staring glass eyes were all the rage, along with the breasts and wings of brightly coloured parrots. Seabirds, ducks, doves and Blackbirds were used to create 'Mercury wings', placed skittishly on either side of a woman's head. Birds of paradise were everywhere.

Etta's campaign was perhaps preceded by that of the famous operatic soprano from Germany, Lilli Lehmann (1848-1929). She abhorred the fashion of wearing feathers. She campaigned passionately against the practice, offering her fans autographs in exchange for their promise not to wear feathers.

What sparked the fashion of wearing feathers in hats? Fact or fiction we do not know, but reputedly, in the late 1700s, Marie Antoinette wore a bird plume to a ball, setting off an international trend. Fashion magazines became popular in that era, apparently increasing the demand for feathered hats. Whether or not that is true, feathers are such exquisite and colourful items of nature's art, that it was surely only a matter of time before ladies in the West used then for ornamentation. However, for a young Victorian woman to write such pointedly critical letters, singling out women for their dress, was certainly courageous.

Croydon, Surrey, 1889: Etta was there, at the first meeting of the Fur, Fin and Feather Society, held in the home of Mrs Eliza Phillips. Etta was soon to put her organisational skills to good use. So many animal welfare issues needed to be addressed – but she suggested they should sharpen their focus to just one outrage against nature.

As it happened, this meeting was not an all-female affair. It was attended by the well-known Argentine-born nature writer W. H. Hudson. He told the ladies about his recent visit to a plumage warehouse in London. It must have shocked him to the core. In the previous year, in March, a catalogue for a plumage sale fell into the hands of a correspondent for *The Auk,* the journal of the American Ornithologists' Union. The sale resulted from shiploads of plumage from all over the world. The numbers defy belief and bring horror of the scale of the trade: 12,000 hummingbirds; more than 7,000 parrots from India and South America; also from the Neotropics were 6,000 Blue Honeycreepers; 5,000 colourful tanagers and hundreds of toucans. Birds of paradise had been killed in shocking numbers, no doubt wiping out mature males in some areas. Native British species were included: 7,000 starlings, Jays (*Garrulus glandarius*) and Magpies (*Pica pica*) and 14,000 game birds – quail, grouse and partridge. Also, 1,450 birds were labelled as penguins but identified as Great Crested Grebes and Little Auks (*Alle alle*) – a tiny seabird. *The Auk* correspondent learned from one dealer that the man had sold two million skins of small birds in the previous year.

This trade was surely the outrage on which the Fur, Fin and Feather Society could motivate the public. In 1891 Etta visited the headquarters of the RSPB in Jermyn Street in central London with Emily Williamson from Manchester. Emily was born just before Etta and Harriet but her motivation was exactly the same. She had written to the British Ornithologists' Union asking them to campaign against the feather trade, but she was ignored by the BOU. In 1889, when she was 34 years old, she called a group of women to her beautiful home in Didsbury, and asked them to pledge to wear no feathers.

The outcome was that Emily's group and the Fur, Fin and Feather Society were merged to become the Society for the Protection of Birds. Frank Lemon, then a young barrister, drew up the constitution. It included these words:

1. The members shall discourage the wanton destruction of Birds, and interest themselves generally in their protection.

2. That Lady Members shall refrain from wearing the feathers of any bird not killed for the purposes of food, the ostrich excepted.

Despite scathing remarks in the Press about the Society for the Protection of Birds (SPB), it had 50 branches across Britain by the end of the first year. Two years after its formation, it had nearly 10,000 members – nearly all women – who had paid their two pence membership and taken a pledge not to wear feathers. Donations rolled in. Etta lobbied the Press; she was the front-line campaigner, so successful that 60 newspapers and magazines ran stories about their work.

Eliza Phillips, publications editor of the SPB, produced pamphlets on the plumage trade. In the USA Harriet Hemenway wrote in a different vein, that the fashion for avian adornment was also killing women's chances of getting the vote.

In 1892, one year after the society's formation, Etta, now 31, married Frank Lemon. It was a good year for her. Men were welcomed into the society. Influential ornithologists became members and Professor Alfred Newton was the first man to become a Life Associate, with the donation of one guinea. Eliza Phillips was a vicar's widow; she knew how to lobby the Church of England. She targeted influential men, such as the Bishop of Durham, president of the Christian Social Union. Important politicians also became members. Artists and cartoonists set to work with their

Frank and Etta, outside their home, 'Hillcrest', Redhill Common.
Photograph: courtesy of the Lemon family, via Tessa Boase.

talents. George Frederic Watts, often considered the greatest artist of the time, made a large oil painting known as *The Shuddering Angel*. Lifeless plumage lay in a heap on a tombstone, over which an angel wept, head in hands. Exhibited at London's New Gallery, several years later, in 1899, it caused a sensation.

By the autumn of 1892, feathered fashions were on the wane and prices of bird skins plummeted. Alas! This was short-lived and the feather dealers must have foreseen this. One shipment to a London dealer apparently included 32,000 hummingbirds (could this be true?) and 800,000 pairs of wings. A massive number of collectors must have been employed and presumably once the wheels of this trade were turning, they could not be stopped overnight. By 1893 feathers were in vogue again.

The remarkable team of Etta and Eliza and the co-opting of men to their cause, was making the SPB noteworthy. However, the more emotional relationship that women had with birds, in feeding them and watching them, was seen as unscientific in some circles. In 1904 the SPB was granted a royal charter and became the RSPB.

Harriet 1896, Boston, Massachusetts, USA

While Etta's life in the 1880s and 1890s was totally devoted to her cause, Harriet's was typical of a woman of her era. She was rearing five children, all of whom survived to adulthood. Augustus was born in 1882, Charlotte in 1888, Hetty in 1890, Lawrence in 1891 and Mary in 1893.

In 1896, when her children were aged from 14 to three, she read an article describing the plume trade, written by William Hornaday. He was the Director of the New York Zoological Society and, before that, chief taxidermist at the Smithsonian Institute. Major targets of the plume hunters were Snowy and White Egrets, with their pure white plumage and delicate filigree head plumes which they wore in breeding plumage. Because egrets gather in big colonies, their nests clustered together in trees, they were sitting targets for the plume hunters. Hornaday wrote: 'It was a common thing for a rookery of several hundred birds to be attacked by the plume hunters, and in two or three days utterly destroyed.' Chicks were left to die of starvation.

In 1896 Etta Lemon already knew about the Massachusetts Audubon Society and had written to Harriet Hemenway to offer congratulation and support. The American ladies were promoting the 'Audubon hat' which was trimmed with ribbons and with feathers from non-protected birds.

Harriet and her cousin Minna Hall rallied more than 900 women to turn their backs on feathered fashion in support of helping bird populations. Since they did not have the right to vote, they lacked the political power to advance their cause. Hemenway's husband, shipping magnate Augustus Hemenway, was also passionate about preserving the environment. With his help, Hemenway and Hall rallied scientists and business people to their cause.

Hornaday had described London as 'the Mecca of the feather killers of the world'. His calculations reached the figure of nearly 130,000 egrets consumed by the London market alone in a nine-month period. That could have been an under-estimate. One 1902 record from a London auction house showed sales of 48,240 ounces of plumes, which would have required the feathers of nearly 200,000 egrets. But that was not all. Well before that, in 1886, it was estimated that 50 North American species were being slaughtered for their feathers (Sauder, 2013). An estimated 5 million to 15 million American birds were killed annually to supply the millinery trade, according to a US Fish and

Female Heroes of Bird Conservation

Harriet Lawrence Hemenway. Portrait of Harriet by John Singer Sargent, 1893.
Courtesy John Singer Sargent Virtual Gallery via Wikipedia Commons.

Wildlife Service website. Appalled at the volume and cruelty of these massacres, Harriet Hemenway was not going to wring her hands and do nothing. She would take action! A very determined woman, she was also very good looking, as testified in a portrait by the famous painter John Singer Sargent.

Enlisting the help of her cousin Minna Hall, the cousins consulted the *Blue Book*, a directory of Boston's elite, and launched a series of tea parties at which they urged their friends to stop wearing feathered hats. Why tea parties? In this era, 24 years before women had the right to vote, they were not permitted to rent meeting venues; they were absent from professional societies and universities.

The cousins sent out circulars, asking the women to join a society for the protection of birds, especially egrets. Incredibly, in this way 900 wealthy, high-profile women came together to boycott the wearing of feathers. It organised fund raisers and lecture tours on conservation and even audited the millinery industry.

By 1897, there were 111 local Audubon chapters in Massachusetts, 105 of them founded and led by women. To achieve so much within one year was extraordinary! The Massachusetts Audubon Society remained independent, but it helped to organise the National Association of Audubon Societies (incorporated in 1905), which later became the National Audubon Society.

Hemenway and Hall needed male support and leadership. It was men who operated the plumage trade, fashion industry, millinery trade magazines and feather warehouses. Most female consumers had no earning power and no voice. The two enterprising ladies targeted prominent ornithologists to join their cause. William Brewster, an eminent ornithologist, became their president.

Fortunately, the most influential man in the land, President Theodore Roosevelt, was not only a nature lover: he particularly liked birds. In the White House the family kept a Hyacinth Macaw, the largest and most spectacular parrot from South America. The President took an interest in the Audubon chapters. In 1903 he named Pelican Island the first Federal Bird Reservation in the USA. During the next few years he named nine more in Florida. This was the start of the National Wildlife Refuge System which today protects 3.4 million square km (850 million acres) of land and waters set aside for wildlife conservation.

Legislation 1900-1913

What was known as the 'bird-hat' campaign of the Audubon Society in Boston spread to Congress and influenced the passage of the Lacey Act in 1900. It prohibited transport across state lines of birds taken in violation of state laws. Unfortunately the law was poorly enforced and had little effect. The mindset at the time was illustrated by a shocking incident. In 1905 a warden called Guy Bradley was shot and killed in South Florida while attempting to arrest a plume hunter. Equally disturbing was the outcome: a jury acquitted the hunter.

Unfortunately, in 1911 egrets were still being slaughtered in their thousands. It was time for Congress to act more forcibly. In March 1913 a law to end the plume trade and interstate transport of birds was passed by Congress. A subsequent piece of legislation, known as the Migratory Bird Act, was upheld. The sale of migratory birds became illegal and commercial hunting of these species ended, effectively ending the plume trade by the end of World War I.

Did Harriet's life then resume the role of domesticity, concerned with her adult children and soon their own growing families? We do not know. Her time in the limelight was brief, compared with Etta's, but it was highly influential. She died in 1960 at the great age of 102.

Etta: Surrey and London 1911-1913

So what was Etta doing? She was the honorary secretary of the East Surrey Anti-Suffrage League, a women's association *against*, yes against, women getting the vote. By 1910 men were taking over the RSPB – by this time it had royal patronage. In the same year Etta was admitted to the British Ornithologists' Union – one of the first women members. In 1911 her husband, Frank Lemon, became mayor of the borough of Reigate (where the Lemons were then living) – at a time when a mayor held a powerful position. Etta then had to step down from her position as joint secretary of the Anti-Suffrage League, as the stance was too political for a mayor's wife. But she had plenty of other positions: local secretary for the RSPCA, head of Reigate's British Women's Temperance Society and head of the local Red Cross. Etta was in charge of the Redhill War Hospital. The *Surrey Mirror* reported that she was loved by the patients. In March 1920 she was awarded an MBE for her war work. In 1921 she became a JP (Justice of the Peace).

The campaign continues

In 1911, a beautiful actress on the London stage, Gabrielle Ray, starred in a production called *Peggy* at the Gaiety Theatre. She wore a huge hat, brimming over with feathers. *Millinery* trade magazine reported that feathers were still in vogue, partly because of the lower prices. The women of the RSPB needed a new tactic. They borrowed an idea from the suffragettes, parading the streets with sandwich boards. They hired ten men, who were dressed in strange sage-green clothes and carried a billboard above their heads, supported on iron shoulder clamps. The leading man's board announced 'The Story of the Egret'. The next man showed hat adornments made of egret feathers, captioned 'The badge of Cruelty'. He was followed by six men with boards showing the life cycle of the Snowy Egret, including corpses at the nesting sites and chicks starving to death. The same pictures were pasted up at one hundred London and suburban railway stations. It was hard to know what else they could do when the suffragettes were smashing shop windows and grabbing all the headlines. In March 1913, the Plumage Bill was put before the House of Lords for the second time. In June it was shelved again. Too much money was being made in the plumage trade. It continued on a massive scale. In that month the skins of 77,000 egrets, 25,000 humming birds and 162,000 kingfishers were auctioned in Mincing Lane, in the city of London (Boase, 2018). As egrets nest in large colonies and were the best known birds in the trade the figure is feasible. I suspect kingfisher was a generic name for small, brightly coloured birds. Even although there are about 90 kingfisher species worldwide, they nowhere occur in large numbers.

Legislation in the UK

It was not the steadfast commitment of the ladies of the RSPB who slowed down the feather trade, it was the First World War. The men who dyed the feathers and those who trapped native birds were away. Many never returned. Women were now dying feathers black for the hats of mourners. In February 1917 the War Office banned the importation of luxury items such as feathers, but only for the duration of the war.

In 1908 the Plumage Bill had been introduced to Parliament. It had got nowhere. Trade interests came before bird conservation. In 1919 the plumage trade was enjoying a post-war boom. Snowy Egrets and birds of paradise with extravagant and showy tail plumes, such as those of the Ribbon-tailed Bird of Paradise (*Astrapia mayeri*), now classified by IUCN as Near Threatened, were said to be in danger of extinction. Etta and her dedicated workers did not give up. They collected signatures from 150 people urging action, to hand to Prime Minister David Lloyd George. The list of signatories was impressive, including George Bernard Shaw, H. G. Wells, Sir

Arthur Conan Doyle and G. K. Chesterton. But it seemed that whatever they did was not enough. Then along came a young man called Harold Massingham, whose influential father was the editor of *The Nation,* a radical weekly newspaper. He founded the Plumage Bill Group to push the legislation through parliament. In July 1920 the editor wrote a column under his pseudonym condemning not the hunters but the women who so thoughtlessly bought the plumes. The column was read by the famous writer, Virginia Woolf. She responded with an article in the *Women's Leader*. 'The birds are killed by men. Starved by men, and tortured by men…'. The bill had been rejected in the House of Commons. Not by women, she wrote. Sixty six of the 67 members of the committee who scrutinised the bill were men. Her response resulted in a mass reaction, something that Etta and her group had never achieved.

But there was someone waiting to take up the cudgel. In December 1919 Nancy, Lady Astor, a wealthy socialite, became the first woman to take a seat in the House of Commons. She started to investigate why the Importation of Plumage (Prohibition) Bill had been blocked so many times. Due to her influence it became law on July 1 1921. But Etta was not happy. It was illegal to *import* feathers – but not to sell them and wear them.

The Americans controlled the trade more quickly. The Audubon Society urged people to boycott feathered hats and garments. They suggested that women should wear bird friendly hats like the 'audubonnets' decorated with ribbons, fabrics and feather-free ornaments. In Britain, where very many voices were speaking out against the trade, it had taken 30 years for the battle to be won. Britain should be so ashamed of this history. British India had forbidden the export of plumage in 1902, Australia in 1912 and even Indonesia (then the Dutch East Indies) in 1913.

Etta's later years

Some RSPB members believed that by 1930 Etta had become too dictatorial. Frank Lemon died in April 1935. When Linda Gardiner, RSPB secretary, gave up her position after 35 years with the organisation that Etta had founded, all her fellow founders had gone. Etta felt it had changed beyond recognition. An internal investigation committee was formed to scrutinise the running of the society and the position of Honorary Secretary was abolished. In 1939 Etta was out.

She died in a nursing home in 1953, aged 92. She will be remembered for her goal to stop the feather trade which happened thirty years after she started her campaign. Ultimately it would have happened anyway. Times had changed. Ironically she received an MBE for her war work, as did so many other people. Perhaps she should have received it for her relentless crusade to give birds a better chance of survival. Not only did she found the RSPB but she led the way as a protector of the Red Kite (*Milvus milvus*) and other species in the UK that suffered at the hands of egg collectors. She founded a nation-wide system, the Watchers' Committee, in which she and other bird lovers protected birds on the ground, in their localities. She was a remarkably compassionate, persistent and determined champion of birds from her teenage years and for nearly six decades thereafter. How many people can say that?

Emily Williamson

Emily had been a prime mover in the founding of the RSPB, yet her part in this story is seldom emphasised. But the people of Manchester had not forgotten her. To celebrate the centenary of the passing of the Plumage bill, on July 1 2021 plans to erect a statue to Emily were revealed. The monument will stand in Didsbury's Fletcher Moss Park – the garden of her former home. In fact, all three of the campaigning women who endured the long fight for justice for birds, must be revered and remembered by everyone who values the natural world.

References

Boase, T., 2018, *Mrs Pankhurst's Purple Feather,* Arum Press.
Sauder, W., 2013, How two women ended the deadly feather trade, *Smithsonian Magazine,* March.

Also refer to new edition

Boase, T., 2021, *Etta Lemon – The Woman Who Saved the Birds* – Arum Press.

5. Emma Turner
1867-1940
Photographer, Author and Passionate Bird Observer

In this digital age, you need only two assets to produce good photographs of birds: patience and enough money to buy a good quality camera or an iPhone. However, even today men predominate in bird photography, yet few people are aware that Britain's most ground-breaking bird photographer was a woman.

Her name was Emma Turner. She was born at Langton Green, near Tunbridge Wells in Kent, on June 9 1867, the youngest of four children. Her father ran a grocery and drapery store. It was almost certainly a thriving business, as the family had a servant and a governess. Emma's mother died when she was 13 – a difficult age for a girl to lose her mother. Perhaps it was then that she became a weekly pupil at a boarding school. It seems that nothing else has been recorded about her childhood, and her life as a young woman was taken over by family commitments. When she was 24, her older sister died. As so often happened in that era, a daughter was expected to care for an ailing parent or family members in need and the opportunity to marry was lost.

In 1900, aged 33, she 'felt the need of an outdoor occupation', and she took up photography. By a huge stroke of luck, she met Richard Kearton, the pioneering wildlife photographer. He inspired her to start taking photos of birds, even though she knew little about them. She must have been very enthusiastic about her new hobby, as she joined the Royal Photographic Society in 1901. She marked up a lot of 'firsts' during her career and when, in 1904, she gave a presentation to the Amateur Photographic Association it was the first time a lecture had been delivered by a woman. In reviewing the technical and scientific category of the 1908 Royal Photographic Society show, *The Times* reported: 'Miss E. L. Turner had some excellent bird photographs in this section.'

She was already lecturing on birds, using an agency to secure speaking engagements. A leaflet listed her subjects, complete with Press notices and testimonials. However, her health was not good at times and in 1907 she suffered a long period of illness. Her activities were also limited because, as she wrote in 1912, she was unable to be away from home for long. Her father had been ill enough to need a full-time nurse since at least 1907. He died in 1913. Emma

Emma Turner.
Emma Turner Archive at the British Trust for Ornithology; unknown photographer.

was also involved in the care of her brother Frank's children, after his wife died. But domestic duties and bouts of ill health did not stop her photography trips or writing magazine articles about birds. These included 57 articles for the prestigious *Country Life,* spanning the period 1906 to 1934, and for *The Times* newspaper, mainly from 1925 to 1927.

Emma left a lot of letters and they are very revealing. She was self-deprecating and amusing. She once described how she fell into a dyke when alone. Totally covered in mud, she staggered to a nearby house and persuaded the people there to give her some clothes! A true bird lover, her letters were full of references to her observations of Blackbirds, Robins and Blue Tits – 'something that set her apart from some renowned bird photographers of the time' (Parry and Greenwood, 2020).

Emma's field work

In an article in *Bird Lore* in 1915 she declared: 'Patience and a thick skin are the two essential qualifications for successful bird-photography.' By a thick skin she did not mean being impervious to critical remarks but being dressed for the weather. She warned against wearing tweeds because they soaked up moisture. Working in damp places – including actually within reed beds – is not easy and, in an age when a woman had to maintain a certain decorum in her style of dress, it was even harder. Her field clothes included a knee-length coat with big pockets to take large photographic slides. One photograph with her trusted friend Alfred Nudd, with whom she spent hours in the field, shows Emma wearing a hat that would have looked more at home at a garden party than among the reeds! The photo, which was reproduced in *Emma Turner, A life looking at birds,* was perhaps staged, as she is looking into a stereoscope pointed at the reeds. Today, when many women spend more time in trousers than in skirts, it might not be realised that even in the 1950s it was unusual to see a woman in trousers and was definitely not permitted for girls in school.

While within the reeds she was accompanied by Jim Vincent, a local gamekeeper and highly respected field ornithologist. Emma credited him with much of her success, for his 'ungrudging and faithful service'. He attracted widespread admiration for making Hickling Broad a reserve. His system of flooding, draining, and grazing and cutting of the reeds, made it into a sanctuary that today is still famed for its bird life. Now an expanded (from Emma's time) 600ha (1,500 acre) reserve, it is situated 4km (two and a half miles) southeast of Stalham, north of Norwich. Part of the Broadland Ramsar[2] site, it is the broad (a river that expands to cover low-lying ground) with the largest reed bed in England, and the largest water surface in the Norfolk Broads. Cranes are among the rare species to be found there today.

Emma had made close friends with several men on the Broads, especially the gamekeeper Alfred Nudd. A younger member of that family, Cubit Nudd, was her 'most faithful henchman, and a past-master in the art of sailing.' Jim Vincent, who also grew up among the marshes of Hickling Fen, was an excellent field ornithologist. These three men were skilled observers of birds and proved invaluable to her, in punting her through the watery landscape, finding nests of rare birds and helping her to make hides. To negotiate the Broads, she used a dinghy, a canoe and a rowing boat.

Emma had a flat-bottomed houseboat made for her in 1905, which was moored at Hickling Broad. At times the boat was very damp and so cold that she might awake in the morning to find the glass of milk at her bedside frozen! Eventually she built a small hut next to it, which served as a photographic dark room and as a spare bedroom. Friends often came to stay, despite the Spartan conditions and the lack of fresh water. At Hickling Emma was always accompanied by her dogs and other non-human companions. One year these included her pet squirrel Togo, two young Short-eared Owls, also a parrot called Lady Jane, who called to Emma's friends and animals in a refined and ladylike voice.

In 1909 Emma was involved in the two earliest bird-ringing schemes in Britain. In that year she and Jim Vincent were surprised to find a nest of Stone Curlews (*Burhinus oedicnemus*). This is an unusual and rare summer visitor to southern England, with long yellow legs, a large head with large eyes (active at night) and relatively long wings and tail. When the two eggs hatched, she returned to photograph and ring the chicks. Emma apparently took the first images ever recorded of a Nightingale and of a Waxwing.

An extraordinary story is attached to the exciting discovery, made with Jim Vincent, of a young Bittern (*Botaurus stellaris*) in 1911. There had been no

---

[2] A wetland site designated to be of international importance under the Ramsar Convention (Convention on Wetlands), an intergovernmental environmental treaty established in 1971 by UNESCO, which came into force in 1975.

Emma found the nest of a Stone Curlew, a rare summer visitor to Britain. Photograph: author.

confirmed record of this species (a small heron) nesting in Britain since 1886. You can imagine their euphoria! Sunset was approaching; the light was too poor for photography and they feared no one would believe them. Emma had 'worked herself up to a high pitch of enthusiasm at the thought of fulfilling one ornithological dream of a lifetime'. However, her

> 'first impulse on seeing this dream in the flesh was to collapse into the reeds and laugh. The young Bittern was the quaintest little ornithological oddity I had ever seen; he looked more like a small animated golliwog than anything else. A halo of light tan-coloured down stuck out all around his head, and his big greenish-blue eyes glared defiance… He would crouch down and then suddenly shoot up to his full height; or throwing himself on his back, would kick at us with his splay feet, which seemed several sizes too large for him' (Turner, 1924).

Readers will be dismayed to learn what they did next – it would be illegal today, when it is forbidden to disturb nesting birds. They removed the young Bittern and took it to the laboratory of Jim's employer. Very early next morning they cycled back to retrieve the captive bird and to return it to the site where it had been found. The resulting photographs have been described as 'among the most evocative ever taken of the species.' This was a landmark in Emma's career. She went on to study the Bittern, which, is extremely difficult to observe, and wrote articles on its behaviour and ecology in the journal *British Birds*. The Bittern had been ruthlessly persecuted. Fen shooters would kill from 20 to 30 individuals in one morning. Fortunately its numbers have gradually increased; it is still rare but has a UK population of more than 200.

She always wanted to be close to her subjects. Sometimes she would be hidden under a pile of marsh litter that had been piled on top of her. Inexplicably she insisted she was not a patient person and yet: 'Only those who have experienced this method of photography know the pain it entailed. Lying prone for three or four hours produces intolerable sensations in one's back and arms. After an hour or so these nervous twitchings cease, and a kind of numbness sets in.'

She was so well camouflaged that once she had a Cuckoo sitting on her head and when photographing a Reeve on its nest, a Snipe frequently settled on her shoulder and gently prodded her cheek! For her, getting to know her subjects was essential. To do this she often rose at 3am, and either cycled to her location or went by boat. But the time she could spend photographing birds was limited, either on a daily basis (between cooking and housework) and for periods on the Broads, probably due to her father's ill health.

She would not have approved of today's bird photographers whose long lenses enable them to get a shot from a great distance, perhaps after only a few seconds of observation. Then they move on to the next species. In contrast, Emma made many repeat visits to nests, often in very challenging locations, in order to photograph the young at every stage of their development. It was not only the Broadland rarities that interested her.

Emma's writings about individual birds indicated how closely she observed them. Of Short-eared Owls (*Asio flammeus*) she wrote: 'As they hang in

A scan from the negative plate of a young Bittern photographed by Emma Turner in the Norfolk Broads.
Emma Turner Archive at the British Trust for Ornithology.

mid-air with outstretched wings, measuring twenty-four inches from tip to tip, they expand each flight and tail feather, so that the sunlight and blue sky filtering through the soft vane give an added charm to their magnificent pose.'

On occasions she hand-reared young that had lost their nests or their parents, including this owl species. The owlets … 'were far more intelligent than any birds I have ever kept, not excepting members of the Crow family.' She could relate many instances of their sense of humour. The owls shared an aviary with two young Kestrels, one of which was sunning itself on a board, with one wing stretched out so that it overhung the board. One of the owls approached the sleeping Kestrel and gave its wing a sharp tweak. The startled hawk awoke screaming; the owl was standing motionless, with his face turned skywards, looking the picture of innocence. Emma went into the aviary and admonished the owl. He flew on to her shoulder and rubbed his beak against her cheek (Turner, 1924).

Emma the writer

This indefatigable lady had first visited the Norfolk Broads in 1901 or 1902. They cast a spell over her. She wrote:

'Outwardly their charm consists in the limitless horizon, ever-shifting clouds, and brilliantly starry nights, when you seem to stand midway between two Heavens, as every constellation is faithfully reflected in the motionless water at your feet. If to these glories is added their rich and varied wild life, much has been said to account for the fascination of these marshes; but, besides all this there is something mysterious, indefinable, magnetic.'

Few writers have ever captured the appeal of the Norfolk Broads in such an eloquent and evocative manner! In her love of birds she found the perfect outlet for this rare skill. She left a legacy in books (eight in all) and articles which distinguish her in equal measure to that of being a celebrated photographer. She did not care that anthropomorphism was unpopular. She wrote of: '…these shy beautiful wild things, whose emotions and actions are so akin to our own … Who is to judge the intellectual capacity of wild things?'

I admire her for those words which, coming from anyone else, would have evoked ridicule. It took decades for them to be accepted, confirmed by Gisela Kaplan in *Bird Minds* (2015); and by Judy Bond and Alan Diamond in *Thinking like a Parrot* (2019).

Her close and thoughtful observations of bird behaviour are very moving to those who love birds. In *Broadland Birds* she described the grief of a female Snow Bunting (*Plectrophenax nivalis*) when she witnessed her mate taken by a Merlin. 'She left the flock immediately the cock was attacked and flew up and down the sand-hills, uttering wild cries of distress. She continued to do this long after the tragic fate of the male was sealed. I lost sight of her after an hour, but later on, when returning by the eastern shore, I again saw her hunting to and fro all along the shore, and heard her continuous wailing. For two days the eastern and northern shores were haunted by a restless wailing hen Snow Bunting' (Turner, 1924).

New locations, new species

Had she travelled elsewhere? Yes, she visited the Outer Hebrides in 1913 and Scotland in 1914. She was able to visit the Duchess of Bedford in her country estate in Perthshire. The Duchess was not only an ornithologist, she ran the Woburn Boys' Ornithological Club – though it seems regrettable that she had not taken the opportunity to promote birdwatching as an interest for girls also. The Duchess and Emma had shared interests in conservation and in educating young people about the value of birds. Emma designed her 1925 publication *A Book about Birds* specifically for 'Scouts, Guides and Others'. She was way ahead of her time in this publication when she wrote: 'Too late, we in England have set apart small Nature reserves where birds are protected. Other countries, such as Holland and the United States, have learnt wisdom from our want of care, and are reserving large tracts of country…' Nearly one century after penning those words, we know that the potential to protect birds in *small* nature reserves is limited.

The war intervened and Emma's life changed: she became a cook in a Voluntary Aid Detachment hospital in Kent. Her first overseas trip in 1920 took her to the Dutch island of Texel, renowned for its migrating birds. A highlight was finding a nest with chicks of a Golden Oriole (*Oriolus oriolus*). She thought that from a photographic viewpoint they were a failure; without colour they looked like Starlings – but her cup was 'running over with joy at the sight of them and the sound of their song.'

In 1922 she went to Italy via Folkestone – but on the way she complained that she was charged for 180 cigarettes when she only had 100! She participated in an art and architecture tour with friends. In 1929 she was a speaker at the International Ornithological Congress in Amsterdam. Several years later, probably 1933, she took a three-week cruise to Spain, Sicily, Greece, Yugoslavia, Malta and Morocco and recorded 159 bird species, of which 52 were new to her.

In 1924 a new opportunity and adventure occurred – because no one else wanted the job. The remote sand and shingle island at Norfolk's Scolt Head had been purchased by the National Trust in 1923. It was the site of important nesting colonies of terns, Oystercatchers and Ringed Plovers. Unfortunately, it also attracted casual visitors and local people collecting eggs for food. A warden was needed during the breeding season. Emma was then 57 and the job was tough and demanding – but she volunteered. The accommodation was little more than a hut; it lacked water and electricity and, at first, boasted only an open fire for cooking. Her duties began on April Fool's Day 1924 – the irony of the date was not lost on her!

Her domain covered 480ha (1,200 acres), including mud flats, salt marshes and low scrub. As many as 2,000 terns nested there – Common, Little, Roseate and Sandwich Terns. Emma became very interested in their behaviour and courtship.

In 1923 there were only 17 pairs of Common Terns; under her guardianship this rose to 303 nests in 1924 and to a remarkable 800 in the following year. This was a testament to what can be achieved when human predators are eliminated! She was captivated by the terns' elegance, especially when they suddenly rose *en masse*. Then, as she recorded in 1928 in *Bird Watching on Scolt Head*: '… nothing could detract from the beauty of the birds as they rose in a great white cloud or descended like drifting snow.'

On Scolt, with the opportunity to study bird immigration, Emma was privileged to observe numbers which surely will never be seen again. In the autumn of 1925 she recorded that 'dense columns of finches over a mile in length flew over the island.' Other visitors were less welcome. These were members of the Press who dramatised her life in magazines and newspapers as self-imposed loneliness on a desolate piece of land, without any relief except reading or sewing! In fact she often had friends there and even when she had only her animals for company she was too busy to be lonely.

After 1925 she visited Norfolk less frequently; she still lived in Kent but her final home was in Cambridge. It appears that she gave up photography in the early 1930s. In 1936 she visited Norfolk for the last time. Her sight was failing by 1938 and she was very unhappy when a cataract operation failed. She died, aged 71, on August 13 1940, during the Second World War. This unfortunately meant that the scarcity of paper prevented her books from being reprinted. Today they are so rare that when I looked for *Broadland Birds* on the internet I found only one original copy; the price was £450 so I settled on a facsimile for £30!

My admiration for Emma Turner is enormous. She was a woman in a man's world, even though, at 33, she was late to come to birds and to photography. She gained recognition for her skill and knowledge with a speed that has seldom, if ever, been equalled in her fields. Not only an ornithological author, she wrote beautiful prose. She worked for two breeding seasons as a warden on Scolt Head in conditions which were so difficult that when she was succeeded by a man, he lived on the mainland. But above all she loved birds – truly loved them. During the last 38 years of her life she built up an ornithological legacy that deserves to be better known and revered. And today's bird photographers, good as some are, merely touch a button to expose a frame. Emma had a cumbersome camera, focused her shot, removed the focusing screen, inserted a large photographic plate, exposed it, withdrew the plate and replaced the focusing screen. For just one frame! And she specialised in wet and hard-to-reach locations. Yes, Emma Turner was a true heroine!

References

Parry, J. and J. Greenwood, 2020, *Emma Turner, A life looking at birds,* Norfolk and Norwich Naturalists Society.

Turner, E. L., 1924, *Broadland Birds,* Country Life, Ltd, London.

6. Emílie Snethlage
Germany/Brazil 1868-1929
World-renowned Ornithologist and Explorer

Emílie Snethlage is a legend in Brazilian ornithology. She was born on April 13 1868 in the province of Brandenburg, north of Berlin, then part of Prussia. Christened Henriette Mathilde Maria Elizabeth Emílie Snethlage, later she was often known as Emília. The daughter of a Lutheran pastor, Emil Snethlage, and his wife Elizabeth, the family must have had a difficult time when Elizabeth died when Emílie was only four years old. She and her three brothers were reared and educated by her father. Growing up in a masculine household might have given her the confidence that she was equal to any man – and, as she was to prove so decisively, superior to many.

Even as a child she loved birds and, as a portent of what was to come, when she was very young her bird notes were published in the *Journal für Ornithologie* (Cunha, 1985). To be published at an early age was extraordinary and indicated a future direction in her life. She liked to read about travels in tropical countries – but it would be a couple of decades before she lived this dream. It would become her *raison d'etre*.

In 1889 Emílie started to teach at a secondary school for girls, and between 1889 and 1890 she spent a year in Switzerland, learning French. During the next ten years she worked as a governess or private teacher (as was common for women of her background in that era) in England, Ireland and Germany.

Thus far her life was unremarkable. Fortunately, in 1899 she received a small inheritance which enabled her to realise her childhood ambition to study natural history at the University of Berlin, and later in Freiburg and Jena. This was very timely. In Germany, the University of Freiburg was the first to officially accept women, beginning in the 1899/1900 semester. As one of the first women to attend university, she had faced very restrictive conditions. Female students had to arrive 15 minutes before the lecture started and to assemble behind a screen (Junglans, unpublished). They were not allowed to speak during the class. These restrictions can only be described as unacceptable insults. The first women received their doctorates in Freiburg in 1901 and in Jena in 1904, the year of Emílie's doctorate. Her thesis was on the musculature of arthropods.

Her life's work commences

She returned to Berlin in 1904 as a zoological assistant at the natural history museum. The dean was the renowned German ornithologist Anton Reichenow. Through him she learned about the position for a zoological professional at the museum in Belém, Pará. In 1905 she moved alone to Brazil to become the Curator of the Bird Collection at the Museu Paraense which was founded in 1866. By 1914 she was head of zoology and acting director. The museum contained zoological, ethnological and botanical collections, also zoological and botanical gardens.

This was a period of economic strength for Belém, the capital of the state of Pará, allowing investments in education and infrastructure. It was a modern, thriving city of 100,000 inhabitants and the port was a gateway for all commercial and transport movements in the Amazon and over a much larger area. The state of Pará has been described as a pioneer in Brazil and South America in opening the doors for women to enter higher education and public service activities.

Emílie Snethlage in 1906.
Photograph: Wikipedia Commons.

Women outside the museum in 1900.
Photograph: Museu Goeldi.

Emília (the Portuguese spelling) had arrived in Belém in August 1905, aged 37. She immediately started to study the avifauna of the Amazon region. In October she visited Santo Antônio do Prata, to which she returned many times. Her first article about Brazilian birds was published in Berlin in 1906 in the German journal *Ornitologische Monatsberichte* (Monthly Ornithological Report). It was simply entitled Über brasilianische Vögel (About Brazilian Birds). This was the start of a career in which she made an enormous contribution to ornithology which must never be forgotten.

The work for which Emília is best known, *Catálogo das aves amazônicas,* was published in 1914. It combined the information collated by the Swiss zoologists Emil Goeldi (who started to reorganise the Pará museum in 1894) and Gottfried Hagmann, from the material in the Museu Paraense and other museums, and her own work in taxonomy, biology and biogeography. Her descriptions and taxonomic assessments formed the base for ornithological studies for more than 70 years. It was an extraordinary accomplishment, an important source of reference. When Helmut Sick published *Birds in Brazil* in 1993 he dedicated it to 'Dr Emilie Snethlage, pioneer of field research on birds in Brazil.' Sick considered the Catalogue to be the 'ground zero' of Brazilian ornithology.

We must not forget that the strong and active participation of a woman in the world of science, especially in the Neotropics, was extremely rare. However, at first Emílie disguised her gender by publishing and writing letters in the name of 'E. Snethlage'. Sometimes she even referred to herself in the masculine, a strategy which apparently was used by other female scientists of the same period. Emílie contributed many articles to prestigious German journals, such as *Journal für Ornithologie* and the *Ornithologische Monatsberichte,* and was also published in Portuguese.

The intrepid explorer

Obviously fieldwork is important for any ornithologist but at that time women rarely worked in the field. However, Emília was a notable exception and she embarked upon an intensive programme of fieldwork. The most important were the journeys made between the Xingu and Tapajos rivers in 1909, accompanied by Indians. The region had not previously been explored by white men because of the many difficulties in working there – yet Emília conquered it! Field expeditions were hard enough for men but as a woman she endured lack of privacy, bad accommodation and inferior shotguns. She alone had to prepare all the material she collected. And all this while learning Portuguese and Indian languages!

The French explorer Henri Coudreau had suggested that there could be communication between the Xingu and Tapajos tributaries of the Amazon. A supposed connection, even if it was temporary and existed only during the winter, the time of the floods, would facilitate the settlement and economic exploitation of the region. However, when Emília started the crossing, she was already aware of the absence of this supposed connection. The unexpected was to find, during the terrestrial part of the trip, a granite mountain range of approximately 500m (1,640ft) high, which had to be crossed. She was totally unprepared for this from the aspect of equipment.

The result of the expedition was to trace the course of the Jamanxim River, one of the tributaries of the right bank of the Tapajos, which corrected the 'scarce and not always accurate' information left by Coudreau. His route descriptions are full of ethnographic details. Based on his research and notes, Emília was able to publish, in 1912, a comparative vocabulary of Chipaya and Curuahé Indians, demonstrating another aspect of her lively mind.

When in the field the museum's scientists received special support from the owners of farms and rubber plantations. They provided shelter and transport, and contact with Indian guides. These friendly relationships included the acceptance of Emília's presence as a scientist, and increased her reputation. In a book by Raimundo de Morais about the region, she was called the 'German of the Museum who knows everything'.

Helmut Sick, who became Curator of Birds at the National Museum in Rio, recorded: 'She sought out the most inhospitable areas of Amazonia because they were precisely the most promising in poorly known species… In those times it was an extremely arduous task for a woman to penetrate the farthest reaches of Amazonia. Emílie Snethlage almost always travelled without any other assistants than horse wranglers and paddlers. She inspired the respect of the natives by her kindly but energetic personality and by her long, thick hair, which gave her a dignity equal to that of a cacique.' The word cacique means either a native Indian chief – its use here – or a family of delightful large Neotropical birds which enchant with their colours, displays and bubbling vocalisations.

Her work load was prodigious. Pursuing her interests in ornithological

Emília.
Location and Photographer unknown.

research, she travelled to areas never previously explored, facing extreme challenges in her fieldwork. This courageous and self-reliant woman amputated her infected finger when a piranha had eaten the tip. After contracting malaria, she walked for miles in inhospitable forest, shaking with fever.

Emília described sixty new bird species and subspecies (Sick, 1993), such as one from the interior of Brazil. The great ornithologist Dr E. Stresemann dedicated a genus of flycatchers to her (*Snethlagea*). She published more than 40 scientific articles (listed in Junghans, 2009). Those published in the *Bulletin of the National Museum of Rio de Janei-*

ro included articles on the avifauna of Maranhão (1924); Observations on rare or little-known birds in Brasil (1927); new species and sub-species of birds of Central Brasil (1928) and Catalogue of birds in the National Museum (1936). In 1917 the *Geographic Review* of New York published her 'Nature and man in Eastern Pará, Brasil.' Many of her papers appeared in German publications, most of them describing new Brazilian bird species. She had collected thousands of specimens.

The greatest satisfaction she had was in receiving a letter addressed 'To Dr. Emilio Snethlage'. It convinced her that she had done a man's job. However, she did not want to present a masculine appearance and she wore long trousers only when she went into the field. Photographs from that era show an attractive woman dressed in the long-skirted fashions of the time. She kept her hair long.

In 1907 Emilio Goeldi resigned from the Pará Museum and returned to his native Switzerland. In his place came the botanist Jacques Huber, and Emília became the director of the Zoology Section. Huber's unexpected death in 1914 gave her even more status. However, the social and economic situation in the Amazon was to change profoundly. Pará was entering the great depression that would extend until 1930. It hit the institution hard. Nearly all scientists of Germanic origin had left as the politics between Brazil and Germany became difficult during the First World War. In March 1918 she was asked to leave the museum in Pará. According to Junghans (2009), 'Dr. Emília Snethlage was displaced, as a lonely and foreign woman, in a social and institutional space that was hostile'. Helmut Sick wrote that she left when the state of Pará was insolvent due to the collapse of the rubber boom. However she returned to work there between 1919 and 1921.

In December 1921 she sent an important collection of 1,050 specimens of birds and 110 mammals to the National Museum of Rio de Janeiro, with the consent of the new director of the Museo Paraense and the government of Pará. This enriched the collections of Amazon material in Rio, which had been poor (Alberto and Sanjad, 2019).

In January 1922 Emília requested six months leave for her own research purposes. She accepted the proposal of the director of the National Museum for the post of travelling naturalist, for six months from July 1. Covering huge areas, she made numerous scientific trips through the states of Maranhão, Espírito Santo, Minas Gerais, Bahia, and from Paraná to Rio Grande do Sul, in addition to a long stretch of the Araguaia River in central Brazil. She also worked in the field in Argentina and Uruguay. In 1929, at the age of 61, she decided to cross the Madeira River, the only one of the great tributaries to the south of the Amazon that she had not properly explored. She also intended to study the avifauna of Brazil's borders with Colombia and Peru.

The letter she wrote to a female relative near the start of the journey described the hotel in Porto Velho in which she stayed, which was built just before the collapse of the rubber industry. The facilities were grand, the rooms were large and ventilated, and surrounded by wide balconies. The plumbing and electricity were good, ice was available and breakfast and multi-course meals were provided – at a high price. She described the location as '… a nice Brazilian village, mirrored in the electric lighting of its streets shining brightly … the wide and majestic river at the foot of the rapids, have a very pleasant appearance, especially seen from where I am now.'

There was a farm in front of her, on the other bank of the river. She was happy because she had met a lady from England, a butterfly specialist, with whom she greatly enjoyed spending two and a half days. So rarely did she encounter another female scientist – and they sat and smoked together! (Translated in Junghans, 2009, and elsewhere.)

What was she like?

A lot has been written about Emília's achievements but I could find nothing more about her personality except Raimundo Morais's words: 'Within a few hours she conquered our friendship' (in *Os Igaraunas,* 1938). And what of her personal life? Perhaps she was married to science and had no time or opportunity for relationships.

It was evident from her work that she lived a simple and uncluttered life style, probably without the company of fellow scientists for long periods. Her joy was in Nature. The personal details are lacking but a letter she wrote approximately three weeks before she died indicates a contentment in the pleasures of this simple life, an appreciation of the help of others and overall a very positive attitude.

She had been planning to return to Germany and to write an extensive work on the birds of Brazil (Sick, 1993). Her plans were never fulfilled. Emília died alone in the hotel in Porto Velho, on November 25, 1929. She had struggled against malaria since 1909 and died of a heart attack.

Her death was a huge loss to ornithology. There was so much more she wanted to do and to publish. Perhaps to this very day, no woman in natural sciences has achieved so much in the field, in taxonomy and in published works, as the remarkable Emília. In 1926 she had been invited to join the Brazilian Academy of Sciences. She had become the first female director of a scientific institution in South America.

Inexplicably, unlike other scientists and civil servants who contributed to the importance of Brazilian science, she did not have an official tribute in the park of the Museu Paraense Emílio Goeldi. Then the building that currently houses the Board of the museum was named Pavilhão Emília Snethlage. A bust in her honour was displayed at the Menorial Rondon, on the banks of the Madeira River, in Porto Velho. It was installed at the behest of the writer Júlio

Olivar, then president of the Rondoniense Academy of Letters. These were small tributes to a woman who surely deserved so much more.

But her work lives on. Prof. Luís Fábio Silveira is the Scientific Director and Curator of Birds of the Zoological Museum of the University of São Paulo. He reveres her to the point that he searched – unsuccessfully – for her grave when he was in Porto Velho. He told me:

> 'The work of collecting specimens is of paramount importance not only for increasing the knowledge about taxonomy and the biodiversity of the planet, but these samples serve as a testimony of the presence of organisms in a certain time and space. Today, these old specimens can be viewed like messengers from the past, and they tell us about a world that, in many cases, vanished. Among the many scientific contributions of Emília Snethlage, her collections of birds in many of the biomes of Brazil stand out as among the most important. Due to the criminal acceleration of deforestation in the last decades, especially in the Amazon, we know about the distribution of some species only because this brave woman, facing enormous difficulties, had the stamina to penetrate the deep forest to unravel its secrets. The Amazon is a hard place to work even today, with modern medicine, gasoline, motorboats, GPS, good food, and accommodations. We can barely imagine the challenges that Emília faced, and this increases the value of her work and her dedication to science.'

References

Alberto, D. and N. Sanjad., 2019, Emília Snethlage (1868-1929) and the reasons for celebrating her 150th birthday. *Bulletin of the Museu Paraense Emílio Goeldi.* Human Sciences, Belém, v.14, n.3, p.1047-1070, Sept.-Dec. http://doi.org/10.1590/1981.81222019000300018.

Catalog of Amazonian birds, containing all species described and mentioned until 1913. *Bulletin of the Paraense Museum of Natural History and Ethnography,* Belém, v.8, p.1-530. 1914.

Cunha, O. R. da, 1985, Maria Emília Snethlage (1868-1929) – the first female scientist in the Amazon, *Jornal O Liberal,* Belém, 15 nov., News section.

Junghans, M. E., 2009, A trajetória científica da naturalista Alemã Emília Snethlage (1868-1929) no brasil, unpublished Dissertation, Oswaldo Cruz Foundation, Casa de Oswaldo Cruz, Rio de Janeiro.

Sick, H., 1993, *Birds in Brazil,* Princeton University Press, New Jersey.

7. Magdalena Heinroth
née Wiebe Germany 1882-1932
Researcher, Author and Photographer: recorded development of young of 1,000 European Birds

Magdalena Wiebe was born in Berlin on April 22 1882. She was the second daughter of Adolf Wiebe, a construction director from a respected Prussian family, and his wife Helene. From an early age Magdalena's love of animals and plants was apparent. She frequently visited Berlin Zoo, in which her father was a shareholder. Unusually, a natural history teacher showed her how to skin animals and prepare skeletons. As a child she collected small bones and made a little museum. To sharpen her powers of observation, she received special drawing lessons; as a teenager she already had the skills for her future endeavours.

Magdalena left school at 16, in 1898, as the best senior high school student but she did not go on to graduate classes. Her father indulged her ambitions by taking her to the director of the natural history museum for advice on her career. Soon she was employed there under the direction of an excellent taxidermist.

Oskar Heinroth was working there as a volunteer. Heinroth was born in Germany in 1871. In 1895 he obtained his medical doctorate, following the wishes of his father – but he had other ideas. He began to study zoology in Berlin, working simultaneously in the Natural History Museum and the Zoological Gardens. Delightful carvings from this era could still be seen in the bird house a century later.

In 1900 Oskar left the museum for one and a half years to serve as a zoologist and medic to an expedition organised by Bruno Mencke to the Bismarck Archipelago. This is a group of volcanic islands in the Pacific, which form part of New Guinea. In that era it was a dangerous place for researchers and the expedition ended tragically when Mencke was killed by native people. Oskar escaped with a spear wound and ornithology can be very grateful for that…

He returned in 1901 and he and Magdalena became engaged in 1902. Apparently his engagement present to her was not a ring but a Blackcap Warbler (*Sylvia atricapilla*)! In 1904 Oskar became assistant director at the zoo and he and Magdalena were married. It was then that Magdalena's passion for rearing birds developed. Their birdroom was full of Redstarts (*Phoenicurus phoenicurus*), warblers (even Goldcrests,

57

Carving of a hornbill in the bird house at Berlin Zoo.
Photograph: author.

Hand-rearing European birds

Magdalena's goal was extraordinarily ambitious: to rear every bird species native to Germany! She knew that it was impossible to obtain all the details she wanted about the lives of wild birds. Observation of captive birds would provide many of the answers to her questions. The list of species being hand-reared at one time almost defies belief, not only for the intensity of the work involved over a period of months, but because many of the species would even today be considered difficult to rear.

In July 1927, Oskar wrote to his mother:

'Our present bird business is almost too much of a good thing; two Eurasian Bitterns (*Botaurus stellaris*), one Bustard (*Otis tarda*), one White-tailed Eagle (*Haliaeetus albicilla*), three Purple Herons (*Ardea purpurea*), five Gull-billed Terns (*Gelochelidon nilotica*), one Kentish Plover (*Charadrius alexandrines*), four Avocets (*Recurvirostra avocetta*), two Ruffs (*Philomachus pugnax*), two Ospreys (*Pandion haliaetus*), two Grey-headed Woodpeckers (*Picus canus*), two Quails (*Coturnix coturnix*), one Barred Warbler (*Sylvia nisoria*), four Spoonbills (*Platalea leucorodia*). That's enough! … It is a great deal of work for my wife; all these fish-eaters make it very difficult to keep the place clean'

Regulus regulus), Dippers (*Cinclus cinclus*), Tree Creepers (*Certhia familiaris*) and tits. More unusual species resided elsewhere. They were not easy subjects to keep in captivity.

Imagine the scene! 'In a rented apartment in the centre of Berlin, a Black Grouse male is displaying on the balcony; in the dining room a Goshawk is eating a Pheasant, and in the sitting room a pair of European Nightjars is rearing their second brood of the year'. A photograph taken in 1909 shows Nightjars (*Caprimulgas europaeus*) on a peccary rug in the Heinroths' sitting room. There were two fully grown young. The female was incubating her second clutch under a kitchen sieve, and the male was sitting on top of the sieve! Such was everyday life in the Heinroth household! (Schulze-Hagen and Birkhead, 2014).

(unpublished: Heinroth, Staatsbibliothek Berlin; Heinroth, 1971).

From my own experience of hand-rearing much easier bird species and in smaller numbers, I know how demanding and relentless this work is. You cannot take even a few hours off! During the late spring and summer when they were busiest, the Heinroths had only three to four hours of sleep a night for months at a time. Not only was the feeding and cleaning of the birds very time-consuming, but there were records to maintain every day: chick weights, measurements and development. These details were recorded with the greatest accuracy and were vital material for their publications. Chick growth was recorded in photographs that were developed by Oskar in their darkroom. In the Proceedings of the 5th Ornithological Congress, 1910, Magdalena published a paper on 'Room observations, on rarely-kept European birds', and in *Gefierderte Welt* (Feathered World) 'Keeping and breeding the Nightjar in captivity'.

Magdalena was the driving force in this work, always eager to look for nests. At times, especially during the war and post-war years, this was difficult. Usually she cared for the smaller species and her husband for the larger ones. Only the most disciplined and committed people could work at that level. And Oskar had a full-time job at the Aquarium, of which he became Director in 1911. His work was of immense ornithological importance. He

Magdalena Heinroth with Jackdaws. Photographer unknown.

was the first scientist to point out that instinctive behaviour could be used like morphological features to determine the genetic affinities of species and genera. He focused on behavioural displays through which individuals signal to other members of the same species. He also described the behaviour, often attributed to Konrad Lorenz, known as imprinting.

What is truly amazing is that the Heinroths reared 286 species of European birds – and I do mean hand-reared. I doubt that anyone in the history of science or aviculture has achieved an equivalent feat – and in a small apartment, not with specialised facilities!

After nine years of marriage the Heinroths moved to a more spacious apartment in the Aquarium, built in 1913, at the zoo. By that time the Aquarium had become the largest and most modern of its kind. They shared their passion for rearing birds, visited zoos together and greatly enjoyed the company of like-minded people. 'She always stepped back behind her husband and nothing delighted her more than when he was recognised' (Rühl, 1932).

They went to southern Russia, Italy, London, Paris, Copenhagen, Stockholm, the Netherlands and Eastern Europe. She loved to fly on planes, to have an impression of what migratory birds saw.

Die Vogel Mitteleuropas

The Heinroths had no children. Their legacy was *Die Vogel Mitteleuropas* (The Birds of Central Europe). Four volumes were published between 1924 and 1933. Magdalena did all the preparatory work. An amazing twenty-three editions of this work were published between 1926 and 1967, in German and in other languages. It was held by 60 World Catalogue member libraries worldwide. The most important aspect of these volumes, never replicated for so many species, was the detailed summaries of their observations and measurements. Their photographs of life stages and behaviours reportedly numbered in excess of 15,000. They drew or photographed the gapes of nestlings for many species, with the realisation that this was an important signal to parents.

Sadly, the deteriorating financial and political situation in Germany before the Second World War, and the lack of an English translation, meant that these volumes did not then receive the attention they warranted. Paul Rühl (1932) wrote: 'For those who want phylogenetic, psychological and ethological questions in birds the "Heinroth" is an inexhaustible source. This work secures their immortality.'

Their accomplishments included pioneering studies of the relationship between mating systems, plumage dimorphism in waterfowl; navigation and orientation in pigeons; the adaptive significance of moulting strategies in birds; and the relationships between egg size and incubation duration. Schulze-Hagen and Birkhead point out: 'While Oskar Heinroth's name may be familiar to some ornithologists, the full extent of what he and his wives achieved is poorly known.'

Not surprisingly, given the work load, both Oskar and Magdalena struggled with health problems. Magdalena underwent major abdominal surgery as well as an operation for breast cancer in 1931 (Schulze-Hagen and Birkhead, 2014). She died in 1932, from complications arising from the abdominal surgery. Oskar must have been very tolerant of Magdalena's house full of birds. He ceased to keep birds in the home, and he recovered from the asthma from which he had suffered for many years. He was allergic either to feathers or to the mealworms they bred to feed the birds.

The year following Magdalena's death Oskar married zoologist Katharina Berger, another extraordinary woman who was to be the saviour of Berlin Zoo. Her story is told in Chapter 2. One thing is certain about Oskar. His choice of wives was perfect.

References

Heinroth, K., 1971, *Oskar Heinroth – Vater der Verhaltensforschung.* Wissenschaftliche Verlagsgesellschaft, Stuttgart.

Heinroth, K., 1979, *Mit Faltern begann's,* Kindler, Münich.

Rühl, P., 1932, Erinnerungen an Magdalena Heinroth, *Journal für Ornithologie,* 80: 542-551.

Schulze-Hagen, K. and T. Birkhead, 2015, The ethology and life history of birds: The forgotten contributions of Oskar, Magdalena and Katharina Heinroth, *Journal of Ornithology,* 156: 9-18. http://doi.org/10.1007/s10336-014-1091-3.

Also refer to:

Schulze-Hagen K. and G. Kaiser, 2021, Die Vogel-WG, *Die Heinroths, ihre 1000 Vogel und die Anfange der Verhaltensforschung,* Knesebeck Verlag.

8. Margaret Morse Nice
USA 1883-1974
Innovator in Field Ornithology and Ethology

Margaret Morse was born in Amherst, Massachusetts, on December 6 1883. Her parents were Anson D. Morse, Professor of History at Amherst College, and Margaret Duncan (Ely). She had four brothers, and two sisters. The animal-loving Morse family lived in a secluded house surrounded by two acres planted with shrubs and fruit trees.

From the age of nine Margaret was extraordinary in starting to keep records of the birds she saw. Her very first entry related to the Song Sparrow (*Melospiza melodia*) – and how significant this was! This species was to bring her fame and worldwide recognition as an ornithologist. Her book *Studies in the Life History of the Song Sparrow* was published 45 years later! This tome – a weighty 247 pages (Nice, 1937) – was the result of hours and days, months and years of observation and writing.

When she was 12 years old, in 1895, she received Mabel Osgood Wright's book *Bird-Craft,* which featured 200 species. In her autobiography (Nice, 1979) she wrote that it was 'The most cherished Christmas present of my life'. She attended grade and high school in Amherst where her subjects were Latin, Greek and French. Her two passions in life, ornithology and language studies, were thus strongly established in her teenage years. At this time she closely observed the family's flock of one dozen chickens. Their interactions fascinated her so that the 'pecking order' concept materialised in her mind. This idea was not to reach scientific literature until many years later.

On entering Mount Holyoke College in 1901, she found the zoology classes tedious and boring. Their focus was on dissection and taxonomy, which was typical of that time. She wanted a break and took a year out from college to live in Europe to improve her language skills. She spent the winter of 1903-1904 with her maternal step-grandmother in Italy. During the summer of 1904 she travelled with her family in Switzerland, Germany, Holland and England.

When she enrolled at Clark University in 1907 the faculty encouraged her in experimental and observational studies of animal behaviour. Her father did not approve of scientific careers for women but she began to research the feeding habits of the Bob-white Quail.

In 1910 Margaret published in *The Journal of Economic Entomology* 'Food of the Bob-white the result of more than two years research.' (Not until 1915 did she return to Clark to receive her M. A. in zoology.) She was distracted from her graduate studies when she met fellow student, Leonard Blaine Nice. They married in 1909. Blaine, as he was known, received a PhD in physiology in 1911. The couple then moved to Boston, where Blaine was an instructor until 1913.

I find what happened next astounding because so much of her research occurred while she was rearing five daughters! Even more amazingly, she put her scientific and enquiring mind to work to use them as research subjects! When her children were young, she made important linguistic studies of their language development, such as 'The Development of a Child's Vocabulary in Relation to Environment' (Master's thesis, Clark University), published in *Pedagogical Seminary* (22, 1915: 35-64). She published 18 articles on child psychology between 1915 and 1933. Her five daughters were born during a period that spanned thirteen years, from 1910 to 1923, so for 20 years she always had young children to care for. She had the disruption of uprooting her family to move several times, as her husband's academic career advanced. There was little time to publish on birds, except, with her husband in 1914, the delightfully titled short paper 'A City kept awake by the honking of migrating geese'.

1920s – Pioneer of Ethology

By the 1920s Margaret was again publishing many papers. Absorbed in behavioural studies of birds, this was partly as a result of rearing doves, owls and other birds that had been found injured or taken from nests. Her work on behaviour, understanding animals by watching what they did, was part of a new branch of science known as ethology. She was a pioneer – remarkable for the fact that she had no backing from any institution, yet she was leading in a male-dominated field.

In 1921 she published papers in the *Proceedings of the Oklahoma Academy of Science*, in *Condor, The Wilson Bulletin,* and *Bird Lore*. As sole author she wrote about the extension of range of the Robin and Arkansas Kingbird in Oklahoma and also on nesting records from the Norman area between 1920 and 1922, which contained data on the impressive number of 612 nests (Trautman, 1977). In 1924 Margaret published, with her husband, *The Birds of Oklahoma* (122 pages), and they produced a revised edition in 1931.

Althea Sherman of Iowa (Chapter 3) was a strong influence on Margaret's ornithological career. They began to exchange letters in 1921 when Miss Sherman was 68 and Margaret 38, and continued until 1932. After the posthumous publication of Althea Sherman's book *Birds of an Iowa Dooryard,* Margaret published *Some letters of Althea Sherman* (*Iowa Bird Life,* 1952) that show the rapport that existed between

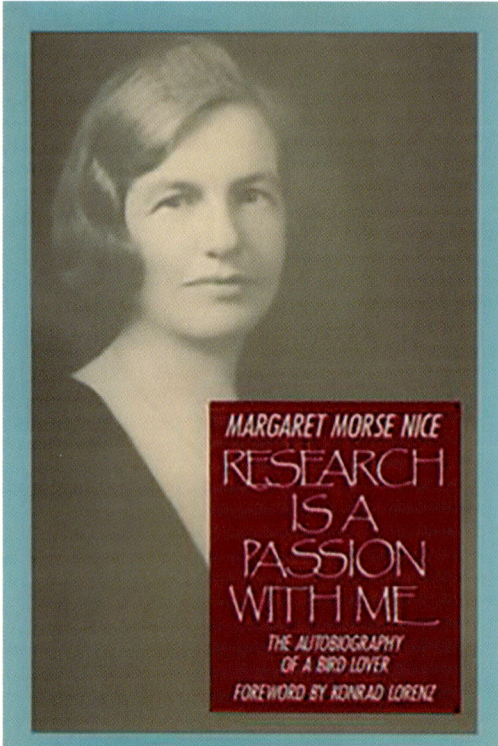

The posthumous autobiography *Research is a Passion with Me* was reprinted in 1979.
Donald Peattie, in commenting on Margaret Nice's writing ability, stated: 'Your art of telling is so good that it conceals how good the science is.'

them. Miss Sherman had ardently advocated a search for truth, to avoid the 'guessing blunders by ornithologists of note' who copied 'ancient guesses as to the length of incubation periods.'

During the summers the family visited Massachusetts, where Margaret studied warblers and other passerine birds. In 1926 she published articles on observations she made during the 1925 summer near Pelham, Massachu-setts. They resulted from 'long hours by the nest in the juniper, recording the doings of the exquisite little birds [Magnolia Warblers] ... the watching of which grew to be my main occupation in life.' Her articles also appeared on the Blackburnian (*Dendroica fusca*) and Black-throated Blue Warblers.

In 1927 she described experiences with cardinals, Pileated Woodpeckers wintering in Oklahoma, new nesting records for Cleveland County in 1925 and 1926, the evening bath of a flock of Scissor-tailed Flycatchers, bird counts and more. During the 1920s, she began to display an ever-increasing interest, eventually a passion, for behavioural studies. Published in 1927, The bird life of a forty acre tract in central Oklahoma (*University of Oklahoma Bulletin*). *Proceedings of the Oklahoma Academy of Science*, 7: 75-93) was typical of her careful observations.

In the autumn of 1927 Blaine joined the faculty of the Ohio State University, as a professor of physiology, and the family moved from Oklahoma to Columbus, Ohio, to remain there until 1936. As in Oklahoma, she had birds flying about the house. Milton Trautman remembered: 'I found it difficult to concentrate upon the subject at hand, especially when a Nuthatch alighted on my head or a Song Sparrow hopped across my dinner plate.'

In Columbus they lived on West Patterson Avenue, several hundred yards east of the Olentangy River. It was prime Song Sparrow habitat, consisting largely of neglected fields of brush, weeds, and scattered trees. During this period, Margaret's first major publication on the Song Sparrow was published in two parts (1933 and 1934) in Germany. It totalled 139 pages.

Travel in the 1930s

The Nice family started to travel further afield. In 1932 they visited the wonderful city of Rome for Blaine to attend the international Physiological Congress and to give their daughters a 'sight-seeing and educational' experience. It was important to Margaret to meet certain European ornithologists, to visit museums and zoological gardens in Paris and Berlin, and to observe birds. The family arrived in Brittany in June, and then went on to Germany, Switzerland and Italy. In mid-September they left Cambridge, England, to return to Columbus.

Another visit to Europe occurred in July 1934. Margaret attended meetings of the Eighth International Ornithological Congress in Oxford and at the Natural History Museum. While in London with her sister Katherine, the sisters spent much time in libraries. Margaret made several excursions to observe birds, including watching seabirds from a destroyer off the coast of Wales.

Her last European trip was in 1938 to attend the Ninth International Ornithological Congress at Rouen and Paris. Highlights in France were the bird collection in the beautiful château at Clères, belonging to the world-renowned ornithologist and aviculturist Jean Delacour, and the Camargue with its flocks of flamingos and white horses. Later she spent a month with the famous naturalist and author Konrad Lorenz at his home in Altenberg, Germany. Dr Lorenz taught her how to raise chicks of altricial bird species.

Promoting an appreciation of birds was important to Margaret. She occasionally gave nature talks to small groups and to radio audiences: 'to help listeners to get more joy out of life'. As a member of the Columbus Audubon Society she served in several official capacities, including vice-president from 1933-1936. She occasionally took part in field trips but after 1936 she had little opportunity to watch birds. She wrote to her daughter, Marjorie, that 'a great city is no proper home for me'. Most of her work was at her desk. She made line drawings of newly hatched and young birds for her daughter Constance's article in *Nature Magazine,* 'Bird Babes of Delta Marsh'. Margaret had taken drawing lessons as a child but 'displayed no aptitude'. Returning to Chicago from

The Song Sparrow.
Photograph: Wikipedia.

Columbus by train in 1946, she spent the journey sketching passing trees. Thus began another interest, resulting in the publication of line drawings and stipplings of plants and animals in several articles. They also appeared in attractive individual Christmas cards and letters to friends.

She became a council member of the Wilson Ornithological Club (later Society) from 1929 until 1931 and was the President in 1938 and 1939 – the first woman to serve as President of any major American ornithological society. She was an Associate Editor of *The Wilson Bulletin* from 1939 to 1949.

1940s and 1950s

In 1941 Margaret continued to publish observations obtained before leaving Columbus. In *1942 Studies in the Life History of the Song Sparrow II* was published and *The Behavior of the Song Sparrow and Other Passerines,* appeared as Volume VI in the *Transactions of the Linnaean Society of New York*. However, it was the three monographs on the life history of the Song Sparrow, published between 1933 and 1943, that established her reputation as an outstanding ornithologist. In 1942 she received the American Ornithologists' Union's Brewster Medal for these publications.

They were influencing many people who were studying bird behaviour, including Louise de Kiriline Lawrence (Chapter 10). In her book *The Lovely and the Wild,* Louise remembered the year before her husband returned from the war – so she was probably writing in 1944. One day she met two bird watchers and learned 'the best and proper way to study birds.' It was an auspicious meeting. 'Through them I was to be introduced into a new intellectual environment which culminated in my first meeting with Margaret Nice. World famous as a student of bird behaviour, this remarkable and gifted friend took hold of my purpose, and my work, and the whole of my thought life in fact, and as gently as the wind blowing from the south in the spring, as gently and as surely, changed all of it'. Alas, that was all she penned about her remarkable friend.

By 1946 Margaret's improved health allowed her to travel outside Chicago to study bird behaviour. She visited relatives and friends and more distant locations including Florida, Louisiana, California, Baja California and Canada. This resulted in 1948 in articles on spring in Arkansas and a trip through Arizona deserts and mountains.

In her seventies and eighties

In 1952 she published excerpts of letters she had received from Althea Sherman and three poems. Her publications in 1953 ranged from why one should love vultures, the incubation periods of birds of prey, and experiences in imprinting ducklings, to the earliest mention of territory. She was one of the first people in the USA (or the first) to analyse a 'deme' (a local population of closely related species). In 1957, the number of annual publications, except reviews, began to decline. In 1965 after a second eye operation, she wrote that she 'must cut down on activities'. At that time, she was 81.

As she grew older, Margaret became increasingly outspoken, especially in correspondence. She was not afraid to give an opinion on those who did not agree with her, including presidents, senators and other politicians, conservationists, and the public in general. She condemned the unrestricted use of pesticides, the widespread use of DDT, other insecticides and herbicides, the killing of albatrosses on Midway Island, and misuse of wildlife refuges.

In 1953, at a dinner in his honour, Ludlow Griscom, a pioneer American field ornithologist, paid tribute to 'that remarkably gifted woman, Margaret Morse Nice, the great student of [bird] life histories. She has no advanced degrees, never had any museum connections, never shot a bird or did any taxonomic work, spent her life running a home and raising four children on a meager budget. No one now fails to call her an ornithologist, and it shows what persistence, determination and interest can do.'

In a letter to the editor of the *Bulletin of the Massachusetts Audubon Society* she replied, 'In regard to Mr. Ludlow Griscom's kind tribute to me, may I make a few corrections? I have an M. A. from Clark University, 1915; I have prepared bird skins and done considerable work on the bird collections in the Museum of the University of Oklahoma; and I have shot a few birds.' It is true that she never earned a PhD, was never a faculty member of a university, and she had received few or no grants and little secretarial assistance. To have made so great a contribution without these presumed necessary requirements makes her achievements all the more noteworthy. She appeared to be very sensitive about this lack and especially resented being referred to as a housewife. She was sometimes heard to exclaim, 'I am not a housewife, I am a trained zoologist' (Trautman, 1977). Undoubtedly she was both.

Publications

Most of her work was scientific. In 1967 she published for a more popular readership *Watchers at the Nest* (Dover Publications). The first ten chapters summarised her work on Song Sparrows.

Milton Trautman wrote:

'If a complete list of Mrs. Nice's publications exists, I have not seen it. The best estimates are that she published more than 250 titles on birds in scientific journals, 7 of book length, and 3,313 (her count) reviews of the works of others. Her need to communicate with others, to tell them what she had learned, knew, thought, and did, apparently was a compelling force expressing itself not only in publications but through correspondence and the spoken word to groups or individuals. In 1952 her correspondence file contained the names of 130 foreigners and 220 Americans. To some she wrote dozens of letters. She could not have accomplished as much as she did without her working knowledge of several languages which enabled her to cover much of the field of natural science and to prepare large and valuable bibliographies, some containing several hundred citations, a major contribution in themselves.'

During her later years she wrote her memoir which was sent to Cornell University Press in 1970, but they returned it. Margaret Nice died on June 26 1974 at her Chicago home, a few months after the death of her husband. He had played an extremely important role, providing great moral support and monies for her travels and research. She was 90 years old. Fortunately, her autobiography was published five years later under the title of *Research Is a Passion with Me,* edited by Doris Heustis Speirs. (Toronto: Consolidated Amethyst Communications, 1979). It contained an extensive but not wholly complete bibliography of her published writings. Forty years later her work found a new audience with the publication of her biography *For the Birds* (Bailey, 2018).

Recognitions and tributes

Many honours were bestowed upon Margaret. She received honorary memberships of the British Ornithological Union, and of the Finland, German, Netherlands and Swiss ornithological societies. During her 50th reunion at her alma mater, Mount Holyoke, she received an honorary D.Sc. In 1962 she was awarded another D.Sc. from Elmira College. In 1969 the Wilson Ornithological Society honoured her by establishing the Margaret Morse Nice Grant-in-aid. The monies were to be given to self-trained amateur researchers. This delighted her as she had always been willing to assist others, especially younger ornithologists.

Her most renowned and important peers, including Konrad Lorenz, Ernst Mayr and Aldo Leopold, acknowledged her as an innovator in field ornithology and ethology. Lorenz wrote the foreword to her autobiography. Milton Trautman recorded in 1977 that he had received a letter from Ernst Mayr about her work and especially of the Song Sparrow: 'I have always felt that she, almost single-handedly, initiated a new era in American ornithology and the only effective countermovement against the list chasing movement. She early recognized the importance of a study of bird individuals because this is the only method to get reliable life history data.'

On her seventieth birthday in 1953 Professor Niko Tinbergen (the Dutch biologist and ornithologist who shared the 1973 Nobel prize in Physiology or Medicine) praised her Song Sparrow work highly. He wrote to her: 'In a long life you have found reward not only in the home circle for all your cares and sacrifices, but with remarkable creative power you have served science. Through your works you have become known to ornithologists throughout the entire world as the one who laid the foundation of population studies'.

The words of Mayr and Tinbergen say it all. No need for mine!

References

Bailey, M., 2018, *For the Birds: American Ornithologist Margaret Morse Nice,* University of Oklahoma Press.

Nice, M., 1937, Studies in the Life History of the Song Sparrow. I, A Population Study of the Song Sparrow. *Transactions of the Linnaean Society of New York,* 4: 1-247.

Studies in the Life History of the Song Sparrow II, 1942.

Trautman, M. B., 1977, In Memoriam: Margaret Morse Nice, *Auk,* vol. 94: 430-441.

Some important works:

The Birds of Oklahoma, 1924, with Leonard Blaine Nice, Norman: University of Oklahoma.

The Theory of Territorialism and Its Development, in *Fifty Years' Progress of American Ornithology, 1883-1933,* 1933, the American Ornithologists' Union, Lancaster, PA, Zur Naturgeschichte des Singammers, 1933, *Journal für Ornithologie,* 81: 552-595 and 1934, 82: 1-96.

The Social Kumpan[3] and the Song Sparrow. 1939 *Auk,* 56: 255-262.

Development of Behavior in Precocial Birds, 1962, *Transactions of the Linnaean Society of New York,* 8: 1-211.

---

[3] Kumpan means companion.

Female Heroes of Bird Conservation

9. Len Howard
UK 1894-1973
Ground-breaking Books on Bird Observations

'Len', christened Gwendolen, was the youngest of the four children of Henry Newman Howard (1861-1929), a poet and dramatist, and Florence Howard, nee Warman. She had three brothers. She was born in Wallington, now in the London Borough of Sutton, but then in the county of Surrey.

Little is known about her early life. Until she was in her late forties she had a music career in London. She gave lessons, organised concerts for children of the poor and played the viola in an orchestra under the most famous conductor of the day, Sir Malcolm Sargent.

In 1942 she moved to Ditchling, East Sussex, to the house she would call 'Bird Cottage'. Her life gradually changed in a way she never could have envisaged. Her observations of the birds in her garden, her extraordinary ability to win their trust, and her talent for writing, unexpectedly brought her fame. She came to understand garden birds as perhaps no one else has, before or since.

Many people – perhaps even most people – who read her first book, *Birds as Individuals*, will never again consider birds as creatures with little or no ability to think and reason. Her writings should be required reading for all ornithologists, especially those scientists who can always give you a good reason why, when we ascribe emotions to birds, we are mistaken.

Theodore Xenophon Barber, PhD, is a research psychologist noted for his pioneering investigations into aspects of consciousness. In his book *The Human Nature of Birds,* he wrote that when *Birds as Individuals* was published in 1953:

'...ornithologists apparently discounted it as anthropomorphic. Because it contradicted the official dogma that birds are mechanistic carbon copies or virtual automata, it has never been mentioned in official texts. However, much of the scientific data gathered in recent years agrees with Howard's basic conclusion that wild birds are much more like people than anyone (especially official scientists) had imagined. Since the scientific data have now caught up with Howard's intensive, intimate and naturalistic observations, each of her contentions must be taken very seriously and tested in further research.'

Since Barber's words were written in 1994, there has been more than enough evidence, scientific and anecdotal, to prove that birds are as highly individualistic as humans. Len Howard's close relationship with birds was not a research experiment. It was her life. She was totally absorbed by the behavior of birds that had no fear of a human – but this applied to just one person – herself. I was in my twenties when I first read this book. It left a very deep impression on me as the only text I had read by someone who related to birds as I did – as individuals. I was twelve when I started to breed Budgerigars. Their behavior and individuality fascinated me. I failed to understand how 'scientists' could deny this aspect. Obviously, they did not know birds as individuals.

Sadly, most copies of this classic, out-of-print book are probably consigned to dusty shelves, their pages unopened for decades. As a young person I loved the book but a move overseas necessitated down-sizing my library – and out it went. In later years I often looked for it on second-hand book shelves. In 2010 I was lucky, excitedly snapping up a copy for £1.20 in a second-hand bookshop that seemed to belong in the same era as the book I bought. An internet search as I wrote this revealed one copy only – for £48.

It was so good to re-read the words of Len Howard and of the intimate relationships she developed with many birds, especially those that freely entered her home. She believed, as I do, that fear was the primary motivating factor in much of avian behaviour as observed by humans. To this end she did everything possible to maximise the sense of security of her avian visitors and to encourage an uninhibited relationship with them.

She starts her second book, *Living with Birds,* with these words: 'For many years about forty Great Tits, twenty Blue Tits, Blackbirds, Thrushes and other species have been in and out of my cottage all day, some of the Tits also roosting indoors. The interior of the cottage is arranged to suit them and my life has become more or less regulated by theirs.'

She has been described as a recluse – discouraging visitors for the negative impact they might have had on her birds. In fact we know very little about her life, before and after she moved to Bird Cottage. Several people have tried hard to discover more – with little success. It is interesting that the only published photographs of her are back view with a Great Tit (*Parus major*) and one side view image with her face obscured by her hair. (How refreshing in this time of daily 'selfies' posted for the world to see!)

The picture rails in her sitting room and bedroom became roosting sites for young Great Tits. One night, one fell from her perch in her sleep so the next night Len gave her a cardboard box on the picture rail. Soon, instead of being enhanced with pictures, the rails were hung with sugar boxes and cereal cartons, the corner boxes being favoured and fought for!

Female Heroes of Bird Conservation

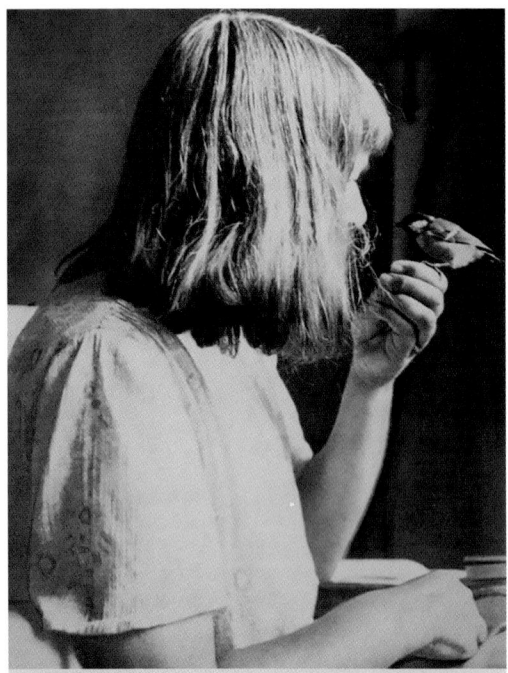

Len Howard with an attentive Great Tit.
Photograph: Len Howard.

When she was ill, she had twenty or more playing on her bed. They flew to the windowsill where newspaper was spread to deposit their droppings, then returned to the bed directly. If she spoke to them severely, for tearing at her book or pulling a blanket to pieces, they retorted by depositing their droppings on the bed, then flying to the window!

She wrote: 'One of the great joys of close and intimate bird-watching is learning the expressions in their eyes…' This is how she learned to read birds' emotions, also through the movements of the beak. 'Birds understand the importance of watching eye expressions, not only among themselves but with the human', she said. When she held food in her hands, they did not fix their eyes on the food or her hand, but gazed searchingly into her eyes. If they were going to steal food and she kept silent, they watched her eyes for signs of objection, while going towards the food and helping themselves.

Eye contact with a human is avoided by most wild creatures but it is achieved when you learn how to make friends with a wild bird. Initially it will probably occur through giving it a favourite item of food but it can develop into something stronger. One of the greatest satisfactions I know is when 'my' Robin or 'my' Blackbird looks into my eyes, without fear, but with curiosity or anticipation.

Tits, especially Great Tits, were very dear to Len. She studied numerous individuals, often over many years, and named each one. Twist was so called because she would roost with her tail pressed sideways, causing it to twist. This much-loved bird seemed to be able to communicate with her mate – or her hearing was extraordinarily sensitive. Sometimes when she was inside the cottage she would suddenly stand rigid, with a tense expression, dropping the food she was eating tucked between her toes. Then she would hurriedly fly out of the window and across the meadows to the copse. Sometimes Len followed her to find that she had flown to her mate. 'The sudden tension of her body and her facial expression, as if vision was centred inwards, her eyes not focusing upon what was in front of them, suggested she was responding to some form of communication from her mate.'

It was insights such as this that made Len Howard's work so fascinating.

In 1950 nine pairs of Great Tits were nesting in her garden. She knew this species so well she was able to publish a genealogical tree documenting the young from two females and their several mates. Some pairs had second nests and one female reared two broods for eight years. The average clutch size was nine eggs and eight or nine would hatch. All the young would fledge but about half would be taken by predators after two or three days. One day she counted sixty young Great Tits in her garden! Such abundance would surely never be repeated after the 20th century. In *Living with Birds,* she chronicled the life history in 70 pages of a Great Tit she called 'Star'. She even taught her to tap the number of times she instructed verbally, with a nut as a reward. And we thought Grey Parrots were clever! (See also Chapter 35.)

Her unique books

In her magical books, *Birds as Individuals* (published in 1952) and *Living with Birds* (1956), Len Howard demonstrated spatial awareness and intelligence in a number of small species, truths about birds that were seldom recognised previously. A wonderful writer, she not only described bird behaviour but conjured up the atmosphere of time and place. On a bleak December day a thrush suddenly 'broke the heavy winter silence by a full, rich song and at the same moment a small shaft of sunlight fell on the smooth peak of Mount Caburn so that its shadowed form was crowned with gold, which slowly spread until this shapely hill stood all alight while everything around as yet remained in gloom.'

A unique aspect of *Birds as Individuals* is Part Two which consists of four chapters about Bird Song. Was she the first person to analyse technique in bird song? The chapter on this topic is technical yet easily understood by the non-musician. In the chapter on Songs of Warblers and Thrush Tribes she describes how a Blackbird actually composed the opening phrase of the Rondo in Beethoven's violin concerto. This was not imitation as she could vouch for the fact that he had not heard this. At first the phrase differed but a few days later he sang the complete phrase twice, exactly as in the beginning of Beethoven's Rondo, only of course in a higher pitch. His interpretation varied. If the tune was sung only once he took it slowly, with smooth phrasing; when sung with the repeat, the pace was quickened towards the end. For those who read music, she transcribed his songs. What an amazing woman! I am lost in admiration!

I wrote a magazine article about her that was published in 2018 because I was so saddened that her work had been forgotten. However, in 2016 Dutch author Eva Meijer published in the Netherlands a novel based on Len Howard's life and work, *Het Vogelhuis*. It became a best-seller. The English

Female Heroes of Bird Conservation

The Great Tit is a very clever species. Photograph: Tracy Farrer.

translation, *Bird Cottage,* was published world-wide in August 2018.

Between 1951 and 1957 Len Howard published articles in *Out of Doors and Countrygoer* (prior to 1950, these were separate publications) and in *The Countryman,* including 'Two Nesting Seasons' in the Spring edition of 1957.

In May 1973 the magazine *British Birds* published the obituary of this 'remarkable personality'. It stated that a decade or so previously, the Sussex Trust for Nature Conservation purchased (through a national appeal for funds) an orchard adjoining 'Bird Cottage' when there were plans to develop the site for housing. This orchard, together with the cottage (bequeathed to the Trust by Miss Howard), was to be sold, and the money used towards the purchase of a new reserve in Sussex, 'a fitting memorial to a dedicated birdwatcher extraordinary.'

It would, indeed, have been a fitting memorial. But it never happened. The Sussex Naturalists' Trust had promised to turn her property into a bird sanctuary. The Trust sold the land and the house for a good price to someone who immediately felled most of the trees in her garden. Only the ancient oak is still standing (Meijer, 2018). This was an unforgiveable betrayal of a wonderful woman. She is buried in an unnamed grave, in the graveyard behind Bird Cottage.

In the Foreword to *Birds as Individuals,* Julian Huxley, a renowned naturalist, wrote: 'There are very few people in existence who love birds as much as she does'. Words to that effect should have been written on her grave. The birds were her passion, the focus of her life, until she died on January 5 1973 at the age of 79. I wish I had known her.

References

Barber, T. X., 1994, *The Human Nature of Birds,* Penguin, New York.

Howard, L., 1952, *Birds as Individuals,* Collins Press, London. Reprinted in 1953 by Country Book Club, London.

Howard, L., 1956, *Living with Birds,* Collins Press, London.

Meijer, E., 2018, *Bird Cottage,* Pushkin Press, London.

10. Louise de Kiriline Lawrence
(née Flach) Sweden/Canada 1894-1992
Self-taught Ornithologist and Conservationist

Louise Flach was born in Sweden on January 30 1894 on a large farm estate located near the Baltic Sea, about 320km (200 miles) south of Stockholm. (Year of birth has also been given as 1896). Her parents were wealthy landowners with connections to the Swedish and Danish royal families. Princess Louise of Denmark, a close friend of Louise's mother, Hilleved Neergaard, was her namesake and godmother. Her conservationist father Sixten Flach helped to found the bird sanctuary on Stora Karlsö, Gotland. Visitors to the estate included ornithologists and nature artists.

When Louise was 17, her father died, and the family moved to the city. How she must have missed the Nordic landscape and the villa where she was born! In *The Lovely and the Wild* she wrote: '… to this land I belong forever. The sky, arched and free, the water spreading in tongues and strips between dark-green wooded islets and promontories, blend with each other in the mood conjured by the current moment. This is the fjord Bråviken that cuts deep into the east coast of Sweden from the Baltic Sea.'

The year following her father's death she was presented to the court of King Gustav V of Sweden. Instead of enjoying a life of banquets and balls, until she married someone of similar social status, she chose a different path. When the First World War broke out in 1914, her aim was to become a Red Cross nurse but, unable to begin formal training until she was 21, she worked on probation at the General Hospital of Norrköping. Her next location was a prisoner-of-war exchange camp in Horserød, Denmark, where she met her first husband, Gleb de Kiriline, an officer in the Russian White Army. They married at the end of 1918 but only three days later he departed to serve with the Army as his homeland was plunged into civil war. In March 1919 Gleb sent for Louise to join him in Arkhangelsk in northern Russia. She arrived after a long journey on April 22. She had barely enough time to unpack when Gleb went back into action. Louise followed her husband, serving as a field nurse just behind the front lines.

She had already seen the tragedy, the tyranny and the terror of war. Now she was to experience this in the most personal and life-shattering way possible. Within weeks, the White Army

Louise and Gleb de Kiriline.
Source: Library and Archives Canada/Louise de Kiriline Lawrence.

front collapsed. Louise and Gleb joined a huge retreating army fleeing by foot or by horse-drawn sleigh through the Russian countryside. After more than a week of living outdoors along the corpse-strewn route, they were discovered and captured by the Bolsheviks. They were sent by train to Petrozavodsk, where male and female prisoners were interned separately. After questioning, Louise and the other women were released, while the men were eventually sent to Moscow for interrogation.

Louise travelled separately to Moscow, where she visited Gleb in prison camp. However, he and the other captive officers were moved without warning in June. Louise eventually heard a rumour that 500 officers, including Gleb, had been executed. Hoping the rumours were wrong, she decided to remain in Russia. She volunteered for a Swedish Red Cross Mission trying to combat a massive famine in the Soviet Union, working with thousands of famine victims and orphans from 1920 to 1924. Her hope of finding Gleb alive slowly faded. In 1924 Louise returned to Sweden, where she attempted to resume her former life as a socialite, but she soon felt bored and restless.

Canada calls

Gleb had told her about Canada. In her book *The Loghouse Nest* she wrote:

'And so one bright day of spring I broke with the old and turned my face toward the new. With enough money in my pocket to travel about for three or four months and – in case of need – for a return passage, I crossed the ocean to find out whether my picture of Canada carried a good resemblance to the original...'

'Thus I came to Canada, not to nurse a broken heart, but to tend to something new that impetuously pressed through to live out the shattered fragments of a lost episode. And of all countries I chose Canada, because she, I knew, possessed the unspoiled soil, the life-giving space, the fresh winds that promote spontaneous growth.'

She had heard about a new Red Cross programme in Canada's north where there was a chronic lack of doctors and hospitals. The Red Cross was opening scores of medical outposts, each staffed by a single trained nurse who would deal with all kinds of medical problems. In addition, the nurses were expected to educate rural residents about hygiene, child care and proper nutrition. In 1927, Louise was assigned a huge territory in north-eastern Ontario. Her ability to speak English, French, Swedish and Russian served her well in an area of immigrants and indigenous Algonquins. She visited patients on foot, by car, on an open boat or by dog sled.

In 1930, Louise came across *The Red Terror in Russia,* a book that confirmed what had happened to her husband. Gleb de Kiriline and 800 other former Imperial Russian officers had been executed and buried in a mass grave by the Red Army only weeks after he and Louise had last seen each other.

In 1934 a new chapter opened in Louise's life. When the world's first surviving quintuplets were born near Ontario, their guardian offered Louise the position of head nurse in a state-of-the-art nursery specially constructed for the 'miracle babies'. She had become renowned for her professionalism and dedication. Louise nursed them through their precarious first year but, as they grew, so did public interest. Now known around the world as the Dionne Quintuplets, a booming tourist complex nicknamed Quintland sprang up around the nursery. Louise disliked this exploitation. It was time to move on.

Louise de Kiriline Lawrence inscribed her gift of The Lovely and the Wild *with the words 'With the fresh winds from the Canadian Shield'.* Photograph: author.

In 1935, she retired from nursing to write her first book, *The Quintuplets' First Year: the survival of the famous five Dionne babies and its significance for all mothers.* She discussed the latest medical breakthroughs in an age when infant mortality was still high.

In 1939, when she was 43, Louise married a local carpenter, Leonard Lawrence. In his spare time, he and two Scandinavian woodworkers constructed a log cabin on a 2.5ha (six-acre) wilderness plot overlooking Pimisi Bay near Rutherglen, Ontario. The couple barely had time to settle in before Louise's happiness was shattered yet again by war. That year Len Lawrence was among the tens of thousands of Canadians who volunteered to serve with the Allies. For the second time in her life, Louise found herself alone. Her husband enlisted at the start of the war. (However, *he* came back – five years later.) Stranded in a tiny cabin in the wilderness, Louise chose to stay and to observe wildlife.

A friend had given her *Birds of Canada* by Percy A. Taverner, Canada's leading ornithologist and Curator of Birds at the National Museum. Louise wrote to him, telling him that his descriptions of birds, species by species, made 'a tale of astonishing fascination and vividness'. She remembered: 'The effect of the letter was beyond all expectations... From the first contact a friendship developed between us... that turned out to be of great significance to me in my new role of serious nature student'. They never met but they discussed many things from politics and philosophy, to war and peace, and always with birds and natural history as the central theme from which the digressions emanated and expanded. 'This was my first real contact with someone who represented the scientific attitude, somebody with the larger vision' (Lawrence, 1968).

Louise joined the American Ornithologists' Union (AOU), a male-dominated association of mainly professional bird scientists. Undaunted by their credentials, Louise began submitting scientific reviews and papers to the AOU about the local birds she observed around her Rutherglen cabin. Her elegant prose and astute observations (see also Chapter 35), honed by her long service as a frontline nurse, stood up to the meticulous standards of the Union. Over the years, she contributed more than 500 reviews and 17 scientific papers to its journal *The Auk*.

The Lovely and the Wild won important awards for natural history writing.

Then, in 1954, Louise became the first Canadian woman to be named an Elective Member.

It is fascinating to observe some similarities in the lives of Len Howard (Chapter 9) and Louise, born two years apart and in different continents and very different circumstances. Both had previous careers and did not start to study birds until they were in their forties. Their studies were centred in their immediate environments. The Black-capped Chickadee (*Poecile atricapillus*) is an American member of the tit family. It used to be in the genus *Parus*, as is the European Great Tit (*Parus major*). The two species are closely related, much alike in behaviour and both have the coal-black cap. The chickadee was one of the species closely observed by Louise.

In 1968, in *The Lovely and the Wild*, she wrote, poetically:

'The chickadees look like fluffballs with beads of frost clinging to their whiskers and to the peripheral tips of their erected plumage. Small cakes of ice stick to the backs of some of them where their breaths froze during the night as they slept with their heads tucked into the feathers of their shoulders. Others appear with their tails twisted and bent sideways.'

Then they visited her feeding station.

'To have a wild bird come to my hand of its own free will seemed for a long time to be an utterly remote possibility… But I did not reckon with the power of the seed. Peet was the first chickadee that introduced himself to me as a unique individual. He sat on a twig and rather in fun, expecting nothing, I offered him a sunflower seed. To my immense surprise, he alighted on my hand, looked me in the eye and curled his feet around my finger with flattering confidence… But from the moment that Peet came to associate me with the seed the bond was forged between us. And it was irreversible.'

Although he could never have seen sunflower seed before, in this remote wilderness, he knew precisely what to do with it. Peet became a regular visitor to her house, entering through an open window. For Louise, his searches for hidden seeds were sources of 'never-palling delight'.

Note that Peet 'looked her in the eye'. Len Howard had written that when she held food in her hands, the Great Tits did not fix their eyes on the food or her hand, but gazed searchingly into her eyes. Their writings are almost interchangeable; it is mainly the favourite species that differ, due to their geographical locations.

I have the impression that Len Turner loved the Great Tits above all other birds. Seven chapters of *Living with Birds*, published in 1956, are devoted to this species. Her books are illustrated with enchanting photos of them in her cottage, even sitting on her typewriter as she worked. For both women, these birds were their friends and they probably saw few people. Louise wrote: 'Peet brought practically the whole chickadee population to my hand that first winter. By his own unpremeditated example he induced others to overcome their timidity to the required degree.'

In 1945, Louise published her second book, *The Loghouse Nest*, an account of her life in the wilderness surrounded by birds and nature. That same year, her husband Len returned from his army service and resumed his job with the township. Louise continued to observe and write about nature, producing seven books in total over a span of 44 years. She died on 27 April 1992 at the age of 98.

On the Uwo.ca website Amy C. Wallace writes:

'Swedish aristocrat, Bolshevik concentration camp survivor, revolutionary widow, world-renowned nurse, gifted linguist, strict atheist, prolific writer, dedicated conservationist, and friend of the birds, Louise de Kiriline Lawrence defeats any attempt at categorization… Her log house, nestled in the forest of Pimisi Bay near North Bay, Ontario, was the visual manifestation of her unique set of experiences. A hybrid of aristocratic opulence and Canadiana, her tiny cabin was adorned with snowshoes and taxidermy fish as well as with precious family heirlooms and antique tapestries that dated as far back as the eighteenth century.'

Amy Wallace quoted two keen bird watchers who arrived on Louise's woodland doorstep to find her 'barefoot, with sapphires dangling from her ears, the very picture of the aristocratic recluse.' Amy Wallace travelled to Library and Archives Canada in Ottawa, where all Louise's ornithological notes, bird diaries, migration charts, professional and personal correspondence, manuscripts, photo albums, and other ephemera are kept. She spent three days in the archives, yet had time to explore only a fraction of the collection housed there.

Honours and Awards

In 1969, Louise's book, *The Lovely and the Wild*, was awarded the John Burroughs Medal for natural history writing and the Sir G. D. Roberts Special Award for literature from the Canadian Authors' Association. She received an honorary Doctorate of Letters from Laurentian University in Sudbury in 1971, and a scholarship was created in her name. Ten years later, she gained the Francis H. Kortwright Award for outdoor writing. In 1991, she was given the Doris Huestis Speirs Award by the Society of Canadian Ornithologists, for outstanding lifetime contribution to Canadian ornithology. In 2014, a local conservation group, the Nipissing Naturalists' Club (NNC), established the annual Louise de Kiriline Lawrence Nature Festival. The NNC was the driving force behind the creation of an Ontario Heritage Trust plaque. It was erected on the shores of Pimisi Bay in 2016, just a few hundred metres from Louise's log cabin.

Louise was a truly extraordinary woman, gifted, passionate and compassionate. What she achieved after the age of 40, especially in the scientific papers that she wrote, would be a lifetime's work for most academic ornithologists. Oh! To have been able to sit down with her and to talk birds!

Her books

- *The Quintuplets' First Year (1936)*
- *The Loghouse Nest (1945)*

- *A Comparative Life History Study of Four Species of Woodpeckers (1967)*
- *The Lovely and the Wild (1968)*
- *Mar: A Glimpse into the Natural Life of a Bird (1976)*
- *Another Winter, Another Spring: A Love Remembered (1977)*
- *To Whom the Wilderness Speaks (1980)*

Reference

Lawrence, L. de K., 1968, *The Lovely and the Wild,* McGraw-Hill Ryerson.

11. Phyllis Barclay-Smith
UK 1902-1980
Of world renown in Ornithological Circles

Ida Phyllis Barclay-Smith was born on May 18 1902. She was the second of three daughters of Edward Barclay-Smith and his wife Ida Mary. Edward was a professor of anatomy at Cambridge University. Phyllis studied at Blackheath High School and King's College in London.

Little is known about her early life but her aunt and uncle, Mr and Mrs Frank Lemon, had a big influence on her when she was in her twenties. Her aunt, the formidable Margaretta Louisa Lemon, known as Etta, was one of the founder members of the Royal Society for the Protection of Birds (RSPB). We have already met her in Chapter 4.

In 1924, Phyllis, as she was always known, joined that organisation as Assistant Secretary. She built up a lot of contacts in the world of bird protection and was very highly regarded. She worked alongside the secretary, Linda Gardiner who, after 35 years' service for the RSPB, was to resign in 1935. Both Phyllis and her co-worker Beatrice Solly, with the society since 1921, expected to jointly succeed to Linda's position. However, the RSPB's Council had already recruited a man to the position. Phyllis and Beatrice were furious and demanded that they should be treated as equals to the contender, Robert Preston Donaldson. They informed the Council that if their requests were not met, they would resign. They were shocked when their resignations were accepted. But that was not all. Etta Lemon believed that a male secretary was needed for the organisation to be viewed more seriously. Furthermore, she would not support anyone getting, as she thought, above their station, not even her own niece. This attitude is hard to understand but it was based on Etta's belief in the authority of men.

Phyllis then joined the International Council for Bird Preservation (ICBP) where her knowledge and talents were appreciated. She stayed there for the remainder of her working life, becoming the secretary in 1946 and secretary-general in 1974. The famous French ornithologist and aviculturist Jean Delacour was a founder member of ICBP in 1922. During his work for the RSPB he came to know Phyllis. He wrote:

'Here, unusual efficiency was already obvious. Her association with all the ornithologists interested in preserving birds all over the world developed gradually, and in 1935 she became an Assistant Secretary of the ICBP. She soon took over a number of the various responsibilities of the Council, and between 1938 and 1958, while I was its President, she actually managed our activities all over the world…' (Delacour, 1980).

In his memoir *The Living Air* (Delacour, 1966) he wrote: 'Thanks to her unusual capabilities and efficiency, to her incessant and unselfish work, we have been able to expand to the whole world.'

After the war Phyllis organised a number of congresses and symposia. Delacour commented: 'Now that hard work appears to have become an oddity, it is difficult to imagine that anyone achieved so much, for so many years. In the course of her incessant activities, she had met all the prominent ornithologists of the world, and many became close friends. She was able to interest them in her pursuits and to gain their support for international bird preservation. She travelled extensively and promoted with a special willing eagerness the causes she had at heart.'

This inspirational lady helped to set up the International Wildfowl Research Bureau, as part of the British Section of ICBP. In 1954 the name was changed to Waterfowl & Wetlands Research Bureau and the scope was expanded to include the protection of wetland areas. She also helped to establish the ICBP

Phyllis Barclay-Smith.
Photographer unknown.

reserve on Cousin Island in the Seychelles, in the Western Indian Ocean. The purchase of the island in 1968 saved the Seychelles Warbler (*Acrocephalus sechellensis*) from extinction. It occurred only on Cousin Island and just thirty were known to survive. Now it has been translocated to other islands and its population numbers several thousands.

Pioneer in ocean pollution

Phyllis was years ahead of her time. Rachel Carson (Chapter 12), a marine biologist, achieved worldwide fame in the 1950s for alerting the world to the dangers of pesticides and of ocean pollution, yet Phyllis Barclay-Smith had done both, many years earlier. She was one of the first to perceive the danger to birdlife from oil pollution, creating a sensation with a lecture on the subject at the VII International Ornithological Congress of 1930 in Amsterdam. She had to wait years for action to be taken. A conference in 1953, organised by Phyllis, had brought together people from thirty or more countries representing 95% of the global shipping fleet. Together with James Callaghan (British Prime Minister from 1976 to 1979), she created the Advisory Committee on Oil Pollution of the Sea (ACOPS), which was instrumental in drafting and bringing to realisation the International Convention for the Prevention of Pollution of the Sea (OILPOL), signed in May 1954. In the 1950s, the normal practice had been to wash the oil tanks out with water and then pump the resulting mixture into the sea. The OILPOL Convention prohibited the dumping of oily wastes within a certain distance from land and in 'special areas' where the danger to the environment was especially acute.

Despite her ground-breaking work, outside the worlds of ornithology and conservation, few knew who she was, yet she was instrumental in one of the most important environmental acts of the era. When she started to advise the Government about the lethal impact of crude oil on seabirds and other wildlife it was probably a subject never previously tackled. Today we all know about it and we have all seen footage of shorelines covered in the lifeless, black, oil-covered bodies of seabirds – but not until 1957 were members of the public able to understand the consequences of oil spills. The tanker SS *Torrey Canyon* ran aground on a reef off the southwest coast of the United Kingdom in 1967, spilling an estimated 25-36 million gallons (94-164 million litres) of crude oil. Around 15,000 sea birds were killed, along with huge numbers of marine organisms, before the 700km^2 (270 square miles) slick dispersed and reached the beaches of Cornwall and many other locations. It was then easy to understand why Phyllis had been such a strong advocate of OILPOL.

Editor of the *Avicultural Magazine*

Her demanding full-time job with ICBP (later to become BirdLife International) did not prevent her from taking on more work. In 1938 the Avicultural Society (founded in 1894 and still existing today) sought a new editor for the monthly *Avicultural Magazine*. David Seth-Smith (Curator of Birds at London Zoo) had retired after editing this magazine for more than 30 years. Ethel Chawner took the role for a very short time. Phyllis had joined the Avicultural Society in 1937 and Jean Delacour persuaded her to take on this job. She did so reluctantly – and the magazine never achieved a higher standard than under her editorship. I have the complete set and I often dip into the fascinating magazines of this era. In an Editorial in 1939 she wrote: 'I have considerably increased the links with other nations, by means of exchange of publications with scientific institutions and societies, and by requesting contributions from aviculturists in other countries.'

She seldom wrote more than brief notes for the magazine or interjected a comment on the Correspondence page. In the May-June 1950 issue Jack Indge penned a short letter: 'Although a lot of words have already been spilled on the above subject, I should like to add simply: Let the Avicultural Society adhere to avicultural matters and leave out ornithology; it will be better for all concerned.' This was too much for Phyllis! Her brief editorial comment was unequivocable: 'I entirely disagree with the views expressed in the above letter. Aviculture has an important part to play in the science of ornithology, and to this end the AVICULTURAL MAGAZINE has always striven. The amount of valuable data that has been lost by aviculturists who have failed to record their observations on birds in captivity is deplorable. – EDITOR.'

This is a view that I have expressed many times!

In that year, 1950, she reported that membership of the Avicultural Society was 679, the highest on record during the Society's 56 years of existence. It had not been easy for Phyllis to edit the magazine throughout the Second World War, especially as she had demanding jobs, first as a secretary to the business manager of the Bristol Aeroplane Factory and, from 1943 to 1945, in the Ministry of Labour. Her strengths were in building organisations, ensuring communication, collaboration and participation within and across an international network of scientists, civil servants and politicians.

Phyllis Barclay-Smith's workload was prodigious. She was Honorary Secretary of the British Ornithologists' Union from 1945 to 1951 and also found time to write. In 1946 King Penguin published her slim volume on *Garden Birds* and she also wrote the text of *British Birds on Lake, River and Stream* to accompany sixteen colour plates after the originals in *Birds of Great Britain* by John Gould. She penned book reviews for the *Avicultural Magazine* and translated into English the works of French and German ornithologists.

Edward Max Nicholson was a brilliant man – ornithologist, ecologist, co-founder of the World Wildlife Fund and of the BTO, private secretary to a deputy prime minister and chief editor of *The Birds of the Western Palearctic* 1977-1994. On her death he wrote:

'By virtue of her skill and personality, she was always the Queen Bee in her global hive; everything revolved around her. Always respected, widely loved, and sometimes dreaded, she rejoiced in her affectionate nickname 'The Dragon', and took most seriously her mission to keep order, make progress and ensure the efficient conduct of business. Ever a loyal and warm friend, she established relations of trust with outstanding active personalities in her field.

Richly endowed with a sense of drama, but equally of humour, of character reading and of means of inducing action even among the inactive, she enjoyed living in an atmosphere of imminent disaster, which was, however, always to be averted in the nick of time by the prompt and heroic interventions of her colleagues and herself. Life with Phyllis could be challenging and crisis-ridden, but it was always also amusing, stimulating and very much worthwhile. Quintessentially English, she was instantly at home anywhere in the world. She fascinated many foreigners. On one occasion, at a conference which the Hungarian delegate was prevented at the last minute from attending, she agreed without demur to stand in for him, and performed with aplomb the extra role of representing Hungary' (Nicholson, 1980).

Male Red-legged Sugarbird, photographed in Costa Rica. Photograph: www.wildparrotsupclose.com.

She edited the *Avicultural Magazine* from 1938 to 1973 without any financial reward. For many years she chaired the Council meetings of the Avicultural Society. The British Aviculturists Club was the dining club of that society, usually held in a hotel in South Kensington, five times a year. There would always be a guest speaker, a distinguished ornithologist or aviculturist or natural history film maker. Often there was a Guest of Honour, sometimes from overseas – thanks to her numerous contacts. Phyllis would always be in the chair. I remember her at meetings I attended in the 1970s. Of medium height, thin and gaunt, she seemed to me to be a very formidable person.

On August 31 1974 Phyllis was a guest on the popular BBC Radio 4 series *Desert Island Discs*. In this programme the chosen person talks about her/his life and picks eight favourite recordings. Phyllis's favourite was Chopin's Nocturne in E flat Major (Opus 9, No. 2). She also chose a recording of birdsong and, as her 'luxury item' a pair of binoculars.

Her home was in Warwick Avenue, Maida Vale, in north-west London. She often gave dinner parties there, entertaining ornithologists from many countries. But it was not only people who occupied her home! Phyllis kept a few birds, notably a pair of Red-legged

(Yellow-winged) Sugarbirds (*Cyanerpes cyaneus*) which lived with her for many years. These beautiful little nectar-feeding birds brought colour and joy into her life.

So what did she do when she was not working? We know little of her private life. She enjoyed travel but this was probably mainly in Europe. In 1979 she visited her nephew Roger in Malawi. He wrote that when she asked his cook for 'two eggs boiled for six minutes each' and received six eggs which had apparently been boiled for only two minutes she decided there and then to assist Malawi to educate its people! (Howell, 2009).

Her work was recognised with a number of prestigious awards. In 1958, she became the first woman to receive an MBE for work in conservation, and she was made a CBE in 1971. She also received the gold medal of the RSPB, the Delacour Medal of ICBP and the most Excellent Order of the Golden Ark by Prince Bernhard of the Netherlands. She was honoured posthumously by the World Wildlife Fund, which included her name in the WWF International Conservation Roll of Honour.

Phyllis Barclay-Smith died on January 2 1980, at Islington's Whittington Hospital, aged 77. Five days previously, on Christmas Day, 1979, she suffered a severe stroke and went into a coma. She had devoted her life to birds, not in a sentimental manner but in practical ways that she would probably never have achieved, had she stayed with the RSPB.

Whatever she did she did well. Her aunt had founded the RSPB to end the plumage trade, yet it took 30 years of banner waving and public speaking before that happened. Phyllis's achievements in the sphere of bird conservation were more fundamental and very important. If she had been a writer, like Rachel Carson, she would have been eulogised on the same level. She should be remembered for her commitment to the organisations she served: 24 years as assistant secretary to the RSPB, with ICBP/BirdLife International from 1935 until her retirement, and editor of the *Avicultural Magazine* for 35 years.

References

Delacour, J., 1966, *The Living Air,* Country Life Ltd, London.

Delacour, J., 1980, Miss Phyllis Barclay-Smith, CBE, *Avicultural Magazine,* 86 (1): 46-48.

Howell, J., 2009, The legacy of Roger Barclay-Smith, *Once a Caian,* 10: 14-15.

Nicholson, E. M., 1980, Obituaries, *British Birds,* 73 (5): 215-216.

12. Rachel Carson
USA 1907-1964
Author of *Silent Spring* – started Environmental Movement

Carson remains an example of what one committed individual can do to change the direction of society. – Lear, in Carson, 2002.

This is not a story of someone whose life was dedicated to bird conservation: her influence on the birdlife of the USA and across the world was indirect – yet immensely powerful. Rachel Carson was born on May 27 1907 in the village of Springdale, near Pittsburgh, in western Pennsylvania. She was the youngest of three children of Robert Waden and Maria McClean Carson.

Her family's two-story clapboard house was situated on a 158ha (64 acre) farm with an apple and pear orchard. As a child she was greatly influenced by her mother who was interested in the so-called 'nature study movement' which had its roots in natural history and theology. Growing up near the Allegheny River she was fascinated by the natural world and she would scramble down rocks and wade into tide pools. She enjoyed wandering among fields and hills with her mother, who taught her the names of plants and birds. When she was eight years old, she wrote a story about two Wrens searching for a house. In her teens she described the Bob-white Quail's nest, tightly packed with eggs, the oriole's aerial cradle and the lichen-covered home of the hummingbird.

Unlike her siblings, she graduated from high school (in 1925) and was then educated at what is today called Chatham College. She later won a scholarship but, even so, her parents' financial contributions to her education were not easily made. Rachel's first subject in college was English but she changed her course to biology in 1928 and graduated in 1929. After her full scholarship for graduate study at Johns Hopkins University in Baltimore, she supported herself.

Her career

Teaching and laboratory work during a summer appointment at the Marine Biological Laboratory at Woods Hole in Massachusetts were her occupations. She counted deep-sea fish in dangerous currents south of Nova Scotia, and, wearing an extremely heavy

Rachel Carson.

In 1936 a part-time job as a radio script writer on ocean life for the federal Bureau of Fisheries in Baltimore started a more secure career. She was so successful that she was soon one of only two professional women with a full-time position as an aquatic biologist with the Division of Scientific Enquiry. Rachel wrote for the *Baltimore Sun*, describing the pollution by industrial run-off of oyster beds at Chesapeake Bay.

She was promoted through the agency, which became the US Fish and Wildlife Service (USF&WL) in 1939. Her work included writing booklets publicising departmental preserves and programmes and editing field reports, thus broadening her scientific knowledge. By 1949 she was editor-in-chief of all the USF&WL publications.

Rachel's books

Her first book, *Under the Sea-Wind*, was published in 1941. It included the story of the Sanderling (*Calidris alba*) of whose habitat she wrote: 'To stand at the edge of the sea, to sense the ebb and the flow of the tides, to feel the breath of a mist moving over a great salt marsh, to watch the flight of shore birds that have swept up and down the surf lines of the continents for untold thousands of years, to see the running of the old eels and the young shad to the sea, is to have knowledge of things that are as nearly eternal as any earthly life can be.'

Her talent for writing was obvious but her demanding job had left her lit-

diving helmet, she explored Florida's coastal waters. Noticing how more garbage was being dumped in the ocean, she was one of the first to wonder how rising sea temperatures affected living creatures.

The Great Depression, starting in 1929, brought hardship to countless families. The number of unemployed Americans rose from 1.6 million in that year to 12.8 million in 1933. Rachel's father was forced to sell off some of their farmland. In 1932 Rachel completed an M. A. in zoology but in 1934 she was forced to look for work. When she was 28, in 1935, her father died. She had to support her mother, sister and two nieces. Her part-time teaching jobs and writing newspaper articles, mostly about marine life in Chesapeake Bay, provided income for her and the family.

tle time for this occupation. In 1951 she became 'an overnight literary celebrity' when *The Sea Around Us* was serialised in *The New Yorker*' (Lear, in Carson, 2002). *The Sea Around Us* became an Oscar-winning documentary film in 1953. It won the National Non-fiction Award in 1952 and was on the *New York Times* best-seller list for more than 80 weeks – an extraordinary achievement. This brought her enough financial security to resign from her job with the USF&WL to concentrate on writing. The issues of ecosystem conservation and environmental protection became her foremost concern. The popularity of her books enabled her to buy a few acres of land along the Maine coast, where she built a summer cottage. With the publication of her next book, *The Edge of the Sea* in 1955, Rachel was the foremost science writer in America.

As early as 1945 she had tried to interest the popular magazine *Reader's Digest* in the alarming evidence of environmental damage. The widespread use of the new synthetic chemical DDT and other long-lasting agricultural pesticides were to blame. The magazine was not interested. She knew then that this must be the subject of a book. In 1958 Rachel started to gather reports from a wide variety of sources – including many women – members of gardening clubs, bird watching societies, renowned scientists, journalists and politicians. From these sprung *Silent Spring*. This remarkable woman had been ill with breast cancer for the previous two years and she was exhausted from radiation treatments. She worked on the book for four years, struggling to finish it when, sadly, she was terminally ill, but determined to do so. After its publication in June 1962, it quickly became a best seller.

In *Silent Spring* she wrote:

'Since the mid-1940s over 200 basic chemicals have been created for use in killing insects, weeds, rodents, and other organisms described in the modern vernacular as "pests"; and they are sold under several thousand different brand names.'

'These sprays, dusts, and aerosols are now applied almost universally to farms, gardens, forests, and homes – non-selective chemicals that have the power to kill every insect, the "good" and the "bad", to still the song of birds and the leaping of fish in the streams, to coat the leaves with a deadly film, and to linger in the soil – all this though the intended target may be only a few weeds or insects.'

Rachel thought that the barrage of poisons on the surface of the earth would make it unfit for all life. She said that they should be called biocides, not insecticides.

Worldwide poisons and habitat destruction

Her warnings about the use of DDT and other pesticides stimulated wide-

Bald Eagle populations were decimated by the use of DDT and other pesticides. Photograph: author.

spread public concern because of adverse environmental effects on wildlife and on humans. However, it was not until 1972 that the use of DDT was banned in the USA. Today it is classified as a probable human carcinogen (cancer-causing) substance.

In the UK Sparrowhawk populations crashed in the 1950s. DDT, found in prey, and other organochlorine pesticides, thinned their eggshells, killing the embryos. In the USA populations of Bald Eagles and other birds suffered the same fate. In *Silent Spring* Rachel wrote about Charles Broley who banded more than 1,000 young of this species from 1939-1949. In 1947 many eggs failed to hatch and between 1952 and 1957 about 80% of nests failed to produce young. In 1958 Mr Broley searched over 160km (100 miles) of coast before finding a single eaglet. By 1957 the Hawk Mountain Sanctuary recorded only one young eagle for 32 adults. From 1935-1939 40% of the eagles counted had been juveniles.

In St. Louis, in Michigan, residents later complained for years about the numbers of dead birds in their backyards. When the bodies were tested, they were found to contain very high levels of DDT, banned 40 years earlier.

This was the legacy of a former chemical plant.

The chapter in *Silent Spring* entitled 'And No Birds Sing' was too painful for me to read. In the UK there had been a change from treating farm crop seeds before sowing, a change from fungicides to insecticides. Suddenly landowners and farmers were picking up dead birds – hundreds of them – 600 on a single estate in Norfolk; another report there: 'The place is like a battlefield'. Pigeons were dropping out of the sky, dead. There were huge bonfires to burn the bodies of birds.

Rachel Carson knew that insects had evolved to become immune to the insecticides used, hence a deadlier one always had to be developed. Enormous numbers of people had come into contact with these poisons, without their consent and often without their knowledge. The chemicals had been used with little or no advance investigation into their effect on soil, water, wildlife and on man himself. In less than two decades of their use, the synthetic pesticides had been so thoroughly distributed throughout the world that they occurred virtually everywhere, including in the bodies of birds, fish, reptiles and domestic and wild animals. And, of course, in man.

Rachel decried 'the bludgeoning of the landscape'. She cited the 'tragic example' of the sage brush lands, destroyed to substitute grasslands. She wrote:

> '... here the natural landscape is eloquent of the interplay of forces that have created it. It is spread before us like the pages of an open book in which we can read why the land is what it is, and why we should preserve its integrity. But the pages lie unread.'

The sage lands cover the high western plains and the lower slopes of the mountains that rise above them, a land born of the great uplift of the Rocky Mountain system many millions of years ago. It was a harsh place in which to survive but the evergreen sage plant had adapted, with its small grey leaves, to hold moisture to defy the winds. Two creatures had thrived there – the pronghorn antelope and the Sage Grouse (*Centrocercus urophasianus*). But in the name of progress, the land management agencies set about destroying the huge areas of sage to grow grass for cattle grazing. In the Bridger National Forest in Wyoming 4,000ha (10,000 acres) of sagelands were sprayed. This eliminated the sage, the willow trees that followed the streams, the moose that lived in the willow thickets, the beavers that fed on the willows and felled them for their dams, and the Sage Grouse that fed on the sage; all died. The trout in the mountain streams seldom grew longer than 15cm (6in) and without the beavers to dam the lake, the lake drained away. The living world was shattered (Carson, 1962).

Rachel Carson was very readable, writing in a style that was easy for the layman and pleasing to the scientist. She was credible. *Silent Spring* was the starting point of the environmental movement as we know it today. The book sold more than six million copies in the US alone and has been translated into 30 or so languages. Government entities sprung up around the world to study the issues and regulate them. Prior to her publications, few individuals concerned themselves with the environment.

Her approach was based on stubborn and remorseless presentation of scientific facts. Over and over again she has been proved right in her predictions. Her warnings were not heeded for long enough. Her words reverberate again today. In the 21st century in the UK we needed to be reminded that bees are absolutely necessary for our own survival, an obvious 'discovery' that gained a lot of media attention. In *Silent Spring* she wrote: 'These insects, so essential to our agriculture and indeed to our landscape as we know it, deserve something better from us than the senseless destruction of their habitat.' She warned that the chemical destruction of hedgerows and weeds were eliminating the last sanctuaries of these pollinating insects and 'breaking the threads that bind life to life.'

The mowing of roadside verges is a great source of annoyance to me. Valuable pollen-bearing plants such as dandelions, so important to bees, scarcely have time to flower in my immediate locality before local council contactors move in and destroy them in the name of tidiness. Yet councils claim there is not enough money to fill in the ruts in the roads!

Her story

What do we know about Rachel's personal life? Heavy family responsibilities had included being a source of income from a young age and, from the time she was 50, taking over the care of her niece's five-year-old son, Roger. Her generous, caring nature had found another purpose when her niece died from diabetes. Her efforts to support her family were enormous.

Rachel did not marry. In the summer of 1952, when she was 46, after building her summer cottage on the coast of Southport Island, she met neighbours, Stan and Dorothy Freeman. Thus began a very close and deep relationship with Dorothy that lasted until Rachel died. The two women loved nothing more than walking in the woods or exploring the crevices in the rocks lining Southport's shore. Dorothy had reservations about 'the poison book', as they called *Silent Spring* when they were apart, but Dorothy's letters 'brightened even the darkest days' as Rachel struggled with her investigations against DDT. They had previously filled their letters with 'news of plants in bloom or the desire to spend time together spotting birds or even the occasional whale in the bay'. Now Rachel hoped that Dorothy would understand how much she believed in what she was doing. She told Dorothy: 'There would be no future peace for me if I kept silent' and 'I wish I could feel that you want me to do it.' Dorothy was concerned. Her friend was 'at heart a gentle soul, with little taste for the public spotlight' and the enervating controversy her new book might provoke. Rachel had 'nagging health problems' that already sapped her energy (Lytle, 2007).

She was fighting two battles – that for her own life and the relentless battle against the chemical companies and agribusinesses who feared major financial losses if her warnings were heeded. In an era when any criticism of them or of the governmental policies relating to them was virtually unknown, it was a uniquely brave stand to take. The industrial chemical industry spent a quarter of a million dollars to malign her character and discredit her research. They labelled her hysterical and unscientific.

Rachel Carson was undoubtedly one of the most influential scientists, worldwide, of the 20th century and a writer of extraordinary moral and ecological vision. I believe that her impact and influence were greater than that of any other woman featured in this book. She died on April 14 1964 – much too soon. She was only 57. She posthumously received the Presidential Medal of Freedom in 1981. (Why did it take so long?) This award is bestowed by the president of the United States on people who have made an especially meritorious contribution to the security or national interests of the United States, to world peace, or cultural or other significant public or private endeavours.

References

Carson, R., 1962, *Silent Spring*, Houghton Mifflin Co. Lear, L., 2002, in Carson, first published 1962, Introduction, *Silent Spring*, Mariner Books, New York.

Lytle, M. H., 2007, *The Gentle Subversive. Rachel Carson, Silent Spring and the Rise of the Environmental Movement*, Oxford University Press, New York.

Also refer to:

Freeman, M. (edit), 1995, *Always, Rachel: The Letters of Rachel Carson and Dorothy Freeman 1952-1964* (Concord Library), Beacon Press.

Lear, L., 2009, *Rachel Carson: Witness for Nature*, Mariner Books, New York.

13. Anne LaBastille
USA 1933-2011
Documented Extinction of the Giant Grebe

Maybe there's little basic difference between insects and humans. One attacks prey directly to eat and survive; the other captures natural resources and the financial wealth of its victims. – Anne LaBastille in **Beyond Black Bear Lake.**

Mariette Anne LaBastille (she never used her full name) was born in Montclair, New Jersey on November 20 1933. She was the only child of Ferdinand Meyer LaBastille, a language professor at Columbia University, and Irma Goebel, a German-born actress and concert pianist.

As a child she longed for the wilderness, the nearest thing to which were the roughs of the local golf course and the nearby woods where she loved to venture. In *Woodswoman II, Beyond Black Bear Lake,* she wrote 'But for many years I didn't go farther than my suburban backyard. I yearned for a tent and pack yet had to be content with a treehouse in a white pine and lunch in a brown bag. At Christmas I asked my parents for stout boots and a .22 rifle – only to receive silk stockings and a dictionary. I was dragged to dancing school and art lessons rather than taken fishing and hunting.' She was told by her mother: 'Girls don't go camping!' and 'You must not walk in the woods alone!'

She thought her love of the outdoors and the lure of the wilderness might have been in her genes. Her adventurous English-Yankee grandfather made his fortune treasure-hunting in the Caribbean and a paternal French forebear pioneered a plantation there (LaBastille, 1987).

Her first 'real job' out of college was with the National Audubon Society. It ran two-day trips in south Florida around Lake Okeechobee and through the Everglades and Florida Keys. Anne was hired as a wildlife tour leader – the first woman ever in this role for the Audubon Society. She enjoyed showing people Snowy Egrets and other birds, while cruising among mangrove islets (LaBastille, 1990).

As an 'unworldly' teenager she took a summer job teaching horseback riding in the Adirondack Mountains of New York. This, for her, was 'the real introduction to and infatuation with wilderness'. At the rustic lodge at Big

Lake Atitlán.
Photographer: unknown.

Moose Lake where she worked, this attractive blond-haired girl fell in love with the innkeeper, Morgan Brown. She worked there for a few summers before they married. They then spent the winters organising nature tours outside the United States – probably the first Americans to do that. Leading tours to the Caribbean and to Central America, they experienced famed wildlife spectacles, such as Scarlet Ibis in Trinidad's Caroni Swamp, Oil Birds in the caves of Tobago and Flamingos on Bonaire's salt pans.

In 1960, Anne and Morgan were boating along the shores of south-western Guatemala's Lake Atitlán, the biggest tourist attraction in the country. Located in the Sierra Madre mountain range, it is the deepest lake in Central America. German explorer and naturalist Alexander von Humboldt called it 'the most beautiful lake in the world'. Something happened there that was to change the course of Anne's life. They saw a strange water bird. It was not identified until they visited the Museum of Natural History in Guatemala City. The bird was an Atitlán or Giant Grebe (*Podilymbus gigas*), found only on that lake. Grebes are water birds with round bodies, tiny tails and legs set far back on the body.

Almost nothing was known about this flightless species. Its population had been estimated at about 200 individuals in 1929 and in 1958. That day they returned to the lake with the museum's director and made their own count, actually seeing 99 birds and also estimating a population of 200 or more.

Back in the USA Anne and Morgan's marriage fell apart and in 1965 they were divorced. Free to do anything she wanted, Anne built a little cabin in the woods in the Adirondack Mountains. She lacked electricity and indoor plumbing. As the weather became cold, she thought increasingly about Guatemala. So she went back there, to Panajachel, to the lake, at an altitude of 1,500m (5,000ft) where wavelets lapped incessantly at the edge of the beach. Thunder rumbled over the Pacific coast far behind the distant volcanoes which rose to 3,350m (11,000ft).

She stayed with a friendly woman called Rosa, who let out rooms. She also rented a rickety wooden rowing boat. When a storm blew up on her first day of exploration she discovered why a dozen or more people drowned there every year. At one point the engine failed. When she reached Panajachel she was shaking with fright, sunstroke and exhaustion. She was lucky. She met Don Emilio, who had lived there for seventy years. He was 82 and his youngest child had been born on that birthday! He said 'You are the crazy bird lady… who goes barefoot and wears pigtails like an Indian woman and loves animals.'

The *poc* (Giant Grebe)

Don Emilio's friend Armando found a new engine for her boat and helped her search for the giant grebes, known locally as *pocs*. They found only 82 birds. There were no conservation officers anywhere in Guatemala and none of the universities had environmental science departments. She went to the only official, the Secretary. 'There are only 80 *pocs* left alive', she told him. 'And what difference does that make?' he responded. 'There is nothing that can be done about it.'

The Indians' houses lacked modern furniture. Anne knew that the *poc*'s population decline was partly due to the cutting of reeds in which they nested. The Indians' made sleeping mats and seats from them. All the reed beds were rented out to reed cutters. But the introduction of large-mouthed bass (*Micropterus salmoides*) to the lake in 1960, for local people to eat, also contributed to the decreasing population. These huge fish were food competitors and preyed on young grebes. They caused the decline of more than two thirds of the native fish species.

Anne was determined, fearless – and yes, foolish – in her fieldwork. After close observation of a pair of grebes, one day she decided to force her way into a 5.4m (18ft) reed bed, among the densest on earth. She wrote: 'I swam through the tallest stalks in ten feet of water. The bottom was firm here, but as I shoved my way through matted patches of reeds, and it got shallower, it turned to oozy mud. The water became murky, fetid gases bubbled up around me. I paused often to look for snakes and scorpions, although common sense told me they probably could not survive on this rough lake. My heart was pounding with apprehension and exertion. The sun beat fiercely on my wet head.'

Anne and Armando were elated to find the nest. It measured about 45cm (18in) across and was anchored to a few reed stalks. Only 8cm (3in) protruded above the surface; the rest hung down in a 1m (3ft) long funnel. There were no eggs inside.

Anne was not going to give up. She went, with Armando, to Guatemala City to meet the Minister of Agriculture. She explained to him her idea for Operation Protection of the *Poc*: enforcement, habitat management, education and appreciation, and finally a reserve. Armando suggested that he and Anne should be appointed as wardens of the lake. This was accepted, the education programme was a success, reed cutting was limited and *poc* nests and eggs were protected. Local artisans crafted objects with *poc* motifs – and life was good.

Part of the lake was made into a reserve where a few captured Atitlán Grebes survived safely. A small visitors' centre was constructed by Armando. Anne was commissioned to write an article on the grebe for the prestigious *National Geographic. Prensa Libre,* an important national newspaper, ran the story about the conservation campaign. Her next aim was to try to get rid of the large-mouthed bass. She had the idea, inspired by Sir Peter Scott, to produce a postage stamp and this was agreed by the National Postal Director. Unfortunately, the $123,000 the stamp raised went to the Government of Guatemala. The introduced fish were poisoned and 6,000 small native fishes were introduced into the reserve part of the lake, which covered 121km (75) miles of shoreline.

One day Anne saw a *poc* with six chicks. Normally they raised only two or three. She looked closely. This was a hybrid between a Giant Grebe and the smaller Pied-billed Grebe. Now there was another fear. They could hybridise themselves to extinction.

In 1966 Anne and Armando were in love. Anne wrote: 'He was a typical Aries, I thought, always on the go, full of courage and vigor.' With him she always 'felt safe, always cared for'. Then, after a year in Guatemala and ten months with Armando, Anne returned to the USA, to study at Cornell University. Anne wrote: 'I cried for him all the way back to New York'. She did not adapt easily to campus life. She missed Armando. She nearly gave up on her degree. One of her professors told her: 'You must go on. That degree will be your credit card in conservation for years to come.' He added: 'Go back to Guatemala and gather more information for your thesis. Get your campaign reactivated. You have seven years in which to complete the requirements for your degree.'

Anne returned at once to Lake Atitlán and to Armando. In the spring of 1968, Anne counted 116 *pocs* – an increase from the low of 80 in 1964-1965. That winter Armando flew to the USA for two weeks. He could barely tolerate the penetrating cold. When he went home, she wrote, 'some of the magic went with him'. Anne was grieving. She realised at last that they could never live together in the USA: he belonged at Lake Atitlán.

In the summer of 1969 Anne was working hard to finish her thesis. She taught for two years at Cornell. When she returned to Lake Atitlán Armando had gone. In March 1989 she returned after a long absence. During a visit to Panajachel (a town now often overwhelmed by tourists), while trying to find a vet to treat an injured dog, by chance she ran into Armando. They had an amicable meeting.

Disasters in Guatemala

On February 4 1976 all hope for the survival of the *poc* evaporated with the terrible 7.5 magnitude earthquake. More than 26,000 people were killed in Guatemala and the lake bed was fractured. As soon as she could, three months later, Anne was back in Guatemala to see how she could help. All her friends had survived but the lake had lost so much water that the few *pocs* in the refuge had to be released. They could not live in less than 60cm (2ft) of water. But that was not all – pollution and development, including a 14-storey three tower condominium on the lake's edge, blighted the landscape. Years later it had not been finished.

The *poc* population fell from 232 in 1975 to a maximum of 130 in 1980. In 1985 an agreement was signed for a captive breeding programme at Roberto Berger's Auto Safari Park, not far away. Permission was given to take *pocs* or eggs. Sadly he died before this could take place. At the same time Gary Nuechterlein counted 56 adult birds. He discovered a major potential cause of *poc* mortality. Nylon fishing nets were a new phenomenon on the lake. Now they were cheap and the fishermen could double their catch by using nets instead of hooks. The Indian population around the lake had doubled in 20 years; the people needed protein.

Over the years a local farmer, Edgar Bauer, gave Anne every assistance and became a close friend. He built a small house for her. He was paid a small salary as warden of the lake. Several years later he was murdered at his farm. Anne was devastated by his death. Another of her close allies, Father Alberto, had also died.

The *poc*'s extinction occurred between 1983 and 1986. By then 39% of the lake's shoreline was occupied by chalets, 10% by crowded Indian villages, 10% by working farms and 10% was uninhabitable terrain. By 1989, when Anne returned, the water level in the lake had dropped by more than 6m (19ft). The number of weekend houses there had increased from 28 in 1965 to 449. What had been good grebe habitat had decreased by 83%. The lake was heavily polluted and filamentous green algae grew like cotton candy among the aquatic plants. Plastic littered the surface (LaBastille, 1980). No *poc* could have survived there. In September 1989, a Commission for the Conservation of Lake Atitlán was established by presidential decree. Too late. Anne had worked so hard over a period of

20 years in her passionate attempt to save this very important bird. Her work had included master plans and maps to Guatemalan government officials, setting up Operation Protection *Poc*, writing numerous magazine and newspaper articles about saving it and the lake, and raising funding from major international conservation organisations, such as WWF.

Fame at a price

Anne had achieved a BSc in Conservation of Natural Resources from Cornell University in 1955, an MSc in Wildlife Management from Colorado State University in 1958 and a PhD degree in Wildlife Ecology from Cornell University in 1969.

It seems that she never really found personal happiness. In the USA she fell in love with a surgeon – but it was the same story of incompatible lifestyles. He was at home in the city hospital in an operating theatre. She could not live outside the lakes and the hills of the Adirondacks.

In the USA Anne's name is forever linked with the Adirondacks Mountains, where she purchased land on the edge of a mountain lake. Inspired by Henry David Thoreau's work, *Walden*, published in 1854, she built a log cabin in 1964. Thoreau's book describes the two years he spent in his cabin by Walden Pond, deep in the woods outside his hometown of Concord, Massachusetts. A philosophical treatise on labour, leisure, self-reliance and individualism, it was an influential piece of nature writing. Paul Grondahl, an award-winning American journalist, described Anne as having a rock star's charisma and a movie star's allure. She was only 1.54m (5ft 1n) but she 'packed a wallop in the public imagination as a fearless woman who in some ways out-Thoreaued Thoreau.'

In the 1970s Anne became a licensed New York State Guide and led backpacking and canoe trips into the Adirondacks and was on the Adirondack Park Agency Board of Commissioners for 17 years. She gave wilderness workshops and lectures for over forty years. A charter member of the New York State Outdoor Guides Association when it was reorganized in 1981, she was among a few pioneering women who broke into this male-dominated field. As an Adirondack guide Anne led and conducted workshops for various academic institutions. For her, guiding women was highly rewarding. She explained: 'What the wilderness did for these women is remarkable. First, they came to value a place where they could go safely without fear of rape, robbery or harassment. Secondly, the wild outdoors was a stage on which they could test their physical strength and practice new skills. I have seen exquisite moments such as when a sixty-year-old grandmother went skinny-dipping (first time ever) with a flock of loons [known as divers in the UK, such as the Red-throated] on a crisp dawn' (LaBastille, 1987).

Anne the author

Anne had started to write in 1971, as a contributor to several wildlife magazines, including *Sierra Club* and *National Geographic*. She had more than a dozen books published (see below). The most popular were those of the *Woodswoman* series, four memoirs spanning four decades of her life in the Adirondack Mountains. The final two books, *Woodswoman III* (1997) and *Woodswoman IV* (2003), were produced by her own publishing company, West of the Wind Publications.

She described the increasing difficulty of balancing freelance writing (more than 150 articles and 25 scientific papers), academic teaching, and conservation consulting with her desire to retreat into the wilderness. A keen photographer, her pictures appeared in various nature magazines. She became so well known that she appeared in numerous newspaper and TV interviews.

Her books elicited a huge response from readers and at book signings. Her German shepherd dog Pitzi would carry their letters from the mail boat to her cabin. 'At times Pitzi could barely carry up the mail sack.' Anne eventually made a rule that she would answer only those 'from young people interested in improving their education and from people who were hurting'. She reached out to advise girls in college or in the Peace Corps on choices in conservation careers. She was compassionate and practical.

Where and how did she write those letters? In *Beyond Black Bear Lake* (1987), she described how she built her smaller second cabin, *Thoreau II*, without electricity or running water, on a remote area of her property to obtain a more Walden-like experience. She wrote of her working day in her cabin:

'Time at the desk or on the sun deck is the equivalent of an executive's hours in an office composing letters, writing memos, researching, and editing. However, instead of coffee breaks and committee meetings, my work is broken by such distractions as meeting the mail boat, tramping to the outhouse, putting fresh wood in the stove or admiring the hummingbirds. I am alone with time yet never really alone. On sunny, calm days I may even work in the bottom of my canoe, floating on the lake. My portable typewriter just fits on the seat like a stenographer's desk. And a yellow pad works anywhere. No word processors for me! I want

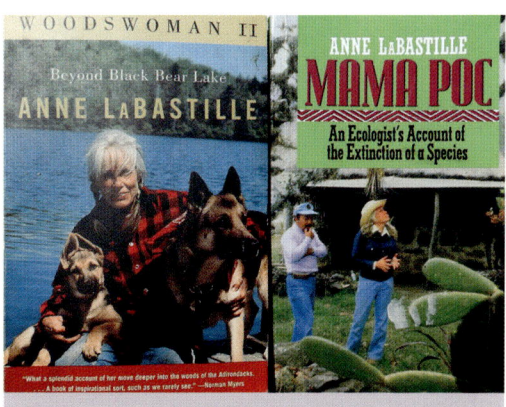

Two of Anne's highly popular books.
Photograph: author.

no machinery or electricity between my brain, hand, pen and paper' (LaBastille, 1987).

Said Grondahl: 'She found all the philosophy she needed in the still, crystalline waters of a mountain lake at dawn.' Anne could transport you there. She described coming across a Hooded Merganser:

'The male preened quietly among a flotilla of cow lilies. His pure white crest and chest flashed in the late-afternoon sun and his sleek body looked like black laquer against the green pads. With his yellow eyes matching the yellow flowers, I was reminded of a Japanese painting: *Mandarin Duck Among Lotus Blossoms*.'

And at sunset one day: 'The lake was cloaked in austere purple and seemed larger than by day. In the last light a pair of hooded mergansers whirred down from the silvery sky and parted the water in a long V for their night's rest.'

Anne was honoured by the World Wildlife Fund and the Explorers Club for her pioneering work in wildlife ecology in the United States and Guatemala. She travelled around the world and worked with various non-profit organisations to study and alleviate the destructive effects of acid rain. She saw how the waters of Black Bear and other mountain lakes were becoming acidified and damaged by chemical fallout. Around her lake, 35% of the trees were dead or dying. In 1978 *Outdoor Life* magazine asked Anne to write a story about acid rain. Scientific awareness of this started in the United States in the mid-1970s. She collected (even snorkelling underwater) and analysed water samples on her own property. Finding an old report, she discovered that her lake was roughly a hundred times more acidic than 50 years earlier.

She went to Scandinavia, where the countries were harder hit by acid rain than in the USA. In 1979 *National Geographic* commissioned an article on the same subject. This was the most complicated piece she had ever written, 'necessitating a working knowledge of chemistry, meteorology, hydrology, physics, politics, biology and more'. Her research took two years. Acid rain was causing forest dieback in Europe. She found that Swedes and Norwegians were trying to mitigate the problem, much of which was caused by smoke from electrical generating plants, steel plants and factories from the UK and Germany. These European countries denied that was a cause. Since then, acid rain in Europe and North America has abated because of stronger controls on sulphur dioxide emission (SO_2) and nitrogen oxide (NO_x). These included the U.S. Clean Air Act of 1970, the Canada–United States Air Quality Agreement in 1991, and similar measures in Europe.

Not everyone was sympathetic towards Anne's stance against the development of the Adirondack Park. She unfortunately received death threats, her remote cabin was broken into and, in 1993, in an arson attack the barn on her property in Westport was burned down. This was perhaps not surprising as she routinely took environmentalist positions that clashed with the agendas of property developers, snowmobilers and sportsmen. She had fought so hard and so long for the protection of the environment, and had taken a very strong stand against pollution and other man-made destructive forces. She deserved nothing but praise for what she had achieved. She influenced tens of thousands of people to value the natural world and to live more sustainably within it.

Woodswoman: Living Alone in the Adirondack Wilderness had launched her writing career and sold more than a hundred thousand copies. Decades, yes decades, after its 1976 publication, sacks of fan mail continued to arrive by boat, forwarded from her publisher (Grondahl, 2011).

It saddens me that the end of the life of this remarkable woman was not a happy one. After some years of partial memory loss, she died of Alzheimer's disease at a nursing home in Plattsburgh, New York, on July 1 2011. She was remembered as an inspirational voice for women and for the environment. Her close friend Doris Herwig said: 'When she put her mind to something and wanted it, you better move aside. Her tenacity was remarkable.'

So was her intellect, her compassion and her writing skills: a true heroine.

Anne LaBastille's books

- *Bird kingdom of the Mayas.* Van Nostrand, Princeton, NJ., 1967.
- *White-tailed Deer.* National Wildlife Federation, 1973.
- *Wild Bobcats.* National Wildlife Federation, 1973.
- *The Opossums, Ranger Rick's Best Friends.* National Wildlife Federation, 1974.
- *The Seal Family.* National Wildlife Federation, 1974.
- *Woodswoman.* E. P. Dutton, New York, 1976.
- *Assignment: Wildlife.* Dutton, New York, 1980.
- *Women and Wilderness.* Sierra Club Books, San Francisco, 1980.
- *Beyond Black Bear Lake.* Norton, New York, 1987.
- *The Wilderness World of Anne LaBastille.* West of the Wind Publications, Westport, N.Y., 1992.
- *Birds of the Mayas: Maya Folk Tales: Field guide to birds of the Maya world: Complete check list of birds.* Written and illustrated by Anne LaBastille. West of the Wind Publications, Westport, N.Y., 1993.
- *Woodswoman III: Book three of the Woodswoman's adventures.* West of the Wind Publications, Westport, N.Y., 1997.
- *Jaguar Totem.* West of the Wind Publications, Westport, N.Y., 1999.
- *Book four of the Woodswoman IV: Book four of the Woodswoman's adventures.* West of the Wind Publications, Westport, N.Y. 2003.

A parallel history – almost

Lake Junin, in the Peruvian highlands, also had a species of grebe (Podiceps taczanowskii) *found nowhere else in the world. The history of the lake almost exactly mirrored that of Lake Atitlán. It became polluted by runoff water from mining and sewage. The grebe's nesting area dried out as water was extracted to supply hydroelectric plants. By 1993 only 50 Junin Grebes survived. Then, in 2002, the Peruvian government passed an emergency law to clean large areas of its waters and place greater restrictions on water extraction. The lake was designated a Ramsar Wetland of International Importance and an Important Bird and Biodiversity Area. Birdlife International's High Andean Wetland project helped the Peruvian conservation group ECOAN to set up long-term research and education programmes. The grebe became a flagship for High Andean wetland conservation and its numbers increased. In 2020 it was downlisted from IUCN Critically Endangered to Endangered. It then had a fluctuating population of about 300 individuals.*

References

Grondahl, P., 2011, Anne LaBastille, 1933-2011, *Adirondack Explorer*, August 22.

LaBastille, A., 1987, *Woodswoman II, Beyond Black Bear Lake*, W. W. Norton & Co., New York.

LaBastille, A., 1990, *Mama Poc: An ecologist's account of the extinction of a species*, W. W. Norton & Co., New York.

14. The Amazing Female Authors

How different were most of the publications of the heroic ladies of the past to those of today! Several were extremely talented writers and book after book flowed from their pens. The writing energies of most of the living ladies are channeled into producing scientific reports. Two, Neiva Guedes and LoraKim Joyner, are authors of books, another has produced a field guide and others have contributed book chapters.

Some of the celebrated authors discovered the joy of writing at a very early age. In her childhood, Rachel Carson (Chapter 12) wrote and illustrated *Wild Creatures are my Friends* as a present for her father. Her literary ability was outstanding. Her short stories were published in the popular monthly *St Nicholas* children's magazine. It had previously published Mark Twain and Rudyard Kipling.

Rachel went on to achieve worldwide fame with the publication of her book *Silent Spring*. Her first book, *Under the Sea-wind*, was said to be her own favourite. It was overshadowed by World War II, causing it to be a commercial failure, but Rachel knew it was good. She never gave up on it and saw its re-publication to great acclaim in 1952. In 2007 Penguin Classics published a new edition.

The French philosopher and scientist, René Descartes (1596-1650), proposed the idea that animals act purely on instinct and deal with daily life only in response to immediate and visible or perceived stimuli. He declared they had no feelings: they were automatons. Perhaps he was the worst enemy birds have ever known because this idea persisted well into the second half of the 20th century.

It took a number of inspirational women to contradict this theory. But before them came, in 1902 a landmark ornithological publishing event: *Handbook of Birds of the Western United States*. This book remained a standard reference in regional ornithology for at least 50 years. Without sacrificing technical precision, it included vivid descriptions of behaviours, such as feeding, breeding and vocalisations – information that is only briefly described in most field guides. The author was a woman! And this was 1902! And this was Florence's work!

Florence Augusta Merriam Bailey 1863-1948

Her bird-watching guide, focused on living birds observed in the field, is considered to be the first in the tradition of modern, illustrated bird guides. It drew on the best available published work, the study of specimens with Robert Ridgway of the Smithsonian Institution, 600 illustrations from numerous sources, and her own field work.

Florence was born in Leyden, New York, on August 8, 1863, to Clinton Levi Merriam and Caroline Hart Merriam. Florence and her brother were encouraged to study natural history and astronomy; both were interested in birds from an early age. At this time emphasis was on studying skins in museums but Florence was fascinated by the behaviour of living birds. She was incensed by the fact that millions were being killed to decorate women's hats. In 1885 she wrote several newspaper articles on the subject. She was then only 22 – and this action was similar to that of Etta Smith (Chapter 4) in England who at the age of 18 in 1878, was writing to women in her church, imploring them not to wear feathers. They were two of several women in that era who had a passion for birds and found what was happening to them appalling and unacceptable. She later became an active member of the Committee on Bird Protection of the American Ornithologists' Union.

Florence Merriam's publishing output started when she wrote *Birds Through an Opera-Glass* at the age of 26, adapting a series of notes that first appeared in *Audubon Magazine*. The book, directed at women and young people, described 70 common species. Before her 1902 field guide was published Florence was travelling widely in the US, resulting in *My Summer in a Mormon Village* (a travel narrative, 1894), *A-Birding on a Bronco* (1896), *How Birds Affect the Farm and Garden* (1896) and *Birds of Village and Field: A Bird Book for Beginners* (1898). In 1899, when she was 36, Florence married Vernon Bailey, a friend of her brother and the Chief Field Naturalist for the United States Bureau of Biological

Florence in 1916 From Bird Lore. Unknown photographer.

Survey. This was surely a meeting of minds which was to greatly influence her publishing output. Over the next three decades, Florence and Vernon explored much of the American West. The results of their field work in 1917 were published jointly in 1918 as *Wild Animals of Glacier National Park*.

Florence also played an important role in the US Congress passing the Lacey Act, which banned wildlife trafficking in 1900. In 1903 and for the next three summers, the couple carried out substantial field research in New Mexico. A decade later Florence was asked to complete Wells Cooke's work on the birds of that region. Drawing on her field notes, she wrote *The Birds of New Mexico*, which was finally published in 1928 and recognised with the Brewster Medal in 1931. She had visited the Arizona Territory in the 1890s and what became the State of Arizona several times during the 1920s. Her last published work was *Among the Birds in the Grand Canyon Country*, published by the National Park Service in 1939, ten years before her death in September 1948.

In a memorial essay, Paul Oehser described her as 'one of the most literary ornithologists of her time, combining an intense love of birds and remarkable powers of observation with a fine talent for writing and a high reverence for science.' Her approach to the study of nature was one of gentle, quiet contemplation. She wrote: 'Cultivate a philosophic spirit, be content to sit and listen to the voices of the marsh; let the fascinating, mysterious, bewildering voices encompass you and – hold your peace.' (From the Wikipedia entry for Florence Augusta Merriam Bailey.) She was a truly remarkable woman.

Born in the 19th century

The very rare combination of 'an intense love of birds and remarkable powers of observation with a fine talent for writing' was to notably repeat itself four more times within four decades. In England Emma Turner was born in 1867 (four years after Florence), Magdalena Heinroth (Chapter 7) in Germany and Margaret Morse (Chapter 8) in the USA, both in 1883, and 'Len' Howard (Chapter 9) in England in 1894. These four women had in common the passion for birds and the gift of expressing it in very enjoyable prose that keeps one captivated, page after page. The literary output of Margaret Morse was unique in covering two spheres. A pioneer in the science of ethology (understanding animals by watching their behaviour), she also wrote on language development in children, while rearing five of her own.

The writings of the quartet of Bailey, Turner, Heinroth and Howard seem to me to have a wonderful quality that belongs to their era. It is not sentiment – it is a tenderness that is difficult to achieve in words and can be gained only with intimate knowledge and understanding of the birds they are writing about.

From the aspect of observation, Magdalena had it easy; she hand-reared all her birds. They were very tame and they were always in front of her. Len Howard studied the birds in her garden and knew them as friends as many entered her house and some even roosted above her bed! She needed time, patience and an unusual understanding of their behaviour to achieve this degree of intimacy. It was, to a degree, similar for Emma Turner, except that her observations were not made in the comfort of her own home but in a different kind of bed – the reed beds and often knee-deep in water. They all knew birds as individuals and could reveal and publish previously unknown details of the species' behaviours.

Lucy Evelyn Cheesman (Chapter 2) was surely one of the most remarkable female scientists who ever lived. She supplemented her small income by writing 16 popular books chronicling her adventures and discoveries. She was never short of material! Her books included: *Everyday Doings of Insects* (1924), *Hunting Insects in the South Seas* (1932), *Camping Adventures on Cannibal Islands* and *Six-legged Snakes in New Guinea* (1949), a novel: *Landfall The Unknown* (1950), *Insects Indomitable* (1952), *Charles Darwin and his Problems* (1953), *Things Worth While* (1958) and *Time Well Spent* (1960).

During her travels in the New Hebrides she stayed with a tribe of cannibals who had rarely been approached by Westerners. She was able to establish such good relations that in 1930 she received diplomatic gifts for King George V from King Ringapat of Malekula, the leader of the cannibals. Her final expedition was to Vanuatu in 1953, at the age of 73 after a hip replacement.

This intrepid traveller collected 70,000 specimens of insects and animals for the Natural History Museum, some of which were new to Western science. More than 40 years after her death, scientists were still identifying new species and making discoveries among the specimens she collected. Among the many plants, a pressed flower in the Museum's collection was found in 2013 to be a new species of orchid. The blue colour of its flowers makes it unique among the approximately 26,000 known species of orchids.

The ladies from Scotland

Reference books are often thought of as the domain of men yet *The Birds of Scotland,* a two-volume landmark published in 1953, was the work of two women. It remained the definitive reference on Scotland's birds for more than 30 years. Evelyn Baxter (1879-1959) and Leonora Rintoul (1875-1953) were celebrated figures in Scottish ornithology. Inseparable lifelong companions, they founded the Scottish Ornithologists' Club and co-authored many articles. They studied migratory birds on the Isle of May from 1907 to 1933. Their study of migration routes being affected by wind was influential in developing migration theory. Both were elected as Fellows of the Royal Society of Edinburgh in 1951, and Baxter was the first woman to receive the Union Medal from the British Ornithologists' Union.

The two ladies built up a collection of 1,200 bird skins, which they later donated to the Natural History Museum in London. These included first records of some species in the Firth of Forth, as well as the first Pied Wheatear (*Oenanthe pleschanka*) found in Britain and the first Common Nightingale and Melodious Warbler (*Hippolais polyglotta*) in Scotland. Some of their specimens were shot and many were salvaged by light-keepers from the Isle of May and other Scottish lighthouses.

The musicians

It is interesting that two authors were also musicians who understood bird song. Len Howard (Chapter 9) was a professional musician and she could transcribe bird song. While she was observing her beloved Great Tits, another professional musician, Clare Kipps (1890-1976), was working as an air-raid warden in London, not so far away. On July 1 1940, returning from her duties, she found a tiny newly-hatched bird on her doorstep. Fortunately, she was a friend of the poet and author Walter de la Mare, who persuaded her to write the life story of the sparrow. Published in 1952, *Sold for a Farthing* is a very touching piece of writing, in a similar vein to that of Len Howard. However, unlike that of the other authors in this chapter, Clare Kipps' life did not revolve around birds and I believe she had previously published nothing. The fact that this sparrow learned to sing is unique. Musician Clare was able to recognise the mathematical structure of an aria in bird song. But it is the love that Clare and her sparrow have for each other and her ability to relate this that make this book extraordinary. Note that it is difficult to hand-rear a House Sparrow and to do so from day one is remarkable. It is easy to find this book on the internet. If you love birds, you need to read it.

In her review of this book, Sally Read wrote:

> The two, woman and bird, develop a close, loving relationship, sharing a bed and establishing routines that he learns quickly (when she returns from her nights out as air-raid warden he breakfasts with her, then leads her to bed where he snuggles down with her to sleep). The book is full of winning anecdotes about his moods, love for her, jealousy towards other people who intrude on their Eden; how he sits on her hand while she plays the piano and sings in a very unusual way for a sparrow. He lives to the astonishing age of twelve, having become quite famous in Blitz-weary London, performing card tricks and singing to audiences.

Twentieth century writers

The style and personality of the writers I have mentioned seem to belong in the late 19th and in the 20th century. One of the latest examples of this style known to me is Linda John's *In the Company of Birds*. Published in 1995, it was the second book of this American artist; her first was entitled *Sharing A Robin's Life*. Among the birds reared in Linda's home were two cockerels called Bubble and Squeak (dubbed Burble and Shriek when they started to learn to crow!). They were very affectionate and loved to cuddle up with her in the evenings. She wrote:

> 'I gently slid my fingers through Squeak's beautiful handwoven-like plumage, the silky feathers rippling with fluid grace. His eyes were totally closed except when he'd part them a fraction to peer up at me, his whole facial expression resonating enjoyment. Beside him Bubble drowsed deeply, eyes closed, his long iridescent tail feathers flowing over the chair's edge in complete relaxation…'

She reflected on the fact that chickens were 'considered to be more of a joke than a type of creature with personality and dignity, fully entitled to fulfil their own potential; a species abused daily in unspeakable ways, whose defeathered bodies are wrapped in plastic, barcoded and slung into grocery bins.'

Few of my heroes wrote books that brought them fame. Anne LaBastille (Chapter 13) was an exception. Betsy Folwell, creative director at the magazine *Adirondack Life,* watched Anne attract hundreds at public readings and

Much-loved books by Linda Johns, Clare Kipps and Len Howard in the author's library.
Photograph: author.

writing workshops. They would queue up to ask her to sign the *Woodswoman* books. At the annual Author's Night in Long Lake most of the writers sat next to stacks of unsold books, feigning disinterest, while LaBastille's corner was mobbed and she sold case after case. She was commissioned to write *Women and Wilderness*. When it was published in 1981 it was used in many college courses (resulting in speaking invitations for Anne), in women's studies and in American literature.

21st century books

Most female authors in the 21st century with titles on birds naturally reflect the era, in which huge advances in ornithological research have occurred. In *Bird Minds – Cognition and Behaviour of Australian Native Birds* (2015), Gisela Kaplan demonstrates how emotional and intelligent birds can be, using Australian species as examples. The complex behaviours she describes include grieving, deception and problem solving; they show how wrong were Descarte's assumptions. Of course, bird keepers have never had any doubt that he was wrong as they see complex behaviours in their aviaries, even if they don't understand them all.

In a detailed academic account of bird behaviour Gisela Kaplan presents recent changes in our understanding of the avian brain and links these to life histories and longevity. The author is a Professor at the University of New England and an Honorary Professor at the Queensland Brain Institute. Her impressive publishing history includes more than 20 books on birds, primates and other topics. It includes *Bird Bonds*, published in 2019, about sexual selection, mate choice and emotions in Australian birds.

Nearly all 21st century female ornithological authors I have read write with a different voice to those of the previous era. One exception, which just qualifies for the 21st century, is Joanna Burger in her touching book *The Parrot who Owns Me* (2001). It is sub-titled *The Story of a Relationship*. Yes, a relationship between a bird and a human can be very strong and enduring. Authors who describe this, as does Stacey O'Brien in *Wesley the Owl,* deserve applause for again bringing to our attention the individual emotions and personalities of birds, in the Len Howard tradition. Perhaps more people would take a sympathetic attitude towards avian lives if these aspects were better understood.

Joanna Burger is a professor of biology at Rutgers University and her speciality is ornithology and animal behaviour. She has written or co-authored more than 25 books, including *A Naturalist along the Jersey Shore* (1996), *Whispers in the Pines* (2006), *A Visual Guide to Birds* (2006), and *Birdlife of the Gulf of Mexico* (2016). Her style is eminently readable, but it is her empathy with her Amazon parrot Tiko and her ability to interpret his feelings and behaviour that make *The Parrot who owns Me* remarkable. As I read it, I realised its significance. It had the potential to

Joanna Burger and Tiko.
Photograph: Michael Gochfeld.

change the way people perceive their parrots and to provide owners with a deeper understanding of their bird's needs. This can improve their quality of life to an unimaginable degree.

Tiko's elderly owner had died, and Tiko adopted Joanna. The way Joanna unfolded his story provides an insight into what an unwanted parrot suffers and can perhaps make owners act more responsibly. Her remarkable perception of what Tiko needed has surely given many people entry into a hitherto unknown world. The story of how Joanna won Tiko's heart is inspirational. They remained together for 36 years, until Tiko died aged 66. He was the oldest known Red-lored Amazon (*Amazona autumnalis salvini*) in the world. 'Care, companionship, and love clearly matter to a parrot', said Joanna.

A more sympathetic attitude towards birds and their environments will be essential if the huge declines in most bird species worldwide are to be halted. Emotive writers have the power to reach out to huge audiences and to influence decisions, perhaps in a way that is not so effective in more scientific writers. That is why the women in this chapter are all heroines in my eyes.

Present-day Female Heroes

Colleen Downs

Bernadette Plair

Andrea Angel

Nicola Crockford

Neiva Guedes

Judith Mirembe

Sara Lara

15. Careers, Marriage and Families

The remarkable achievements of women in ornithology are recounted in these pages. What they accomplished is even more extraordinary when considered in the context of the times. The women described in the first part of this book had no privileges at all. For American women even travelling overseas might have been impossible in the 1920s. Passport applications could be rejected based on the name they used. A married woman was issued a joint passport with her husband; her name was not included – she was demoted to 'wife of'. If she applied for a separate passport the application could be rejected. Between 1907 and 1922 American women who married non-citizens automatically lost their American citizenship. This was disastrous during the First World War as they were forced to register as 'enemy aliens.'

The big change did not occur until the 1970s. *Time*'s article *Who's Come a Long Way, Baby?*, from August 31, 1970, pointed out of American women: 'They want equal pay for equal work, and a chance at jobs traditionally reserved for men only. They seek nationwide abortion reform – ideally, free abortions on demand. They desire round-the-clock, state-supported child-care centers in order to cut the apron strings that confine mothers to unpaid domestic servitude at home.'

The most radical feminists aimed to topple the patriarchal system in which men by birthright control all of society's levers of power – in government, industry, education, science, the arts. In Europe and the USA, where women had more rights than in other parts of the world, changes were slow to come, even with the strong suffragette movements. In Europe, before the Second World War, the absence of men who were fighting overseas, catapulted millions of women into the work force.

In the UK, by 1971, 53% of women aged 16-64 were in employment. By 2013 this figure had risen to 67%. By the end of 2019 this had risen to 72.4% – a record high – while that of men was 80.6%. In the USA, in 1972, 51% of women aged 25 to 54 were working and by 1979 the figure was 74%. However, salary discrimination against women was a huge issue and remains so, although the pay gap decreased in the 21st century, when it attracted a lot of media attention.

Female scientists earned about 12% less than similarly qualified male scientists in 1972 but, surprisingly, 14% less in 1982; and black scientists earned about the same amount as white scientists in 1972, but 6% less in 1982. (Source: *Industrial and Labor Relations Review*, Vol. 44, No. 1 Oct., 1990).

It was not only salary discrimination that was an issue. Many positions were not even open to women. For example, up to the 1980s the London Symphony Orchestra banned women from becoming members.

Families and marriage

The achievements of some of the women profiled in this book are all the more extraordinary because they had very demanding family commitments. These either occupied the years before their involvement with birds or limited the time they could devote to writing or conservation. Margaret Morse Nice and Harriet Hemenway both had five children. Althea Sherman, Emma Turner and Rachel Carson had to spend much of their lives caring for family members and, in Rachel's case, even supporting them financially. Because of this Althea did not even start to look at birds seriously until she was 42 and Len Howard, due to her work as a musician, until she was 48.

For Neiva Guedes the field work came at a very high cost – she suffered two miscarriages. In 1998 Neiva had married artist Joacilei Lemos Cardoso and in 2002 her daughter Sophia was born. She was determined to continue with her field work. She was often away but her very supportive family and friends looked after her daughter. Money was short but she always had *'em abundância em amor'*.

Natalia Luchetti introduced another important topic. She related:

'Well, I am not married, but I was. I started my PhD in November 2012 and I got married in March 2013. I met my ex-husband in biology graduation, so it was expected he would understand my work, but no. Some weeks after we got married, he started to ask me about having a baby, but I was collecting the material for my PhD in Amazonia. I had about six field trips every year, so it was impossible for me to think about children at that time. He insisted, his family was asking too. I also had problems with him complaining about me travelling to congresses and sometimes being in the lab more than eight hours a day; he did not understand the unpredictable processes with specimens in the laboratory. I asked for a divorce and moved on in April 2014. I have no regrets. It was a hard decision at that time, but today I see it was the best thing I did.'

I believe that this was the correct decision. It can be harder to leave a relationship that is not working for the reason she described than to stay. Ul-

Natalia Luchetti in Porto Velho, Rondônia, close to the Madeira river. Photograph: Natalia Luchetti.

timately, resentment will build against the partner so the relationship will fail. And it becomes more difficult to leave with each passing year.

Sometimes sacrifices must be made to take a good position. Barbara Tomotani from Brazil is married and has a very supportive partner but, she said, 'We also have a somewhat strange family situation. We are both researchers and we did our PhDs in different countries (Germany and the Netherlands). Recently, my husband got a job in New Zealand and I had a large personal grant approved in the Netherlands. So, we are currently living very far away in different continents. It was not made easier with Covid. We are unwilling to live apart forever but we decided to do so until my grant ends.'

Patricia Zurita, who has the very important position of CEO of BirdLife International, wrote: 'For a woman, especially from a developing country, getting to where I am now was difficult, but not impossible. It requires a lot of patience, and you do have to work harder. Being a working mother is an extra challenge. You need to make sure you build a good team underneath you that you can rely on, and also have a supportive team of loved ones at home' (Peris, 2021).

Itala Yepez is Head of Conservation for BirdLife International Americas. Originally from Ecuador, in 2018 she moved to Mexico and worked in the American conservation organisation RARE. She remembered: 'Without a doubt, that was one of the most challenging moments in my career. I was divorced, had two young children and the new position required me to move to Mexico. Accepting a management job with a great deal of responsibilities and constant travel to the USA and Latin America, and trying to balance it with family time was challenging, but it helped me build my career and I am passionate about what I do, so I took the job and learned a lot along the way' (Peris, 2021).

Ana Veiga is from Cabo Verde, an archipelago consisting of ten volcanic islands in the central Atlantic Ocean. Since childhood she wanted to be a scientist and today she coordinates BirdLife's Cabo Verde seabird project. After completing a MSc course in Conservation and Biology, she returned to Cabo Verde, and worked for six years at the National Directorate of Environment.

She said: 'The biggest challenge I faced was when I decided to leave my job at the Government, as I did not want to work just in an office.' She did not have support from some of her relatives and friends. They thought a government job was synonymous with financial stability and that it would damage her career to leave it. 'I just wanted to follow my dreams and implement my own project ideas. It was not easy, but I can say that it was worth it.' She has developed partnerships with other NGOs, and is contributing to improving knowledge of the biodiversity of Santiago island, and the sustainable development of its communities (Abiadh, 2019).

Women working in wildlife conservation face tough challenges, especially if they have a partner and children. Those who need to be in the field for part of the year have my enormous admiration. They are very special people and they deserve extra support from colleagues, supervisors and families. To those around them I would say do not under-estimate their difficulties but give them all possible assistance.

References

Abiadh, A., 2019, Meet the women inspiring change in the Mediterranean, *BirdLife Magazine,* April-June, 42-45.

Peris, M., Women in Science, 2021, Worldwide News, February www.birdlife.org/worldwide/news/womescience-meet-birdlife.

16. Françoise Delord
France 1940-
Founder, ZooParc de Beauval

Delve into the history of a zoo or bird park and more often than not there is an extraordinary story relating to its founder! As a child Françoise Doucet had a passion for animals. Born on January 30 1940, she was raised alone by her mother, a teacher. She was educated at the Lycée Jeanne d'Arc in Orléans. As a young woman of great style and beauty, she was a student at the Conservatory of Dramatic Art in Paris and dreamed of playing Phèdre and Andromache. 'I was too sweet, too flirtatious,' she said. 'In fact I was not made to be an actress… but I do not regret anything'.

Françoise was living in Paris in a maid's room when a friend suggested, as a small job, she could present a show in the Paris Bobino music hall. She had a three-week contract and stayed for six years. She became a celebrated star. It was there that she met and married the magician Jacques Delord. The marriage failed but resulted in two wonderful children.

The gift of a pair of Silverbills (small finches) in 1971 started her passion for birds. After five years there were two hundred feathered inmates in her Paris flat! A photograph from that era shows her family dining in front of a large aviary, a cockatoo perched on her shoulder and an Amazon Parrot with her husband, while their two young children looked on, birds already part of their lives.

A few years later there was only one answer to accommodating her collection: start a zoo! This she did, single-handedly in 1980, with 5ha (12 acres). 'At the time, I was called crazy' says Françoise, who greeted the visitors and put the entrance money in a plastic box. Her husband's parents, who lived in Tours, had introduced her to a place called Saint-Augnan-sur-Cher. There she opened her park, which is skilfully incorporated into the landscape on a small tributary of the River Cher.

Now, 41 years later, ZooParc de Beauval is said to be among the top ten zoos in the world, and listed in the 15 most beautiful. With exceptionally large and well planted enclosures and a scenic setting, it would get my vote in the top five. This is a huge collection: 4,600 plus animals and birds of more than 500 species, with many interesting ones seldom seen in zoos. It is the most visited tourist site of the central Loire Valley region, and one of the five most visited zoological institutions in France.

Parrots have always been very special to her. In 1978 her book *Perruches et Perroquets* was published, describing how to choose, breed and care for parrots and parakeets.

In her memoir *Instinct,* she wrote about her macaws, her first large parrots, acquired while she still lived in her Paris apartment. The male Blue and Yellow Macaw (*Ara ararauna*) called Caroline, was very beautiful, sweet and intelligent. He paired up with a Scarlet Macaw (*Ara macao*) called Aurore. When the bird park opened these two birds lived in a large aviary and were totally devoted to one another. When Aurore died, years later, Françoise's keepers told her that Caroline looked ill but he was quite aggressive towards them. So she went to see him. Although it was 15 years since she had touched him, as soon as he saw her he flew the 8m (26ft) length of the aviary and landed directly on her shoulder and put his beak and his head against her cheek. In the spring she tried to introduce a young female of his species to him, but he would not accept her. So she built an aviary in her house for him, and there he lived until he died. Françoise and Caroline had been together for nearly 40 years.

When I visited the park in 2013 Françoise took me on a tour. There were welcomed interruptions by visitors, who recognised her authoritative presence and trademark large dark glasses, and stopped to congratulate her on the wonderful haven she has created. She is known and loved by staff and visitors alike. This was touching to observe. She introduced me to some of her favourite animals, such as an orang utang. Behind the scenes she fed him yoghurt on a spoon! Her total delight in her animals cannot be disguised.

Her influence is so great that the French president intervened to acquire pandas for the zoo. Each one eats its way through 40 kilos of bamboo daily! Unlike some zoos, where you might

Françoise and a panda – a great crowd-pleaser and easily viewed.
Photograph: author.

queue for a long time to see pandas, here they are close and easily observed.

The superb tropical house includes separate aviaries around the perimeter housing such eye-catching beauties as deep red Cardinal Lories, elegant Red-flanked and Stella's Lorikeets, rare Papuan Mountain Pigeons (*Gymnophaps albertisii*), and a magnificent pair of Rhinoceros Hornbills. A path meanders past the aviaries and around the central area which is contained within large rocks; there are no barriers to spoil the view of palms, philodendrons, ficus and flowering plants and little rocky pools. Nicobar and Victoria Crowned Pigeons, a Red Lory, touracos and stilts, are free to fly and to walk around the area.

Outside, a flock of Sun Conures and Golden Parrots made even the sunshine look dull! In the same range, which has planting inside and outside, are brick-built enclosures. Outstanding were big black Palm Cockatoos in superb condition – their bare cheeks fiery red. In adjoining aviaries were various species of parrots, including Festive Amazons, Black-headed Caiques and Keas (*Nestor notabilis*), those iconic, mischievous, brainy parrots from New Zealand.

Nearby was a range of aviaries for macaws, Galahs and white cockatoos, including Greater Sulphur-crested and the beautiful Philippine species with its red under tail coverts. The conservation of the latter endangered species is one of the many projects supported by the zoo. Well placed information boards highlight these projects.

The enclosures and the park are profusely and attractively planted. Photograph: author.

Opened in 2020, le Dôme Equatorial houses around 200 different species underneath a one hectare and 38m (125ft) high dome with a glass roof. It is constantly heated to a temperature of 26°C (79°F). Stars of the exhibit include the pygmy hippopotamus, the giant otter and the Harpy Eagle. Elsewhere in the exquisitely and profusely planted grounds, all the usual park birds can be seen: a large flock of flamingos, waterfowl including endangered Néné Geese originally from Hawaii, cranes, pelicans and large stately Ground Hornbills.

This is a family-run business; Françoise's son Rodolphe and daughter Delphine play important roles and her many employees are part of that big family. You can feel the difference from a zoo that is owned by an institution even although staff numbers are so high – in 2020, there were 600 permanent employees.

Conservation projects are administered through the Beauval Research and Conservation Association. The zoo takes part in EEPs (European breeding programmes) for many endangered species, such as the Blue-throated Macaw (*Ara glaucogularis*).

She calls the zoo 'mon troisième enfant' – my third child. She is a remarkably strong and determined and passionate woman. Her single-handed initiative grew into something of extreme importance in the world of zoos. My admiration for her is immense.

ZooParc de Beauval is in the area famed for its chateaux, between Tours and Vierzon.
It takes approximately 2½ hours to drive from Paris.
Address: 41110 St Aignan.
Telephone (33) 025475.
www.zoobeauval.com

17. Bernadette Coutain Plair
USA 1943-
Reintroduced Blue and Yellow Macaw to Trinidad

Bernadette Plair was born in a poor rural village of Trinidad on December 18 1943. From very early childhood she was fascinated by plants and animals. Until she was four years old she lived with her grandmother in Sangre Grande, near the northern edge of the Nariva swamp – a fascinating place for a lover of wildlife. Trinidad lies south of the chain of Caribbean islands, only about 14km (9 miles) off the coast of Venezuela.

At the all-girls Catholic high school she attended in another town she was disappointed that there were no biology classes. She had the initiative to approach a teacher about this – so, with the Principal's approval, the first biology classes ever held in this Catholic girls' school on Trinidad took place.

After graduation, Bernadette learned of a priest from Texas who was looking for talented girls to apply for scholarships he had obtained at Catholic women's colleges in the USA. One of these colleges was Mount St Joseph in Cincinnati, Ohio. Bernadette had no idea where Cincinnati was, but she won the scholarship! Never having had the opportunity to study maths, chemistry and physics, she needed to be tutored in these subjects. Without the help of The Sisters of Charity, who founded the College, and of her professors, she could not have majored in biology, leading her to gain a Master of Science degree from the University of Cincinnati. She said: 'Their dedication and example instilled in me the determination to do the same for others who need help. I made every effort in my professional and personal life to help students who need extra coaching, and I continue to strongly advocate for women and under-represented and disadvantaged students.'

After graduating from college, Bernadette taught high school in Trinidad for a year. She then returned to the USA and moved on to clinical and scientific research (including animal and human reproduction), environmental education and finally to global wildlife conservation at the Cincinnati Zoo and Botanical Garden. She made a behavioural study of the first endangered Sumatran rhinoceros to be conceived and born in captivity for 112 years. This took place at the Cincinnati Zoo in 2001. Meanwhile she had married her best friend from college days and raised her family in Ohio.

Trinidad and its swamp

When Bernadette left Trinidad in 1963, she remembered the childhood thrill of seeing Blue and Yellow Macaws flying over the Nariva swamp. Until about 1959 flocks numbering up to 15 birds could be observed. It was a tragedy that, in the 1960s, the macaw was trapped to extinction on Trinidad for the pet trade. By then, 20% of the Nariva Swamp had been destroyed by rice farming.

The 60km^2 (23 square mile) swamp is a permanent brackish lagoon on the east coast. It has an extensive complex of freshwater swamp forests, permanent herbaceous swamp and mangrove forest (separated from the Atlantic Ocean by two parallel sandbars) and a large area of seasonally flooded marshes. The 1,544ha (3,860 acres) Bush Bush Wildlife Sanctuary was established in September 1989. It remains a prohibited area under the Forest Act of Trinidad and Tobago; a government permit is needed for visitor entry (Plair *et al.*, 2013). The swamp became a protected wetland under the Ramsar Convention[4] in 1993.

The Blue and Yellow is unusual among large macaws in not being in a threat category. This is because it has a huge range – over most of the northern and central part of South America. However, its numbers are almost certainly declining, mainly due to habitat loss. Resources seldom exist to study species which are perceived as common. In fact, little is known about populations of the Blue and Yellow Macaw, with the exception of those in south-eastern Peru.

Due to its proximity to South America, Trinidad was the only island in the region where the Blue and Gold Macaw, as it is often called, was found. A few other Caribbean islands had large species of macaws but sadly they are long extinct.

Macaw reintroduction

In 1992 Bernadette conceived the idea of reintroducing the macaw to the Nariva swamp. She was then a scientist at the Cincinnati Zoo and Botanical Garden; its support was of crucial importance for the implementation of her idea. Consultation occurred with the Head of the Wildlife Section of the Forestry Division of Trinidad's Ministry of Agriculture, Land and Food Production. It was agreed to attempt the reintroduction through the zoo's Centre for Research of Endangered Wildlife (CREW). At that time there was no precedent for wildlife conservation on Trinidad; there were few wildlife officers but an abundance of poachers supporting the illegal wildlife trade.

---

[4] The Convention on Wetlands, signed in Ramsar, Iran, in 1971. This treaty, with more than 150 participating countries and 1,800 sites, provides a framework for national action and co-operation for conserving the world's wetlands.

Bernadette Plair: scientist, conservationist and educator.
Photograph: author.

With the cooperation of Government officials, representatives of the business and private sectors and the support of local communities, Bernadette started CRESTT – The Centre for the Rescue of Endangered Species of Trinidad and Tobago. One of their first projects was the reintroduction of the Blue and Yellow Macaw.

This determined lady worked hard to overcome several difficult problems. The idea to use confiscated birds for reintroduction was not accepted. To try to keep her plan alive, at official and community levels, she set up educational opportunities for local veterinarians, and an exchange programme for zookeepers and wildlife officers. Then, with the Cincinnati Zoo involved as a consultant, her project started. She obtained permission, in August 1999, to legally import into Trinidad 18 wild-caught Blue and Yellow Macaws from Guyana where the species was regularly trapped for export. On arrival, some of the macaws could not be released for several months until their flight feathers had re-grown. Sadly, four would never fly due to the barbaric way trappers removed their flight feathers – with a machete. For such highly intelligent creatures, that hours before had been flying with their families in the forests, this does not bear thinking about.

In Trinidad a comprehensive conservation education programme was started in local communities. This applied especially to the children at the Plum Mitan Presbyterian Primary School. Without the help of the Nariva residents, human predators would be the macaws' greatest danger. Under constant monitoring from well-trained local people, who had begun to take a great interest in protecting them, the macaws were quarantined for four weeks in a pre-release flight cage in the swamp.

In 2001 I read a story about Bernadette's vision in an American magazine. Excited, I wrote to her. I remember my surprise when she telephoned me and invited me to participate in her next visit to Trinidad in May that year. Bernadette met me there and I was immediately impressed by her quiet determination and gentle demeanour. When she made up her mind to do something, she overcame any adversity. She told me then: 'I grew up near the swamp. Every morning I would see flocks of magnificent Blue and Gold Macaws passing overhead to their feeding grounds. Every evening I saw them flying back again. Young people today have never seen such a wonderful sight. But now I am in a position to do something about that.'

Bernadette wasted no time in introducing me to the Nariva Swamp and to a remarkable group of men who manned a camp around the clock. They protected the area from forest fires and poaching. Mainly of South Asian origin, they kept watch, night and day, preventing entry by strangers. They had nothing but a roof over their heads – very simple wooden shacks, some raised up on stilts – and their families. I was touched by their dedication to the project. They welcomed us and cooked us a delicious camp meal of cascadoux fish, under an open shelter with a corrugated roof.

On another day, smoke was drifting over the impoverished area when their boat took us through a narrow channel lined with mangroves. Wattled Jacanas (*Jacana jacana*), small aquatic birds attired in black and chestnut, trod daintily across the densely-packed lily leaves. Gregarious Yellow-hooded Blackbirds (*Agelaius icterocephalus*), the glossy black males conspicuous with their bright yellow heads, frequented the swamp edges. Fragmented stands of smooth-trunked moriche (*Mauritia*) palms provided nesting sites for the small Red-bellied Macaws (*Orthopsittaca manilatus*) that were flying overhead. No large macaws were seen that day. Only the wind-battered remains of the release aviary testified to their existence.

Small, poor villages, lacking some of the most basic facilities, border the swamp: Kernahan to the south-east, Plum Mitan to the north-west, Biche to the west and Manzanilla/Cocal to the east. Their men played a leading role. The data collected on the released birds was dependent on these nearby communities, with supervision from trained project personnel. Although wildlife poaching had not been eliminated, its frequency at that time had been minimised by their involvement. Due to their then limited range, the Nariva Swamp was a good location in which to study the larger macaws during their breeding season, between January and June. They nested in the hollow cavities of dead *Roystonea* and *Mauritia* palms. Soon the first young Blue and Yellow Macaws for nearly 40 years in Trinidad fledged into the swamp. Between 2001 and 2005, 26 fledged. Bernadette's dream was succeeding against all the odds.

Men of the Nariva swamp.
Photograph: author.

Female Heroes of Bird Conservation

Education

In the community centre in Plum Mitan, close to the swamp, I attended Bernadette's workshop and witnessed conservation education first hand. I visited the village school and met Marissa and Ganesh, enthusiastic young teachers who had incorporated an environmental education programme into the curriculum in an imaginative way that made it fun. I was greatly impressed. Every morning 140 children assembled to listen to an authoritative talk on the swamp or on environmental issues. I wondered how many teachers in British schools would initiate a programme to emphasise the value of their own environment!

We took our seats for a touching and tuneful performance. Pupils sang a song they had written about the swamp: a girl played a steel drum accompanied by a boy on keyboard. I was elated when I left the school, confident that the young generation of swamp people had pride in the habitat and in the macaw. In 2003 CRESTT launched a new conservation workbook for young students, and the Plum Mitan school dedicated a conservation trail, naming it after Bernadette.

In April 2006 I revisited Trinidad to spend three days with Bernadette. Everywhere we went she was recognised and greeted with hugs or waves of the hand. She loves her native island and its people! She had returned on

Suddenly there was a shriek and a pair of Blue and Yellow Macaws flew overhead! Photograph: Rosemary Low.

several occasions to conduct conservation workshops in the swamp villages.

By then there were four teams of macaw 'guardians', totalling 24 men. We walked on the Bush Bush trail, and suddenly there was a shriek and a pair of blue macaws flew overhead. In a second they were gone. But I had seen them! In the swamp settlement of Kernahan I found a new Forestry research station. A steel observation tower had been erected and we ascended to view the wide vista of the flat landscape. Far away, three blue macaws, tiny specks in a palm tree, were feeding, and in a distant stand of trees one pair were nesting.

Twenty more macaws were imported from Guyana in 2007 in order to increase the genetic diversity. Seventeen could be released and survival was 100%. By 2008, 33 young macaws had fledged from eight breeding pairs, to give a total population of 59 birds. By June 2011 about 48 young had left their nests, and the population numbered 74. In 2009 Emperor Valley Zoo on Trinidad controversially released eight captive-bred birds. Their fate is unknown as they were not monitored. In the next three seasons fourteen more young fledged. By the end of 2013, 26 of the 31 birds released had survived – an 84% success rate. The population had increased to 86 individuals.

In January 2017 Bernadette's news was mixed. She told me:

'A lot has changed politically and ecologically in the last eight to ten years, making research on the macaws much more challenging. However, the opportunity has come up for me to attempt a new effort to get some current data on the status of the Blue and Yellow Macaws, as well as some Scarlet and Green-winged that have been released from the illegal wildlife trade. To the best of my knowledge, the population of reintroduced Blue and Yellow Macaws could now be over 100.'

The numbers had unfortunately been augmented by illegal importation. In 2021 Bernadette told me that macaws could be seen feeding in backyard fruit trees in villages and nesting in palm trees. When Venezuela suffered a political crisis, poverty increased. People were desperate to earn money in any way they could. The illegal wildlife trade mushroomed and illegally caught parrots entered Trinidad from Venezuela. To avoid risking detection, owners or smugglers released illegally accessed macaws – and possibly some were even released at sea to avoid detection by coast guards. The unauthorised release of Scarlet and Green-winged Macaws was deeply worrying. They are not native to Trinidad and they compete for food, habitat and nesting sites with the native macaws. They also posed a risk of hybridisation. Large macaws hybridise readily and unfortunately some hybrids are fertile. Releases should always follow established IUCN protocols. This did not.

To try to address the developing crisis of unauthorised releases, in January 2018 CRESST funded Team Macaw. This is a group of young Fellows and Advisors within the Conservation Leadership in the Caribbean (CLIC). Together with Phoenix Landing from the USA, Bernadette organised a meeting with Trinidad's Forestry Department officials. The aim was twofold: to educate the people of Trinidad about the importance of the native macaw population and to teach them how to look after the captive parrots already in their homes. Bernadette and Team Macaw spent two days with forestry officials, game wardens and conservation representatives discussing the needs of captive birds, including suitable diets and veterinary support. The information was shared during four days and more than 130 people attended the meetings. In 2021 Bernadette told me: 'I cannot give up on my conservation efforts or in mentoring young people. I have to keep CRESTT alive.'

Bernadette's guiding hand, local education programmes, especially in schools, and the guarding of the released macaws, had been major factors in the success of the release programme. Trinidadians can be proud of what they have achieved so far. The reintroduction of a parrot to a habitat where it was extirpated by man is difficult to achieve and rarely attempted. Education is a vital factor. In this case, the relatively good condition of part of the original habitat, with suitable natural nest sites for large macaws, added to the success of the reintroduction. However, without Bernadette and the way in which she won the confidence and the love of the swamp people, it would never have happened. It was a lucky day for Trinidad when a far-sighted man came looking for scholarship candidates…

Bernadette retired from the Cincinnati Zoo in 2011. She served as a trustee, from 2010-2018, of Mount St Joseph College, from where she had graduated. She brought a valuable science perspective, a different culture and a different socio-economic background to the board. She represents the little girl from Trinidad who wanted to do something for her country. I count myself very fortunate to have spent time with her on her beloved island.

Reference

Plair, B. L., L. Motilal, A. Ramadhar and S. Ramsubage, 2013, Status of Blue-and-yellow Macaws *Ara ararauna* Reintroduced to the Nariva Swamp, Trinidad and Tobago, *Living World*, Trinidad and Tobago Field Naturalists' Club.

18. Anna Croukamp
Brazil 1946-
Bird Park founder and Atlantic Forest conservation

Anna Sophie Croukamp was born in Hiddesen, Germany on August 11 1946. She was a pretty blond-haired, blue-eyed child. 'I had the best of all parents', she told me. Her father was a Doctor of Philosophy and of Theatre Science. He produced opera, operetta and drama at an important provincial theatre in Germany. He created magic on stage and designed the scenery in his own productions. Music was important in his life, as a pianist, and his voice was trained as a tenor. Nature and gardening were his other interests. Her mother was a teacher and she wrote theatre plays and short stories.

Anna told me: 'The first experience which influenced my life came when I was three years old. Three riders, one on a white horse and two on brown horses, crossed a path in front of me. That was magic! So, my mind was set. At ten years of age, I saw riders on horseback in our small town. I followed them back to the stables and I became a stable girl. I worked and saved to pay for riding lessons, because we were a poor family. Working in the theatre means poverty. Poor, yes, but very educated and intellectual!' Her family lived in rented accommodation and no animals were allowed. But at fourteen, she overcame the lack of pets. She gave a Budgerigar to her mother for Christmas. 'He was called Piccolo – my big small friend, a great love.'

For Anna, school was 'a waste of time', because she wanted to be outdoors, in the forest, spotting birds, building dams, making wooden huts or climbing trees. Eventually a very persuasive teacher convinced her that there was no other way: if she wanted to become a veterinarian, she must sit and learn. So she did.

Parallel to Anna's love of horses and the outdoor life, she lived for the theatre and became her father's assistant during holidays. 'I was torn between a theatre career or a life as a veterinarian. The vet side won. With 48 super interesting subjects to study, I became a study-holic. The students were examined in groups of four. We were three boys and a girl, the closest of friends. I coaxed, bullied, pulled, pushed and coached them through the subjects, because in veterinary medicine you have to sit down and learn, learn, learn, and the boys were slow starters. However, they all became highly successful later in life.'

Anna went on to study veterinary medicine and graduated in 1972. Her doctorate was about the morphology and function of the Bursa Fabricii. This is the organ which in birds produces the B-lymphocytes. The equivalent organ in mammals was not known at the time. Later Anna worked in the Institute of Histology.

Her next aim was to work in the field so in 1973 she went to Harare (formerly Salisbury), in Zimbabwe, to work as a field veterinarian. She treated animals, big and small, but mainly cattle and horses. In the 1990s the terrorist threat had become serious. The terrorists – from their point of view the freedom fighters – would enter from Zambia or Mozambique. They would ambush farmers in the late afternoon and withdraw, so the security forces would not be able to follow them in the dark. Anna remembered:

> 'One farmer told me: "You can't travel like that on your own. Here is a gun". He handed me a revolver. I went to the village police station: "What do I do with this?" The policeman showed a rather relaxed attitude. "See that coke tin over there? O.K. This is how you hold the gun … this is how you aim and shoot." So I travelled by car to the farms with a revolver in the glove compartment, with mixed feelings. The more I heard about another farmer dead or another land mine which had gone off, the more nervous I became. I went through a steep learning curve. Not only was I fairly green as a vet, I also learnt at record speed how to speak English.'

Anna typified the 'can-do' attitude of many of the women in this book. She had to learn how to drive a pick-up truck on dirt roads in heavy rain, and to cross running rivers on fords. Many times she was stuck in the mud and had to be rescued by kind farmers. 'You must be Anna!' they said, when they found a foreign young female standing helplessly next to an old Peugot pick-up.

She moved to South West Africa, today called Namibia. Anna's life changed when she met Dennis Croukamp. He was a mining engineer from Rhodesia, who was invited to open an old German copper mine in the Khan river valley in the desert. Anna recalled: 'His friends called him "larger than life"; he had a strong charismatic personality, and he was an ingenious engineer and a great organiser. He treated the Minister of Mines of Rhodesia or visiting Members of Parliament from England with the same relaxed friendliness as his employee sweeping the mill floor.'

After getting the old copper mine to function, he built up his own mine. Anna and Dennis fell in love, married and had two daughters, Anna-Luise and Carmel. By the beginning of the 1990s, Dennis had retired and the family were living on the Isle of Man in the UK. The gift of a young Grey Parrot changed their lives and opened their eyes to the fascinating world of parrots.

The spectacular Iguaçu Falls.
Photograph: author.

They needed a new challenge. A friend made the strange suggestion that they should move to Brazil to open a crocodile farm! He had visited a beautiful area – just the right place for such a venture, he said. Crocodiles – no! Birds, yes! said Dennis, so they visited Foz do Iguaçu, Brazil's most scenic and spectacular tourist attraction. The Iguaçu Falls make Niagara pale into insignificance. Named as a World Heritage Site in 1984, they drop 80m (270ft) in a series of cataracts and span 2,700m (nearly two miles). The surrounding rainforest is home to about 400 bird species. Could there be a more perfect area for a bird park?

A new life in Brazil

In September 1993 the Croukamps moved to Brazil – with *Portuguese in three months* in their hands. It takes great strength of mind to move a young family to an unknown country, whose language you do not speak and where you know no-one. Bravely, they bought 40ha (16 acres) of land next to the Iguaçu National Park. In November, construction started on Parque das Aves, using Anna's hand-drawn sketch as the plan. Its layout was carefully designed so that no trees would be cut down. The funds from the sale of the mine, plus everything else they could scrape together, including the children's education money, paid for the bird park.

Life was not easy. They tried, without success, to find investors when their only business associate pulled out, leaving them almost bankrupt. They sold everything they owned to get the bird park started in a small way in 1994. Two years later Dennis died.

Anna told me this as we sat surrounded by birds in a café within the park on a stormy but sunny September day, with thunder rumbling overhead. She told me of her struggle to bring up her two children, to cope with the opposition to the park and to enlarge and promote it. She said: 'The fact that the bird park survived is due to the foresight and courage of my husband and a team of Brazilians who helped me, picked me up when I stumbled, and dusted me off, while I lived under constant fear that the park might fail.'

On entering the park, the lush planting, inside (shrubs, ferns and epiphytes) and outside the aviaries (flowering yellow shrimp plants and red gingers), is immediately pleasing. The aviaries are large and high, flanked by trees, and set along a path which takes the visitor on a journey of almost one mile. The highlight is a massive, spectacular enclosure – so large and naturally planted and landscaped that one forgets one is enclosed. More than twenty species live in this paradise for toucans, Scarlet Ibis (*Eudocimus ruber*) and visitors alike. A raised, railed walkway meanders above a lake. Herons and spoonbills perched high in mature trees and a cheeky Bahama Pintail duck (*Anas bahamensis*) rested on a rail close to the path, along with several Toco Toucans (*Ramphastos toco*). Five species of the charismatic big-billed birds have been bred there.

Anna entered with a bowl of grapes. The toucans formed a line, eagerly surging forward to gently take the fruit, toss it, open the bill and swallow it whole.

Anna's joy in the toucans' friendliness and the beauty of the other birds surrounding her was evident. An admiring group of visitors formed with their cameras. The close proximity of many tame birds was an obvious delight. Imagine having a Blue-fronted Amazon (*Amazona aestiva*) – in another enclosure – perch on your camera when all you want to do is to take a photo of it!

Atlantic Rainforest projects

Anna's emphasis gradually changed from birds that make a wonderful display for the public to Atlantic forest species, and especially those known to be endangered. Even older than the Amazon rainforest and much more threatened, the *Mata Atlântica* was inhabited by Amerindians 10,000 years ago and was the first place in South America to be colonised by Europeans. Extensive forest clearance to exploit the Brazilwood tree (*Paubrasilia echinata*) occurred in the 16th century, and later vast areas were cleared and burned for cattle pasture. The Atlantic forests once covered 1.23 million km². Now only about 13% of the original vegetation survives, most of it in small, isolated fragments, many of them not far from the great urban sprawls of Rio de Janeiro and São Paulo.

Cattle ranching, coffee and sugar plantations and towns have paved over what was the richest forest eco-system in the world, with more than 23,000 species of plants discovered so far, 40% of which

Anna and Carmel.
Photograph: Anna Croukamp.

cus all our efforts on the birds of the Atlantic Rainforest is Carmel's idea. This applies to research, *ex-situ* and *in situ* conservation, education, communication, public awareness and commercial activities such as the shop and restaurant – *A one biome zoo*. It was a family decision to do this, as it involved a financial risk. We had to consider a possible loss of income, as visitors might not be impressed by "only" looking at and learning about birds of the Atlantic rainforest. But the visitors were delighted! Carmel had been right. The logistic of working in our back yard are excellent.'

Carmel set up the Centre for Conservation of Birds of the Atlantic Rainforest, which focuses on fieldwork with critically endangered avian species. She also founded the IUCN Species Survival Centre Brazil, in partnership with the Species Survival Commission of the IUCN. 'As 72% of the Brazilian population lives in the Atlantic Forest, and Parque das Aves receives more than 800,000 visitors per year, we have the possibility to inspire many people to make small changes that can make a direct difference in the lives of many animal and plant species', said Carmel.

In the park there is a section of attractive aviaries just for endangered *Amazona* parrots of the Atlantic forest. Each one is planted, has a small pool and information on the conservation projects for them, which are supported by the park. *Projeto Charao,* for the Red-spectacled Amazon (*Amazona*

are endemic. Sixty per cent of Brazil's endangered species live here. The bird life is especially rich and vulnerable. Of Brazil's approximately 1920 bird species, at least 891 are found in the Atlantic forest – and some species will depend on captive breeding for their survival.

In 2021 Anna told me:

'The fact that the bird park is a success today is due to the greatest gift I personally received, when my daughter Carmel and her husband decided to leave academia in 2009 and to move from Oxford to Foz Iguaçu to help me. After a steep learning curve Carmel took over in 2014 as CEO.'

'The conservation projects have been planned and executed by her. To fo-

The Atlantic Rainforest – a treasure drove of biodiversity.
Photograph: author.

pretrei), commenced in 1999. There are few of these striking parrots in protected areas – most live on private property where conservation education and the installation of artificial nests is very important for their survival.

Parrots whose habitats have been reduced so drastically that they are now in an IUCN threat category include three other Brazilian *Amazona* species: the Red-browed (*A. rhodocorytha*), listed as Vulnerable, and the Red-tailed (*A. brasiliensis*) and the Vinaceous-breasted (*A. vinacea*) which are Endangered. The park's work includes financial support for the Red-tailed, and funding initial expeditions to map the occurrence and threats to the Red-browed Amazon Parrot in the states of Rio de Janeiro and Minas Gerais. Today the project is financed and run by Parque das Aves. It is also the main financial provider for the Blue-fronted Amazon project (see Chapter 25).

The Alagoas Curassow (*Mitu mitu*), a handsome turkey-like bird, is already extinct in the wild. However, in 2019, it was the subject of a reintroduction programme using captive-bred birds. This illustrates what is possible with committed and knowledgeable breeders and zoos. As a participant in the captive breeding programme, in June 2015, Parque das Aves received 10 pairs of these iconic birds from a breeding facility in Minas Gerais. Since then, many chicks have hatched in the park. When official permission is given, they will be part of the reintroduction programme.

A more recent project is to breed the Grey-breasted Parakeet (*Pyrrhura griseipectus*) from north-east Brazil. By the early years of this century its population was reduced to probably only 100 birds, due to illegal trapping and deforestation. The NGO Aquasis has worked hard to bring back the popu-

Vinaceous-breasted Amazon Parrot at Parque das Aves.
Photograph: author.

lation to several hundred birds and is seeking areas to repopulate with captive-bred birds.

Anna told me: 'I often wonder what is behind the success of the bird park, considering that I have no special talents. However, I like to see friendly faces of staff around me. And as I did not know the proper way to build up and run a company, I did it my way – with a soft touch, giving credit without interest, bailing my people out when they ran up debts which they could not pay back, letting them feel they had a safety net underneath them.'

Well, Anna, you just told me a very important reason why the bird park is so successful! And Anna is someone who is loved by everybody, for her friendly and kind personality. When visiting zoos, I can often *feel* the difference between an organisation run by largely faceless individuals and a family business whose employees are part of that family. If the staff are happy, that is reflected in everything on those premises. And visitors can feel the good vibes. That is one reason. Another is extremely important: the deep love Anna has for birds and animals. It is not always the efficient business person who creates the best business. It is the heart and soul behind the venture.

The aims of the park are to make a significant contribution to the survival of some of the Atlantic forest birds. As a major tourist attraction, it is in a position to bring awareness of the problems faced by the forests and its fauna and surely impresses on visitors the need to conserve Brazil's unique avifauna. This also takes place through partnerships with other institutions and field workers.

Many people achieve great things during their careers: Anna Croukamp, one of the most inspirational people I ever met, did something remarkable some years *after* she retired. She ran a bird park in a country where, at the time, it was notoriously difficult for expats to succeed. She did not speak the language and she had no business experience. She faced unwarranted setbacks – private individuals and even government organisations that put obstacles in her way.

Opening a bird park is generally considered by the zoo community as a game for optimists. Unlike many zoos, they generally start in a small way and as a family-run business. But it is a very tough business – and zoos, with their popular large mammals, are more likely to succeed. In the UK many bird parks opened, especially during the 1960s and 1970s, but very few have survived and most were short-lived. However, a major problem in the UK is the usually short span of good weather which encourages zoo visits. Many of these bird parks originated as substantial private collections, with founders who were not failing in avicultural expertise but often lacked design skills and the imagination to attract the public. Another important aspect is continuity. Some good parks have closed when the founder has died and there is no family member or reliable person to carry on.

Female Heroes of Bird Conservation

At Parqe das Aves, Carmel has followed in her mother's footsteps and the whole family are committed to the future of the park.

Sadly, birds alone are not an attraction for most people, who want to see large and spectacular animals like lions and giraffes. How many times do we see people walking past aviaries without even stopping to look? I think the size of the creatures displayed is another factor. Perhaps most people cannot be bothered to look at diminutive creatures. In the end, most bird parks either close down or they end up as zoos because without mammals they cannot get enough visitors! The notable exceptions are Vogelpark Walsrode in Germany and Parque das Aves! If you have the opportunity, please visit them to see what can be achieved, especially in the reproduction of difficult species.

Anna succeeded against all the odds and now has the most visited – and probably also the most beautiful – bird park in Latin America. Today it is a thriving concern, supporting conservation and research, educating teachers and playing host to 35,000 schoolchildren every year, to give them a feeling for the natural wonders around them. Anna is a very determined and focussed lady whose love of birds overcame all the difficulties. She is a true heroine in my eyes.

Today the park employs 150 people, including biologists, bird keepers, customer relations personnel and construction workers. The park cares for about 1,300 birds (many of them had been seized by the authorities) of 130 species.

Awards

Anna's work has been recognised with various awards. In 2013 she received the *Medalha Mérito Legislativo* from the Brazilian Parliament. In 2015 she received Honorary Citizenship of Foz do Iguassu. In 2017 the World Association of Zoos and Aquariums presented Anna with the Heini Hediger Award given annually to leaders within this community. She received another accolade in November 2019, when she was made an Honorary Member of the Brazilian Air Force for her services to society.

Anna says: 'Our goal is conservation; our base is enchantment.'

Parque das Aves,
Avenida das Cataratas, km 17.1,
Foz do Iguacu, Paraná, Brazil.
www.parquedasaves.com.br

19. Lorin Lindner
USA 1955-
Unites traumatised War Veterans and mistreated Parrots

Lorin Lindner, PhD, was born in Queens, New York on August 30 1955. When she was growing up she divided her time between the city and the country. In the open spaces she learned to revere Nature and carried that with her for the rest of her life. However, when she returned to her childhood tree house she found the forest razed and shopping malls in its place. The vulnerability of Nature had a profound effect on her.

Her childhood was not easy. The family moved sixteen times in sixteen years; her mother was ill and her father worked long hours. Lorin loved animals and posters of dogs and horses decorated her bedroom walls. Pets were her comfort as she was often alone. When they moved once again to Florida, her beloved 'Halfmoon' Conure (*Eupsittula canicularis*) did not go with them. She had missed that parrot ever since and longed for another. However, she never wanted to repeat the experience of giving up a pet.

It was Christmas Eve, 1987. Lorin was studying for her Psychology Licensing Exam when a friend who worked for an animal rescue group told her that a carer was urgently needed for a parrot. Lorin offered to keep it until a good home could be found. An Animal Control officer took her to an empty mansion that was for sale. An airy central atrium contained tall potted palms and a cage housing a Moluccan Cockatoo (*Cacatua moluccensis*). This big bird's salmon tones and magnificent crest complemented the pastel colours of the expensive home. Is that why the wealthy owners had purchased her, to match their décor? The cockatoo was alone, with droppings piled up like a pyramid to perch level. The seed bowl was full of empty husks. In her book *Birds of a Feather*, Lorin had written: 'I felt as if I were looking directly into a tortured soul… I felt an immediate bond with this bird.' She called her Sammy.

This cockatoo was just one of thousands snatched from their Indonesian home, the island of Seram, in the 1970s. The Moluccan or Seram Cockatoo is highly intelligent and sentient – a very difficult and misunderstood subject in human hands. Lorin traced Sammy's history. She was sold straight out of quarantine in 1977 to an 80-year-old woman for US$5,000. Subsequently the cockatoo had several more homes. Unfortunately multiple owners and, sadly, abuse,

Female Heroes of Bird Conservation

Lorin with Sammy, the Moluccan Cockatoo.
Photograph: author.

was the fate of so many of the literally millions of parrots stolen from the wild in that era. In just one year, 1986, more than 800,000 parrots were imported into the USA. Many soon became unwanted – and this is where Lorin ultimately found her mission. She asked the question: 'What if we were looking at a Bald Eagle in a cage? We might be enraged at the image of our national birds being denied their freedom, yet we think nothing of taking other countries' resources to put in little zoos in our own homes.'

Unexpectedly, she found a way to combine easing the suffering of some of these parrots with that of war veterans. She put her training in psychology, public health and eco-therapy to work in order to help both groups – by creating an environment where part-wild animals and wounded war veterans together found a path of healing from their mutual traumas.

Lorin Lindner had taught psychology at Santa Monica College in Los Angeles for many years. She was also a health advisor, and an advocate for the homeless, for the environment and for animal rights. In 1990 she met a Vietnam veteran called John Keaveney who was campaigning for justice and help for the many war veterans, men and women, who had become homeless. Unable to adjust to life back in the United States, they turned to drink or drugs. They lost their homes, their families and their jobs and ended up on the streets. John began knocking on every door at the West Los Angeles VA Healthcare Center. This property of almost 162ha (400 acres or just over a half square mile) included a hospital, theatre and baseball stadium.

John thought there should be room for homeless veterans. He found a huge building, unused for 75 years; veterans had broken in and were already squatting there. It needed an act of Congress to achieve it but John got a 50-year lease on the building for one dollar. After years of struggle and work, the 156-bed, one-year residential treatment facility opened in 1997. It was called New Directions. Lorin became the Clinical Director. She was working 12-hour days – demanding work with difficult subjects. By now she had two Moluccan Cockatoos, after finding a partner for Sammy; they would not get enough attention at home – so she placed two spacious cages outside her door and a T-stand in her office.

The effect on the veterans of these appealing and lovable birds was miraculous. These men could not trust humans but they trusted the cockatoos, shared

Vietnam veteran Bill Seale with an Umbrella Cockatoo.
Photograph: Courtnay Robbins.

their apples and oranges with them and scratched their backs. Some of these veterans could barely speak to a human being yet they talked to the cockatoos.

Lorin had a friend who also owned a cockatoo – but the neighbours were complaining about its screams. They decided to set up a parrot rescue sanctuary. In 1997 they met a couple from Ojai in California who already had aviaries. The couple was willing to build more on their spacious property. They also wanted to educate people about plants and animals and especially about the unsuitability for most people of parrots as pets. Reluctantly, but for their own benefit, Lorin took her beloved cockatoos there. She visited them every weekend, taking veterans with her to build more aviaries and to interact with the birds. Lorin wrote: 'These tough marines, sailors, and soldiers were practically cooing back to them with soft, calm and tender voices'. She had never seen such good emotional progress in the men in a clinical setting.

At the VA Healthcare Center, New Directions, gardening was integrated into the treatment of returning veterans. The 6ha (15 acre) therapeutic garden would make a perfect site for a parrot and veteran sanctuary. Lorin drew up a petition to bring parrot therapy to the VA and, to her surprise, the heads of the departments signed it. The idea won Lorin many admirers and generous donors. An architect drew up the aviary plans for free and students from an engineering firm provided much of the labour as a community service. A wealthy entrepreneur provided half the cash for the construction materials and other donors followed.

Serenity Park opens

It took a long time but in 2005 Serenity Park opened, so named for its tranquil aura among ficus and plum trees, and the luxuriant purple verbena, fragrant pitcher sage and winecup flowers. Lorin described it as her version of healing: being connected to the natural world. It is far outside the conventional office setting where mainstream 'medical model' healing usually occurs.

The aviaries began to fill up and more volunteer veterans cared for the birds. One morning Matt Simmons walked in. He had served in Iraq. The constant trauma of seeing charred bodies and broken buildings left him unable to adapt to life back in the USA. He suffered from PTSD (post-traumatic stress disorder), turned to drugs and left his wife and small son. Matt ended up at New Directions where his therapist suggested he should volunteer at Serenity Park. He later admitted that he fell in love with Lorin as soon as they met. At that moment she was hosing down aviaries, wearing overalls and rubber boots. He knew nothing about birds but he told Lorin he was available to do anything she needed. He kept his distance. Eventually Matt opened up to Lorin, about his past; she was not his therapist but he found it easy to talk to her as a friend.

Soon Matt had formed another bond, this time with two Lilac-crowned Parrots (*Amazona finschi*), a Mexican species; they had been ejected from the nest as chicks, probably by a predator, and were found badly injured. Several species of Amazon parrots have become naturalised in the Los Angeles area, thriving in the streets lined with big trees that provide all the parrots' needs. One of the young ones, named Ruby, needed to have her wounds dressed. Matt quickly learned how to handle her in a towel, give her medication and clean her wounds. She had endured pain during these processes to make her well – yet one day Ruby flew onto Matt's shoulder. He was her friend now – and that moved Matt to tears.

The parrots were healing in other ways – healing each other. A mature Double Yellow-headed Parrot (*Amazona oratrix*) called Joey lived in the aviary next to Ruby and her sister. Matt noticed how Joey watched the two young birds and told Lorin that Joey wanted to be with them. Lorin was doubtful. Joey was a big strong bird, but Matt said he would be there all the time and watch the three Amazons together. A few days later, Matt led Lorin to their enclosure. Joey was feeding the young ones – regurgitating food to them, just as they would be fed by their parents. The three parrots were now a family.

Drugs are the first method of treatment for people suffering from psychological disorders and, says Lorin, the benefits may not be real, but the side effects are, and they include weight gain, loss of sex drive and even long-term health concerns. 'We need to teach people to solve their own problems'. At Serenity Park this was done by restoring psychological balance by being at one with Nature. The bonds the veterans have with parrots have great restorative effects. The veterans learn the profound

The tranquil setting of the aviaries at Serenity Park.
Photograph: Lorin Lindner.

powers of empathy and compassion, crucial factors in psychological wellbeing. Matt had found ways to persuade the veterans to interact with the birds, just as he did.

In 2007 I was speaking at a parrot symposium in Los Angeles when an attractive blond lady introduced herself to me. Her name was Lorin Lindner. She asked me if I would like to visit the parrot rescue facility she had founded at Serenity Park. Later that day she drove me there, just outside the city. Her ideas and her achievements amazed me. This was no ordinary parrot rescue. I saw happy, active macaws, Amazons, cockatoos and Ringneck Parakeets in aviaries filled with branches, toys, cargo nets and other occupational items to enrich their environment. These birds had the company of other parrots and, if they needed it, much focused attention from volunteers. The aviaries were maintained to a very high standard and the generous height ensured that nervous birds could retreat from humans, should they so wish.

I saw how Lorin's love and understanding of parrots (and all animals) displays itself in deep compassion for them – sadly often lacking in today's self-obsessed society. But that is instinctive. I also saw how her training as a psychologist gives her a different perspective. For example, she described limited food choices as a source of depression in animals in captivity because foraging is a psychological imperative for them.

I also met Matt, with a Goffin's Cockatoo nestling in his arms. I saw at once that he played an important role there. One afternoon Lorin and Matt were shopping in a store. Matt left her side to fetch something – she thought. Moments later his voice came over the loudspeaker with a marriage proposal. She said yes. He went down on one knee and handed her a ring. They were married in June 2009 at Serenity Park. Sammy was the 'flower girl' and her feathers and those from another Moluccan Cockatoo, collected over 22 years, were made into a beautiful bouquet.

Lorin had achieved something remarkable. She used unloved, abandoned parrots to restore to health veterans of the Iraq war, and other conflicts. Unable to trust any human being, they turned to the parrots, many of whom were suffering in the same way. And in their turn, the parrots began to trust people again. Serenity Park is a model for other parrot rescuers, with its loving carers and spacious aviaries. It lives up to its name.

A piece of land in the mountains, north of Los Angeles, eventually became Lorin's home, where she lives with numerous rescued animals at the Lockwood Animal Rescue Center, which is not open to the public. It employs wounded heroes to care for similarly traumatised wolves and wolfdogs in the Wolves and Warriors programme. Lorin continues to practice clinical psychology and lectures throughout the country.

Reference

Lindner, L., 2018, *Birds of a Feather*, St Martin's Press, New York.

20. LoraKim Joyner
USA 1957-
Parrot Conservation in Central America

Kim Joyner was born in Atlanta, Georgia, USA, on July 16 1957. Fascinated by birds from an early age, she wanted to be an avian veterinarian. To this end she achieved a degree in Avian Sciences and then studied veterinary medicine, qualifying as a DVM specialising in birds. Later she gained a Master's degree in Preventive Veterinary Medicine at the Davis University of California.

In April 1987 she was working at the Aviculture Institute, a parrot breeding facility in Newhall, California. The senior staff veterinarian told her that 200 Yellow-naped Parrot (*Amazona auropalliata*) chicks had been confiscated from poachers in Guatemala, Central America.

Guatemala

Many of these confiscated chicks were dying. The help of an avian veterinarian was desperately needed. After acquiring the documentation to enter Guatemala, Kim was on her way. This country is bordered by Mexico to the north and west and Honduras to the east.

On one of her early trips there, two friends accompanied her. On their first morning they were assigned a guide called Daniel (not his real name). Daniel was to play a significant role in her life.

She soon discovered that the *finca* where they were staying (where she had previously surgically sexed parrots as part of her professional work for a private zoo) was overrun with guerrillas. This was her first indication of how difficult and dangerous field work can be in Central America. Young men with automatic weapons were not far away as Kim surveyed the area for parrots. The infamous military had killed thousands of innocent civilians. But there was beauty, too, and another kind of danger. In the far distance the volcano Pacaya streaked her sides with fire.

Her initial short stays in Central America were to change Kim's life. Her desire to work with captive birds faded. She wanted to help save parrots in the wild – specifically in Guatemala where she had learned to love the people and its parrots. She returned many times and for many months from 1987 to 1992 when she finally moved there to study the Yellow-naped Parrots. She discovered to her dismay that nearly every parrot nest was poached – hardly any chicks were fledging. No wonder then that in 2017, this desirable parrot received the IUCN status of Endangered. It occurs in disjunct locations throughout Central America, having been trapped to extinction in some areas. Everywhere poaching was and is rife.

Guatemala had suffered more than 36 years of internal conflict, which formally ended with the signing of the Peace Accords at the end of 1996. It resulted in increased poverty, in a country of very low incomes. For some people selling parrot chicks was the only way to augment meagre incomes; for the middlemen it was a lucrative business.

This is undoubtedly one of the most handsome and loquacious of the *Amazona* parrots. Its mimicry abilities are legendary. From singing and whistling to imitating the human voice it is usually more accurate than any other member of the genus. This ability has made it a bigger target for poachers than almost any other parrot in Central America, apart from the Scarlet Macaw. Combined with serious habitat loss, this led to a catastrophic decline in numbers, suggested as about 50% between 1980 and 2000.

The situation was also serious for the Pacific Parakeets (*Psittacara (holochloros) strenuus*) that nested in the vine-covered cliffs. Competition for chicks was so great that poachers resorted to taking eggs and incubating them under ducks. Few of the eggs hatched. Kim told me that these days illegal traffickers are more sophisticated – they have incubators in suitcases. How these people accomplished the difficult task of rearing these tiny chicks from the egg I could not imagine.

The area was denuded of most natural foliage, and covered in fields of sugar cane and in coffee plantations. The parakeets were not safe except for a few pairs that nested in an ancient mausoleum in the middle of a cane field. The local people believed there was a curse on anyone who tried to steal the young. One man was attacked by bees when trying to take the chicks. He fell to his death.

In this brutal environment where guerrillas and robbers lurked around every corner, it was terrifying to go out at night and neighbours were killed in broad daylight. Kim and her small team risked their lives almost daily. To the poachers she was the enemy. To the guerrillas she was a suspicious woman carrying military equipment: in reality the telemetry devices used for tracking parrots. One day Kim and Daniel were elated to discover a roost site of 250 Yellow-naped Parrots. That was, alas, probably the last good news regarding the local population.

There were several strands to Kim's work in Guatemala – monitoring the nests of the parrots and parakeets for scientific purposes (such as taking blood to check for diseases), preventing chicks from being poached, trying to educate the local people about conservation, and looking after confiscated parrots. She also acted as veterinarian to the local zoo and to bird keepers, and to the country's President.

Kim eventually moved to Guatemala in the summer of 1992, building a conservation project with the aviculturist doing field work. She still lived in constant fear, but remained there due to her determination to protect the parrots from poachers. She even confronted armed and dangerous men, one of whom was later convicted for murder. These men were eventually revealed as neighbours, with whom she played soccer. She even organised football teams. She wrote:

> 'I couldn't go anyplace without seeing wildlife poachers and killers. Even though signs prohibiting hunting were posted along the roads edging the *finca* and the forest, the allure of much-needed money was too great. When I spotted someone hunting from the road I chased them away in my best Dian Fossey[5] imitation. One day I stopped with a car of biologists and visitors who dropped their jaws when I approached a gang of men with rifles. Truth be told, I hadn't see the rifles until I was near them. Luckily their incomprehension overruled their anger and they left. This time I accepted that someone could get hurt and our anti-poaching efforts weren't helping,

The charismatic Yellow-naped Parrot. Photograph: author.

"Don't be Dian", I repeated to myself, and "Find a way to love the people"' (Joyner, 2017).

If she helped the women of the *finca*, she thought, perhaps their families would leave the parrots alone. The next town had electricity, so she sometimes drove the women there so that they no longer had to grind their dried corn by hand.

This involved a journey in the dark on potentially dangerous roads and over a bridge which the guerrillas dynamited one night. Nocturnal explosions were not always bridges being blown up: sometimes they were earthquakes. Once there was a sinister reason: *narcos*, drug traffickers, who shot at a helicopter flying low over the *finca*; one passenger died.

Checking nests was dangerous, not only because of the armed guerrillas, but also due to the many bee swarms attracted to them. (Sometimes chicks were stung to death). In one season only eight young fledged from 28 active nests. The poachers were relentless

---

[5] The gorilla conservationist who was hacked to death by, it was assumed, poachers.

– but for Kim's bravery and determination not even eight would have fledged. More than 90% of nests failed.

Conservation education was another tactic. At the zoo three large cages had been built for a wildlife rescue centre. Thirty-five parrot chicks that had been confiscated grew up there. They provided a focus of interest for busloads of children that Kim and her team brought in to learn about the parrots, to receive colouring books, to listen to songs about conservation and to take home a tree to plant.

By 1995 most of the nest trees that Kim had been protecting had been cut down. She wrote: 'It was time to quit playing the naïve role of some kind of saviour and go home.' She had accepted the position of clinical instructor at the North Carolina State University School of Veterinary Medicine. Two months after settling down there, Daniel arrived. One week later he left, to return to his own country. Several months later Daniel came back with the news that the rescue centre (RESCAVES) had been torn down, along with most of the trees on the *finca*, to make way for a sugar plantation. To prepare the area for planting, the vegetation was set alight, killing all the wildlife.

Kim's relationship with Daniel did not survive. Away from his natural habitat their stormy relationship was doomed and Daniel returned to his partner and children. Kim did not come to terms with the grief of this loss. She was 'looking for tools on how to live with a heart cracked wide open.'

A new life – and back to Central America

She found a solution. She was accepted by the Vanderbilt Divinity School, given a full scholarship and a stipend during her three-year attendance. Then she became a Unitarian Universalist minister, serving in parish ministry for ten years in North Carolina, Minnesota, Texas and Florida. In 2000 Kim married Meredith Garmon, also a Unitarian Universalist minister. He supports her work in One Earth Conservation (see below).

But Guatemala called to her once again, despite the disappointments of the past. She returned in 2010 to the same *finca*. She met her friends. Daniel had gone to set up home with another woman. The roost site had gone, with only one or two pairs of Yellow-naped Parrots in the area. To confirm whether the population crash applied elsewhere, she visited the owners of other *fincas* and private reserves. It was the same story. The Yellow-naped Parrots had gone. Surely there was something she could do, somewhere? She consulted Donald Brightsmith of Texas A. & M. University, renowned for his long-term studies of macaws in Peru. He told her about the remote rainforest region of La Mosquitia in eastern Honduras.

Honduras

In 1980, UNESCO placed this rainforest on its list of World Heritage Sites and the Honduras government set aside 5,250km² (2,000 square miles) of tropical forest. However, it failed to implement monitoring and protection, so deforestation was occurring by loggers seeking pine and mahogany, and for cattle pasture and palm oil plantations. Parrot conservation work was needed there, especially in connection with the declining Scarlet Macaw, decreed the symbol of Honduras in June 1993.

The reserve was said to have the last remaining populations of Scarlet and Great Green Macaws (*Ara ambiguus*) in Central America. Tomás Manzanares, a community leader, had led local efforts to protect the area. However, with her plans made and ready to go, Kim received the news that Tómas had been shot four times by criminals who wanted to take over the land. Miraculously, he survived, after many surgeries. Villages in the area had been burned and abandoned and leaders had been murdered.

Nevertheless, a few months later Tómas returned with LoraKim Joyner, now with her changed name (*Lora* is Spanish for parrot) and the founder of One Earth Conservation. The area was so dangerous they needed the protection of soldiers. With the consent and assistance of local people, they built a research station, and a rescue and release centre for Scarlet Macaws. The project is known as *Apu Pauni*, the Miskito name for this magnificent parrot.

The Miskito people have protected more than one million acres and 153 macaw nests. LoraKim describes this as 'the largest community-controlled parrot project in the wild.' In 2020 the people suffered terrible hardships: countless wild fires, which killed macaw chicks, and two hurricanes with floods that destroyed their crops. They lost everything.

Tropical cyclone warnings were issued in November 2020 in Nicaragua and Honduras, which were still recovering from Hurricane Eta just two weeks previously. Heavy rain had fallen on much of Nicaragua, widening flash flooding caused by the hurricane's high storm surge. Mudslides had caused extensive damage and multiple deaths.

One new area after another was torn down, to the sound of chainsaws. Despite this, a pair of Great Green Macaws were able to fledge two young – believed to be the first documented nest in the country. But a pair of Scarlet Macaws was killed by predators. Their chicks were rescued and reared and eventually released from a big liberation cage. Two Red-lored Parrot (*Amazona autumnalis*) chicks fell out of their burnt nest, to which they were later returned. The nest was watched and it was with joy that the protectors saw the young fledge.

LoraKim worked with the local villagers to feed dozens of Scarlet Macaws that appeared after the two hurricanes had destroyed their food sources. She reported at the end of December 2020:. 'The people have had to double the amount of food (and the costs) offered to the parrots twice a day, and they do this at a time when their own food se-

LoraKim treating a Scarlet Macaw chick with Mosquitia villagers looking on. Photograph: One Earth Conservation.

curity is at risk. It takes longer, because there are so many birds – up to 75 Scarlet Macaws reported coming to the Rescue Centre just a few days ago.' Some of these were older liberated birds – and they brought their wild-hatched young! LoraKim commented: 'The people do all this despite threats, wildfires, failed crops, the pandemic, hurricanes and hardship.' No one was killed in the hurricanes and all the birds survived at the centre.

A stark indication of the poverty of the people of Honduras occurred in January 2021. When incoming US President Joe Biden promised 'a fair and humane immigration system', at least 9,000 people, mostly Hondurans, tried to enter Guatemala during the second weekend in January. Security forces tried to repel the caravan of people. Biden had optimistically pledged to tackle the root causes of poverty and violence that drive Central Americans to the USA.

Nicaragua

LoraKim also works with the Yellow-naped Parrot in Nicaragua. The location is the twin-peaked volcanic island of Ometepe, in Lake Cocibolca, the largest fresh water body in Central America. It is approximately 9km (5.6 miles) from the mainland and is comprised of two volcanoes, Maderas and Concepción, joined by a wetland isthmus. The island was officially designated as a wildlife refuge in 2010 in recognition of its ecological value and encompasses a dramatic range of altitude, topography, and climate within its 276km² (107 square miles).

In 2019 I received an email from her:

'I write this as the sun comes up over Lake Cocibolca. I have been working with a group of young people for about six years and their project is really coming along. The young parrots are still flying with their parents and this is the time to make counts in Central America. At midday we meet up with the nearly 20 youths simultaneously spread out over the island. We are here to count, as much as to involve youth in citizen science and support them economically in these tough times in Nicaragua.'

Counts occurred in four principal areas during seven years up to 2020. In July 2020, 1,028 Yellow-naped Parrots were found, also 821 Red-lored Parrots, 35 unidentified *Amazona,* 1,268 Pacific Parakeets, 142 Orange-chinned Parakeets (*Brotogeris jugularis*) and 11 Orange-fronted Parakeets (*Eupsittula canicularis*) (Joyner *et al.*, 2021).

Sadly, later in 2019 a forest fire ravaged the vitally important nesting and roosting site of the Yellow-naped Parrots. Ecological impacts such as fire are wide-reaching for this vulnerable parrot due to its rarity and limited range. Nearly 50% of the nests were destroyed in 2020. The 120ha (300 acres) lost to the fire represented 40% of the most densely forested area within the wildlife refuge. Fires, started deliberately or carelessly, are a fact of life on the island of Ometepe. That particular patch of forest had been struck twice during the previous five years.

The hurricanes affected other work of One Earth Conservation. The two Yellow-headed Parrot (*Amazona oratrix*) projects took a direct hit. One community that protects the bird in Guatemala had to be evacuated for months and their homes were lost. LoraKim said: 'We are trying to help them by increasing project resources so they can earn income while they rebuild. We hope to receive more donations so we can help these families and this very endangered bird (maybe a hundred left between the two countries) in Honduras and Guatemala.'

Fortunately the islands of Guanaja and Roatán were not badly affected. One Earth Conservation was also helping there with the Yellow-lored Parrot (*Amazona xantholora*). Possibly only about 10 survive on Roatán – the only place in Honduras where they exist, along with Yellow-naped Parrots.

One Earth Conservation

LoraKim drew on her experience as a Certified Trainer in Nonviolent

Communication and on more than 30 years as a conservationist and wildlife veterinarian to lead One Earth Conservation. It seeks to empower people trying to save the planet through their international Nurture Nature Program. She wrote: 'The biodiversity and climate crises compel us each to commit our lives to Earth and her beings. This is a fundamental shift from how humans have claimed privilege over other animals. Now is the time for us to recognise that all beings (including, but not limited to, humans) have inherent worth and dignity, and their suffering matters.'

She travels to areas in Latin America to witness the plight of the parrots and people there, and to do what she can. One Earth's projects extend from Guatemala, Honduras and Nicaragua to Paraguay and Guyana. She will strive to build more projects, such as in Suriname and French Guiana, which she explored before the pandemic.

PRG Secretary

In early 2020 LoraKim took on another role: Acting Secretary of the Parrot Researchers Group (PRG). The previous forum at the IOU (International Ornithologists' Inion), which was used until November 2019, had 211 active members. By December 2020 the Google Group, the main communication means of the PRG, has 425 active members. See: https://groups.google.com/g/parrot-spe-cialist-group/c/nVJpcjp9wvE/m/Bu1y2CZDCAAJ.

The focus in conservation

Most people in Europe have no idea of the dangers and problems for people working in the field in conservation, also of the dangers that beset a pair of parrots attempting to produce the next generation. Too often the parrots fail due to human greed and interference. Only rarely does a passionate and dedicated individual like LoraKim come along to try to reverse the decline and to teach compassion towards wildlife to the local people.

A heroine is someone with the courage and determination to fight for what she believes – not necessarily someone who wins the battle. But sometimes the focus is too narrow. A single person cannot fight agribusiness. Food production worldwide (and that includes in the UK) needs to become less damaging to the environment yet at the same time more productive and sustainable. And the second factor that underpinned the need to poach parrots, in Central America and elsewhere, was the human population. In Guatemala in 1977 it was 5.1 million; it had risen to 14.7 million in 2008; it reached 17.9 million in 2020. Alongside conservation education, teaching means of self-sufficiency, such as bee-keeping, and giving women the possibility to limit their family size, are crucial factors. So the story in Guatemala was not one of total success. But it teaches us a lot of things.

References

Joyner, L., 2017, *Conservation in the Time of War,* One Earth Conservation, New York.

Joyner, L., N. Zambrana Morales, L. Hernandéz and E. Urtecho, 2021, Multiple Point Fixed Transects in Parrot Monitoring: A Case Study, Edition 1, March 1, One Earth Conservation.org.

Watch:
www.youtube.com/watch?v=mDRu1qNeLkI.
www.youtube.com/channel/UCmp5TRcV0rNsMIggnfyp2Tg.

21. Neiva Guedes
Brazil 1962-
Saviour of the Pantanal Hyacinth Macaws

Neiva Guedes was born on January 10 1962 at Ponta Porã in Mato Grosso do Sul in central Brazil. Her story is different: she never intended to work in conservation. She wanted to study Medicine; that was not possible so she chose to take a biology course.

In 1987 she graduated from the Federal University of Mato Grosso with a Master's degree in Forest Sciences. A field trip in 1989 completely changed the direction of her life. One November day she was in Brazil's Pantanal. This is the world's largest wetland, with an extremely rich ecosystem, including 650 species of birds and 132 species of mammals. The most important population of the iconic Hyacinth Macaw (*Anodorhynchus hyacinthinus*) occurs there. The wealth of wildlife and habitats resulted in it being declared a UNESCO Biosphere Reserve in 2000.

During a nature conservation course Neiva saw 30 Hyacinth Macaws perched on a dry branch – and she was enchanted. But her professor told her that the species was endangered and could disappear in 50 years. She could not forget these majestic creatures or that they were threatened with extinction.

Known as the *Arara Azul* (blue macaw), this is the largest and most spectacular parrot of the Neotropics; this region can boast about 150 species. Due to trafficking and habitat loss, this macaw had been placed on Appendix I of CITES in 1987, making commercial trade illegal. But illegal trapping continued and this could have decimated the Pantanal population. The area is covered in cattle ranches; the macaws have lived around humans for centuries and they are easier to trap than other large macaws.

When Joseph Forshaw's classic book *Parrots of the World* was published in 1973 it transformed world knowledge about what was then a poorly studied group of birds. However, there was so little information on this macaw that he quoted from papers published in the 1930s, when it was 'fairly common.' He had recorded under 'Nesting': 'I know of no published records' (Forshaw, 1973). In the third (revised) edition of 1989 he wrote about hunting and trapping with 'the consequent decline in numbers now reaching alarming proportions.'

This big blue macaw occurs in three widely separated areas: the Brazilian

Pantanal in the states of Mato Gross do Sul and Mato Grosso, and marginally in eastern Bolivia, and in Paraguay where its conservation status is listed as Critical; in Pará state in north-eastern Brazil (one of the states worst hit by forest fires in 2020), eastern Amazon region; and northern and central Brazil in the states of Goiás, Tocantins, Maranhão, Bahía, Minas Gerais and Piauí. The Brazilian Pantanal, flooded with water nearly a metre deep, for six months of the year, is its stronghold.

Worldwide there were very few parrot conservation projects when Neiva first set eyes on this charismatic macaw. In 1990 the World Parrot Trust, founded in the previous year, established the Hyacinth Fund, and raised money to fund fieldwork by Charles Munn of Wildlife Conservation International to survey the populations. The estimate was 2,500 individuals in the wild, including approximately 1,500 in the Pantanal.

In 1990 Neiva entered the Master's degree programme at Escola Superior de Agricultura Luiz de Queiroz, of the University of São Paulo. Remembering her emotional first sighting, she chose the Hyacinth Macaw for her Master's thesis, and acquired funding from the World Wildlife Fund (WWF-US) for two years. While studying for her degree she started her work in the Pantanal with the help of family and friends. She had no money to hire an assistant. Scientists taught her the necessary climbing skills to reach macaw nests. She did not even have a vehicle! Instead '… she hitched rides with planes, cars, trucks, tractors, boats, horses and carts, even walking when everything else failed' (Corrêa, 2006). Sometimes it was as late as 10pm or the small hours of the following morning when she got back to her field camp. There were no mobile radios or mobile phones and no electric power.

A paragraph from her book *Blue Jewels Across the Pantanal Skies* not only sets the scene in an evocative manner, but establishes her as a talented writer:

'It's 5.40am, and still dark. I'm on the observation post, a leaning tree trunk that lets me sit 6.8 meters (almost 23 feet) above ground. I chose a high spot because I am about to spend a day on my own in this small *capão* [a round clump of palm trees and bushes on a plain]. Up here I am safe from being run over from a pack of white-lipped peccaries or from other animals that might come by. Silence prevails… My target: a couple of preening hyacinth macaws perched on a limb, cleaning each other's feathers with their beaks. The first signs of dawn pour over the horizon. Golden beams of sunlight start filling the sky. The two macaws fly in silence. In a few seconds the sun rises in grandeur, revealing countless shades and colours, filling the view with light, filling the bounty of nature with colour. Howler monkeys, parrots, parakeets and other birds start singing. It is the dawn of a new day: A unique Pantanal show' (Guedes, 2011).

Gradually Neiva received financial support from interested people and organisations. Two funds were set up by aviculturists, inspired by their love for their own macaws. In 1994 Tony Pittman in the UK started the Hyacinthine Macaw Survival Fund and in 1995 Mark and Marie Stafford in California launched the Hyacinth Macaw Fund. The earliest project had been that by the World Parrot Trust which established a fund in 1990 to try to protect remaining populations. In 2007 substantial sums were raised by television viewers in the UK. They were asked to donate to and vote for one of several featured conservation projects – and who could resist supporting this iconic macaw?

Modestly Neiva told me: 'I've never done anything on my own. I've always relied on the support and partnership of many people, companies and institutions; initially from my family, friends, field team and sponsors.' But it was *her* initiative and determination that made it all happen.

In her book, which documents so well the story of her successful bid to save the Mato Grosso Pantanal population, she wrote: 'To reach my goal, I spared no effort, shied from no risk, refused to compromise. I was eager and I thought there was no time to waste. I would brave anything to see a nest, find eggs or chicks, and then see them fly across the Pantanal skies.'

Toyota Brazil lent her a four wheel drive vehicle. This was essential for checking all the nest sites every two to four weeks. But even with a vehicle there

A pair of Hyacinth Macaws playing near their nest in the Pantanal. Photograph: author.

were disasters such as when the Toyota sank into mud and a tractor was needed to pull it out. Neiva's project started in the Nhecolândia area, supported by the Nhumirim Farm of the Pantanal Agricultural Research Center and 13 properties in the region. Neiva covered a very large area. It was a difficult time for her; a social life was nearly impossible and she made many sacrifices to continue her work – but she 'celebrated each new egg found'.

Every year, 3-5% of Hyacinth Macaw nest trees in the Pantanal are lost to storm damage or felling. Ninety-four per cent of natural nests are in the large, smooth-barked trees known locally as *manduví* (*Sterculia apetala*). This tree is a Pantanal key plant, and extremely important in maintaining a viable macaw population. Neiva and her team encourage farmers to protect and plant these trees and to preserve areas where saplings are growing. It takes 60 to 80 years for a cavity to form – and a metre-long macaw needs a large cavity. There were not enough available to increase the macaw's reproduction rate. By 2000 forest cover represented approximately 26% of the vegetation there and the deforestation rate was increasing.

The importance of nest-boxes

Neiva enlisted the help of local landowners. With their permission, in 1995 she started to erect nest-boxes. They were readily accepted by the macaws. She was thus able to tag chicks in the nest; in 2004 she started to microchip them. By 2011 she had marked more than 1,000 chicks – an almost unbelievable achievement which has made it possible to record the histories of many individual macaws. She said: 'Only *I* knew every nest and track. It was like having a GPS map in my brain.'

In 2003 the *Instituto Arara Azul,* a non-profit organisation, (www.institutoararaazul.org.br) had been created in the Pantanal with Neiva as president. It aimed to develop and manage research projects, to raise awareness of the Hyacinth Macaw's plight, and to encourage eco-tourism to promote conservation. The education programme has resulted in trafficking of the macaw being eliminated in areas where the Institute is present. Other studies include the reproductive biology of species that coexist with them, such as the Red and Green Macaw (*Ara chloropterus*), toucans, owls and ducks. The study area covers 400,000ha (1,544 square miles), and more than 600 nests. Nest sites are monitored, and critical habitats for food and nesting are identified.

In 2005 Neiva decided that for the continuity of her research she needed to obtain a PhD. This was difficult; her daughter was three years old. She did not want to stop the fieldwork so she took a course that allowed her to continue, taking the subjects in more concentrated modules. To finish the thesis, this determined scientist spent 40 days away from her work and family to analyse her data and to write it up.

The result of her commitment was that in 2009 Neiva gained a PhD in zoology with her thesis on Hyacinth Macaw breeding biology. She had studied the macaws on more than 50 farms in Mato Grosso do Sul. By 2015 Neiva and her assistants had discovered 350 plus natural nests, 94% in the *manduví* tree. By then the astounding total of 253 artificial nests had been erected in 180ha (450 acres) of the Pantanal. They were maintained and where necessary replaced by Neiva and her team, almost all on privately-owned ranches. This was the key factor in the increasing number of breeding pairs. Red-and-green Macaws also take advantage of the ready-made nests. From July 2015 to June 2016 the team monitored 151 chicks on eleven properties. The importance of artificial nest sites is underlined in these statistics: 64 chicks were reared in these, plus 87 in natural nests.

In November 2019 I was on the Aguape ranch in Aquiduana, 195km (122 miles) west of Campo Grande. I watched in the pouring rain as one of these heavy nest-boxes was manoeuvred into position by members of Neiva's team. It made me appreciate how much work was involved in erecting just one nest site. The dedication and motivation of Neiva and her team – comprising seven people at that time – were extraordinary.

An important field base of the *Projeto Arara Azul* (Blue Macaw Project) was the Caiman Ecological Refuge in the Miranda district. Guests learn about the Project's activities through the visitors' centre, as I did in 2008. I stayed in a superb lodge, picturesquely situated at the edge of a small cove of permanent wetland. Neiva was absent at the time but her project members allowed my small group to accompany them as they checked nest-boxes. Situated at a height of at least 12m (30ft), they can be reached with the aid of mountaineering equipment – a harness around waist and thighs attached to a pulley. The first chick brought down to be weighed and measured was eight weeks old, with glossy violet plumage and huge dark eyes, accentuated by the naked yellow skin surrounding them. Such a

Neiva with Sr Roseno Ataide. The natural nest on his property was destroyed in 2020 so Arara Azul erected a nest-box. When the chicks were three and five days old the area was hit by fire but the chicks survived. With Neiva are two of her assistants, Fernanda Fontoura and, next to Sr Roseno, Luciana Ferreira.
Photograph: Marcos Roberto Ferramosca.

beautiful creature! Monitoring nests yields important information on chick development, and prevents the death of chicks where there are problems such as bot fly infestation or nest flooding.

In 2012, the base of the Arara Azul Project was transferred from the Caiman lodge to Retiro Novo, 17km (11 miles) away. Its comfortable infrastructure can host up to eight researchers and includes a small laboratory for preliminary biological assessments and a visitors' centre. In November 2013, the Sustainability Center opened in Campo Grande. Its construction was donated by the Toyota do Brasil Foundation. The objective is to foster the institution's projects and implement viable alternatives for the generation of financial self-sustainability.

Throughout the entire period of her work with the macaw, Neiva has had the difficult and worrying responsibility of finding sponsors to fund the project. Her success in this is due to her unending enthusiasm and winning personality. One successful idea is to encourage people to sponsor a nest-box, receiving progress reports of chicks hatched within and having the privilege of naming the chick. I have sponsored two nests and I would encourage readers to do the same!

Neiva's far-reaching influence

Neiva has become a sought-after speaker at international parrot conventions, such as those organised by Parrots International, at various venues in the USA. I first heard her speak at the Fifth International Parrot Convention organised by Loro Parque in Tenerife, in 2002. The impressive details she presented on the breeding biology of the Hyacinth Macaw had not been equalled for any other parrot species in Brazil. Some details were fascinating; for example, the macaw chicks have specific vocalisations that they use for communicating with their parents. They respond to their parents' vocalisations in the vicinity of the nest, but not to those of other pairs. Hyacinth pairs never split up, finding a new mate only if one member of the pair dies.

In 2015 I attended the Ninth International Symposium of Parrots International in Campo Grande in Mato Grosso do Sul. When Neiva spoke there she said: 'After 26 years I am still learning about the Hyacinth Macaws and the species that live with them… Although the total population is estimated at 6,500 individuals I still consider them to be an endangered species.' The tremendous amount of respect and admiration accorded to her by everyone at that meeting was so evident, with many of the speakers mentioning her as their mentor.

In 2019 I at last had the great pleasure of meeting Neiva. I was enchanted by her warmth and friendliness and the wide disarming smile. How proud she must be to know that her initiative and work were largely responsible for this increase! She told me:

'I can't express how I feel about the Hyacinth Macaws, but I know that love and passion are certainties. This gives me the strength to never give up the work, which is long term and extremely necessary because we are working in nature, with constant changes and intricate interrelationships. And the more I learn about the Hyacinth Macaws, the more I know they are special because they're more susceptible than the other big macaws.'

This is because in the Pantanal they are not forest-dwelling birds; they are found in more open habitats and in forest edges where the only two species of palm trees grow on which they feed. Unfortunately, the Pantanal did not escape the many thousands of fires that burned across Brazil in 2019 and 2020. The São Francisco do Perigara, a cattle ranch extending over 24,400ha (61,000 acres), sheltered the largest population of the Hyacinth Macaw, probably at least 700 individuals. On August 1 2020 wild fires swept across the ranch and more than 70% of the farm's vegetation was destroyed. Many other areas of Hyacinth Macaw habitat were badly burned. In the areas watched over by the Institute there is confidence that everything possible will be done to minimise the impact of the fires, but the macaw's population growth has been threatened.

Neiva is a Professor at the University for the Development of the State and the Pantanal Region in Campo Grande. She has authored or co-authored more than 50 scientific papers, mostly relating to the Hyacinth Macaw and its ecology, such as that on natural nesting sites (Santos *et al.*, 2007). She has inspired may people to work with her and to apply what they have learned to other species.

Everyone, wherever they are in the world, knows about Neiva Guedes if they are interested in the conservation of the Hyacinth Macaw. She continues to inspire people worldwide to work in environmental education and conservation science. She is a remarkable example of what one individual can achieve after starting with nothing. It is rare indeed for a single biologist to be associated with one project for more than 30 years.

In 2014 the IUCN status of the Hyacinth Macaw was down-listed from Endangered to Vulnerable. The macaw had expanded its range in the Pantanal and its numbers had trebled – and this was due to Neiva's initiative. No one who has been close to a Hyacinth Macaw can fail to be moved by its big gentle eyes, by its overpowering beauty and majesty. When threatened with extinction you would think that a large, influential conservation organisation would have rushed to its aid. But, no, it took a young biology student with no funding and no experience in the field, but with vision, passion and commitment, to achieve the seemingly impossible. Neiva – you are a true heroine! Thank you – from everyone who loves parrots.

Awards

Neiva's work has been recognised worldwide. In 1995 she received the Pieter Oyens Award of WWF-US (designed to encourage young naturalists), for her conservation work in Brazil. In 1998 she won the trophy for Women who make a Difference in the Environment, offered by the Association of Women and Field Business Professionals in Campo Grande-MS. In 2002, 500 projects from all over Brazil were registered for the Super Ecologist Award. The Blue Macaw Project took second place in the Fauna NGO category. In 2004 Neiva was honoured at Soestdijk Palace in the Netherlands with the Grand Master of the order of the Golden Ark. This is – an honorary title awarded by His Royal Highness Prince Bernhard of the Netherlands for outstanding achievement in wildlife conservation. The following week she met the Duke of Edinburgh (an honorary member of Birdlife International).

Neiva received an extraordinary and well-deserved privilege in 2016 when the Olympic Games were held in Brazil. She carried the Olympic torch through the town of Rio Brilhante in Mato Grosso do Sul. Surely no one else could have been more deserving of this honour!

References

Corrêa, M. S., 2006, *Brazil Naturally*, Fundação O Boticário de Proteção à Natureza, Curitiba.

Forshaw, J. M., 1973, *Parrots of the World*, Lansdowne Press, Melbourne.

Guedes, N. M. R., 2011, *Joias azuis no céu do Pantanal/Blue Jewels Across the Pantanal Skies*, Dórea Books and Art, São Paulo.

Santos, A., Jr., W. M. Tomas, I. H. Ishii, N. M. R. Guedes and J. D. Hay, 2007, Occurrence of Hyacinth Macaw nesting sites in *Sterculia apetala* in the Pantanal Wetland, Brazil, *Gaia Scientia*, 1 (2): 127-130.

Neiva met HRH the Duke of Edinburgh in his private library at Buckingham Palace on May 18 2004. Photograph: Buckingham Palace.

22. Colleen Downs
South Africa 1963-
Scientist and Teacher

Colleen Downs was born on November 3 1963 in South Africa, a country with about 850 species of birds, in a wide variety of habitats. How did Colleen's interest in birds develop? At university she went birding with some classmates and started ringing birds for scientific purposes. Her passion for watching birds developed further during three years back-packing around the world.

In 1985 she received her BSc from the University of KwaZulu-Natal (UKZN) in Pietermaritzburg, where she has been a teaching professor in the School of Life Sciences since 1994. In addition to teaching, she ran the Science Foundation Programme (SFP) in Biology from 1994-2001, and was the co-ordinator of various bioscience and biology classes. She also teaches biology, including Vertebrate Biology, and Animal Physiology and supervises Honours projects.

Her research interests are very wide and include the physiology, behaviour, ecology and conservation of southern African terrestrial vertebrates, including ecosystem health in KwaZulu-Natal and the Eastern Cape. This includes conservation, general biology, invasion biology, effects of changing land use (including urban ecology) and climate change on birds, fish, reptiles and mammals.

Her output of research publications is prodigious, with about 400 peer reviewed articles, covering such topics as the impact of invasive alien bird species, the roosting habit of the endangered Cape Vulture, foraging habits of the vervet monkey, and Crowned Eagles in an urban landscape. She has contributed 21 book chapters and more than 50 popular articles.

Professor Downs' work has been recognised in many ways. In 2014 she was Elected Fellow of the International Ornithologists' Union (IOU) for 'the excellence of her scientific work, and of her involvement in promoting ornithology'. In 2016 she was elected to the Academy of Science of South Africa. In 2017 she was awarded the Gold Medal of the Zoological Society of Southern Africa, of which she had been treasurer since 1997. In 2019 she was elected as an Honorary Fellow of the American Ornithologists' Union. She was made the honorary president of BirdLife

Female Heroes of Bird Conservation

*Colleen Downs.
With permission from Colleen Downs.*

tems (since 2016) and of the *African Journal of Ecology* (since 2018). She has acted as the meeting convenor for a number of important congresses, such as the 22nd International Ornithological Congress in Durban in 1998. She is a member of IUCN Species Survival Commissions for the Hippo Specialist Group, the Crocodile Specialist Group and the Stork Specialist Group. This eye-watering workload would make her a heroine in the eyes of most people – but I believe there are two aspects which truly qualify her for this status.

South Africa in 2016 and she sits on a number of committees.

How does she find enough hours in the day to fulfil all these duties alongside a full academic career? Her former student Craig Symes said: 'Colleen is an early riser rather than a night owl, and I think this is what enables her to get so much work done!'

Then there are her editorial positions which include Associate Editor (since 2011) of the *Ibis,* the prestigious journal of the British Ornithologists' Union. After reading the submissions, she seeks reviewers who are experts in the field, and then summarises their recommendations for the editor. She says that in this era of 'fake news' and sometimes doubtful scientific declarations, it is most important for editors to uphold the peer review process.

She is also Associate Editor of the *Ostrich* (since 2002), of *Urban Ecosys-*

Working with students

The welfare of Colleen's students is very important to her. She has published papers on science education problems experienced by Life Science students and the development of appropriate teaching strategies to address these. She is very interested in working with previously disadvantaged young people, who form a high percentage of the students in her classes.

She has supervised and involved black internship and other undergraduate students from 1995, usually up to six students per year. They spend their spare time during the term and vacations assisting Colleen with her research. She acquired funding for an apprenticeship programme for undergraduate biology students, resulting in ten to 12 students working at various institutions during vacations under her management. Many have continued

Male Cape Parrot. There is captive breeding in South Africa.
Photograph: author.

with postgraduate studies. She is also involved in developing women in leadership at UKZN.

Her former student, Craig Symes, told me:

'Colleen's academic achievements are extraordinary but more importantly it is her character that endears her as a scientist. I think this makes her first a great teacher and, in turn, a good research scientist. I first met Colleen when I started working for Olaf Wirminghaus, as a Research Assistant on his Cape Parrot PhD project. When her husband, Olaf, died, she took me under her wing as a research assistant to continue Olaf's work. I benefitted greatly from her mentorship and encouragement.

'I remember coming back from my first field season (a few months in northern South Africa chasing Grey-headed Parrots) and having a meeting with Professor Mike Perrin, who was also involved in Cape Parrot (*Poicephalus robustus*) research. I asked him, "What do you think I should do now?" His reply was along the lines of, "It's your project, you decide." Colleen was much like that; while providing sound advice, she let students mostly make their own decisions. As a supervisor myself, I remembered that and I tried to do the same. It was important to make the students think they were coming up with their own decisions. It was an empowering tactic that gave me more confidence as I developed as a scientist.'

'Colleen is a very compassionate person. I always remember how composed she appeared when Olaf was going through his battle with cancer. I was still a young undergraduate then and I probably never really appreciated the hardships she was facing. The short time I knew Olaf had a significant effect on my life. I always felt so welcome in their home, and even after Olaf was gone, Colleen had the skill of making all her students feel like she genuinely cared, which she did. She always had an open door policy and I never felt that she had no time for me, even though she had a string of other students to supervise as well as all sorts of academic duties.'

'I always enjoyed working with Colleen. While Olaf and I collected most

Female Heroes of Bird Conservation

of the field data on the Cape Parrot research project, Colleen was the one who effectively wrote it all up. I was still some way from publishing my own papers but really appreciated her including me as an author. In total we co-authored 16 papers. She has a very open and co-operative way of working and it is probably the ease with which she is able to work with people that contributes to her academic success.'

'Colleen has a very enquiring mind and the diversity of topics that she has tackled over the years are a testament to her versatility as a scientist. She is very level-headed and can logically work through most "problems" with clarity and clear thought. I always found this calmness of hers useful as a "sounding board" when I faced my own frustrations as a post-graduate, and felt that things were just not working out!'

'However, before I end I'll comment on her smile! Even when I moved from the University I would pop in to visit Colleen at her office. Catching up with news and discussion was good but always the most rewarding part of seeing her would be the manner in which she greeted me. It would always be with a great smile!'

Many female scientists have impressive lists of publications and other academic achievements. So what else qualifies Colleen as a heroine in my eyes?

Cape Parrot Conservation

The Cape Parrot is South Africa's only endemic parrot. Classified by the IUCN as Vulnerable, it is a food specialist, highly dependent on the declining *Podocarpus* forests and moving between patches searching for the irregular and often protracted fruiting of *Podocarpus*. This makes it difficult to estimate numbers accurately and to determine its distribution.

I met Colleen in June 1996 and was immediately impressed by her enthusiasm and knowledge. My interest in the Cape Parrot had taken me to Pietermaritzburg in southern Natal, where Olaf Wirminghaus had been studying this endearing parrot with its over-sized bill. His work was continued by Colleen. I was in the field in Creighton, their study area, with her and Professor

In the field in southern Natal in 1996 – right to left, Colleen Downs, Craig Symes, Mike Perrin and friend, Val Moat and author.
Photograph: Val Moat.

Mike Perrin, both of the University of Kwa-Zulu Natal.

As we climbed up to 1,760m (5,770ft), we looked down into a small area of yellow-wood (*Podocarpus*) forest on which Cape Parrots rely as their food source. A glimpse of distant parrots through a spotting scope elicited exclamations of excitement from me as I looked at their golden heads, decorated with orange feathers on the forehead – but only in the female.

Colleen told me that no logging of the yellow-woods there had occurred since the early 1950s. However, elsewhere most of Natal is covered in grassland or has been converted to agricultural use. From our viewpoint we saw mainly crops and pine forests. By the start of the 21st century indigenous forest comprised only 2% of the land area of South Africa, only a small proportion of which was *Podocarpus/Afrocarpus* forest. This is increasingly fragmented and declining in area.

Colleen summed up the serious problems faced by the Cape Parrot, which vary at different locations. They include 'loss or change in the quality of their preferred forest habitat, food and nest-site shortages, illegal poaching for the pet trade, disease – especially Psittacine Beak and Feather Disease virus (PBFDV), avian predators and accelerated climate change' (Downs, 2013).

Field data collection started in 1993. Information on the population size was urgently needed – and this is where citizen science came in. The annual Cape Parrot Big Birding Day (CPBBD) was initiated as a national census. Volunteers assist in monitoring and counting in the Eastern Cape, KwaZulu-Natal and Limpopo provinces in indigenous forests, as well as sites where the parrots feed outside of forests. The distribution remains largely unchanged from that in the 1970s.

Colleen has been involved with the CPBBD, which started in 1998, and is organised by the Cape Parrot Working Group, of which Colleen has been chairperson since 2008. Large numbers of volunteers monitor the parrots from fixed vantage points. As well as obtaining crucial information, activities which engage local communities in the observation and protection of this rare parrot are important and help to raise its public profile. This has become one of the longest citizen science monitoring projects in South Africa.

In 1999 the Cape Parrot population was estimated at around 500 (Wirminghaus *et al.*, 2000). In 2012 the estimate was at least 1,189 based on simultaneous counts made from 72 locations throughout the range. In 2013 the conclusion was that there were probably fewer than 1,600 but the maximum count was 1,356. In 2016 the count reached 1,499. However, the ability to detect short-term population fluctuations is limited. In 2017 at least 1,409 parrots were seen during the afternoon count, with 1,719 the following morning. The value of public participation in monitoring an endangered species cannot be over-emphasised. A thriving population of Cape Parrots acts as a flagship for the protection and recovery of indigenous forests in South Africa, for the shared benefit of people and nature. At the time of writing, Colleen has been involved for 28 years in monitoring populations of the Cape Parrot. That is true commitment!

She is married to James Wood. They have two daughters, Tori and Emmi.

References

Downs, C., 2013, Cape Parrot, A South African Endemic, *PsittaScene*, Winter: 20-21.

Wirminghaus J., C. Downs, C. Symes and M. Perrin, 2000, Abundance of the Cape Parrot in South Africa, *South African Journal of Wildlife Research*, 30: 43-52.

See also:

Downs, C., 2005, Artificial nest boxes and wild Cape Parrots *Poicephalus robustus*: persistence pays off, *Ostrich*, 76: 222-224.

Downs, C. T. 2005, Abundance of the endangered Cape Parrot, *Poicephalus robustus*, in South Africa: implications for its survival, *African Zoology*, 40: 15-24.

Downs, C. T., 2005, Is A Year-Long Access Course Into University Helping Previously Disadvantaged Black Students In Biology? *South African Journal of Higher Education*, 19: 666-683. http://doi.org/10.4314/sajhe.v19i4.25660.

Downs, C. T., M. Brown, L. Hart and C. T. Symes, 2015, Review of documented beak and feather disease virus cases in wild Cape Parrots in South Africa during the last 20 years, *Journal of Ornithology*, 156: 867-875.

Downs, C. T., M. Pfeiffer and L. A. Hart, 2014. Fifteen years of annual Cape Parrot *Poicephalus robustus* censuses: current population trends and conservation contributions, *Ostrich*, 85: 273-280.

23. Nicola Crockford
UK 1964-
World renowned for Shorebird Habitat Protection

'I have loved birds since before I could talk and knew I wanted to work to save them since I was about 11.'

Nicola was born in Guildford, Surrey, UK, on May 8 1964, the first of three daughters. Her father, a surgeon, gave her mother binoculars as a present to celebrate the birth. How extraordinarily predictive! Her mother was a nurse and a classical singer. Nicola's early months were spent accompanying her and learning to identify birds in the grounds of the house where they rented a flat near Godalming. Her favourite book as a toddler was the Time-Life book *The Birds*. Her first word was duck, and her first sentence 'look at it, it's a bird!' She could soon identify a Tawny Frogmouth and a Hoopoe from the book. Encouraged by her grandparents, she remembers the thrill of watching Nuthatches (*Sitta europaea*) on their bird table.

After moving to Northumberland when she was two, it was a treat to be taken to watch wildfowl on the local reservoirs by her father or grandfather. Before she was born they had exchanged wildfowlers' guns for binoculars. She remembers a special weekend when she was about eleven, when her father took her to see the great flocks of handsome Barnacle Geese (*Branta leucopsis*) at Caerlaverock.

One winter Nicola was inspired by the Young Ornithologists' Club to undertake monthly waterbird counts at Whittledene Reservoir. In the harsh winter of 1977, when the snow on the road was a metre deep, she rode her Connemara pony, Mickey, to the reservoir, and was rewarded by a flock of Greylag Geese (*Anser anser*) and elegant Goosanders (*Mergus merganser*). But it was for waders (shorebirds) that she developed an early passion. A family friend took her, year after year, to help on monthly wader counts on the Northumberland coast between Seahouses and Beadnell.

While at school she lost no time in becoming involved in conservation. For six months, until she started at university, she volunteered with the RSPB. Finding nests and analysing the food of Wood Warblers (*Phylloscopus sibilatrix*) in Welsh oak woods for Tim Stowe was part of her work. She also helped Rhys Green find Snipe nests at the Nene

Female Heroes of Bird Conservation

The Nuthatch intrigued the young Nicola.
Photograph: Tracy Farrer.

Washes, surveyed Merlin food (pipits and Skylarks) in the Berwyns for Colin Bibby and mapped breeding wader nests for Ken Smith. A decade later she was working for them permanently – including closely with all those people.

She was greatly encouraged by the Northumberland Bird Club who had even supported her with a grant to go on an expedition to Greenland after her A-levels. Thus began a great love of the Arctic, where she has spent seven field seasons. The memory was not diminished by a near catastrophe when the battery of the helicopter on which she was a passenger was about to explode.

In trying to decide where to read Zoology, she wrote to Durham University, asking about their bird research. When they outlined the wader work of Peter Evans' group, she was sold! As a Durham undergraduate, she joined cannon-netting trips to the Tees Estuary. This led to being invited on a wader expedition to Balsfjord in Arctic Norway, to determine to which population the large spring staging flock of Red Knots (*Calidris canutus*) belonged. It turned out that it was the same one that she had been ringing on the Tees! Her undergraduate project sought to understand the distribution of the knots on the various mudflats around the fjord. This involved lots of mud sampling and sieving.

Even before graduating Nicola moved to Canada, to work for Guy Morrison and Hugh Boyd of the Canadian Wildlife Service (CWS). She spent two field seasons on Rowley Island in the Foxe Basin of the Canadian Arctic to help survey and ring breeding waders. It is still her favourite place on the planet: 'I have never spent a more sublime few weeks. It further embedded my love of the Arctic, and I returned twice more to the Canadian Arctic – for a third season in the Foxe Basin with Guy and to the Snow Goose camp on Bylot Island. We gathered lots of data on White-rumped Sandpipers, my main study species, but we also had the immense thrill of finding a couple of Red Knot nests.'

Between Canadian field seasons she had a job for six months with the New Zealand Government's Ecology Division. As a field researcher, she worked on various endemic species, especially radio-tagging of Tuis (*Prosthemadera novaeseelandiae*). These beautiful green, bronze and brown honeyeaters, so different to waders, have a distinctive white throat tuft.

While overseas, she was invited to talk at the Royal Australian Ornithological Union about her undergraduate work on the feeding ecology of Red Knots. She had given her first talk on this subject to the annual meeting of the International Wader Study Group (IWSG) in La Rochelle, France, in 1985, when she was 21.

In Australia she had the good fortune to go cannon-netting waders with Clive Minton, the co-inventor of cannon-netting and founder of the IWSG. She says that Clive initiated what – in her experience of global bird conservation – 'is the strongest, most collaborative community of bird scientists and conservationists in the world.' The group's uniquely friendly, encouraging atmosphere – not least to a young female (who were much in the minority in those days) – further embedded her heart in the wader world, making her lifelong friends. Indeed, it was at the annual IWSG meeting in Ipswich in 1988 that she first met Bill Sutherland, who was to become her husband.

She said: 'Minton alumni and other members of the IWSG have percolated into the conservation world from local to global – from the heart of civil society groups counting and ringing birds year in year out, to professors in the top universities of the world, to national civil servants, and to leaders in Convention Secretariats, as well as across the NGO sector.'

While living in a caravan in a New Zealand field full of farmed red deer, she began to realise her interests lay more in conservation implementation, using the science rather than doing it.

On her return to Canada, Hugh Boyd, knowing of this budding interest, included her in the Canadian delegation to the Conference of the Parties of the Ramsar Convention on Wetlands in Regina, Saskatchewan. She says: 'This experience changed the course of my life. I have spent my entire career focused on implementing the Ramsar Convention and other biodiversity treaties, including the Convention on Migratory Species and its daughter agreement, the African Eurasian Waterbird Agreement.'

Career moves and priorities

Her first job back in the UK, in 1987, was working at the Colchester office of the Nature Conservancy Council (NCC, the UK statutory conservation agency), to designate the Blackwater, Colne and Crouch Estuaries as Ramsar Sites and EU Special Protection Areas of international importance for migratory waterbirds. She moved to the NCC national headquarters in Peterborough, where she supported regional staff to conserve protected areas. She became the government expert witness – on the winning side – with the RSPB in the Public Enquiry against the Lionhope development on the Swale Estuary.

With the breakup of the NCC she moved to the UK Joint Nature Conservation Committee, leading a small team of ornithologists working to reduce negative impacts on birds. She completed the first review of the impact of wind farms. In 1992 Nicola was in-

Female Heroes of Bird Conservation

Nicola's is an important voice at international meetings.

vited to return to the RSPB, where she has remained, working on bird species conservation at national level, then at European level and, since 2009, at global level. She says: 'It is the best job in the world for me!' To begin with she coordinated the RSPB's national work on wetland and upland species, including the reintroductions of Red Kite and White-tailed Eagle, and work to combat raptor persecution. She also coordinated the development of a successful European action plan for the Corncrake (*Crex crex*).

In 1997, she moved to the International Directorate to lead the RSPB's species policy work at European level. The RSPB is the UK Partner of BirdLife International, so at international meetings, Nicola usually operates in the name of BirdLife. Her work uses the Bern Convention to resolve a number of national breaches in compliance from damaging developments. These included forestry policy in Iceland affecting breeding waterbirds, wind farms in Bulgaria and Norway, and the Via Baltica road in Poland.

During this time Nicola had two daughters. She was one of the first professional women at the RSPB to keep her job on a part-time basis. The girls, now grown up, appreciated that both parents travelled a lot as they developed independence early. Nicola is certainly well travelled, having visited 63 countries!

Since 2009, her global role has focussed on migratory birds, especially by leading the policy work of BirdLife International's Global Flyways Programme. She now concentrates on supporting governments and key allies to take conservation action in line with BirdLife's objectives for migratory birds.

In 2008, she was appointed Chair of the Slender-billed Curlew Working Group under the United Nations Convention on Migratory Species (CMS). The group had been dormant due to the absence of confirmed sightings in Morocco since February 1995. Nicola wanted a concerted effort to find this curlew (*Numenius tenuirostris*), with the new technologies available, including much improved optical equipment, cameras to find and verify sightings and satellite tags small enough to fit on any bird caught.

'If we couldn't make such an effort, hopefully to prove that this was not the first Western Palearctic bird extinction since the Great Auk in 1844, how could we expect less wealthy parts of the world to look after their rarest species? I couldn't rest easy until we had really, really, tried our best to find the Slender-billed Curlew.

'It was like looking for a needle in a haystack. However, there were formerly records from passage and wintering sites around the Mediterranean. We focussed our efforts on these sites, where birds would hopefully stay long enough for us to tag them. Gradually we managed to recruit over 50 volunteers who we sent to 659 sites in more than 30 countries. We also encouraged existing waterbird counters to look for Slender-billed Curlews.'

From all this effort, the only potential records were from Crimea in August 2010. There were no photos so no one will ever know whether they were the last of the species. This highly motivated lady is keen to ensure that the Eurasian Curlew (*Numenius arquata*), already showing signs of serious decline, does not follow its cousin towards extinction. Nicola ensured that the RSPB and others raised the Eurasian Curlew to one of the top priorities for UK conservation action. An intergovernmental action plan was adopted, coordinated by the RSPB, under the African Eurasian Migratory Waterbird Agreement.

Curlew numbers in the UK fell by 48% between 1995 and 2018 – and the UK holds at least one fifth of the global

Slender-billed Curlew painted by Henrik Gronvold (1858-1940) – a Danish naturalist renowned for his bird paintings.

population of this species. In 2021, 106 eggs were removed from nests on eight military and civilian airfields. These nests would have been destroyed to remove the risk of potentially catastrophic collisions between birds and aircraft. The eggs produced an incredible 84 young at Pensthorpe Conservation Trust in Norfolk. The young Curlews were released at the royal Sandringham Estate and at Wild Ken Hill, also in Norfolk. Some were fitted with GPS and radio tags so that their survival could be monitored.

Besides supporting development and implementation of species action plans for the most threatened birds, Nicola has focussed on the establishment of intergovernmental thematic working groups to strategically tackle – through concerted and cooperative action – key threats to migratory birds. This includes a Task Force trying to eradicate the illegal killing of birds in Europe and particularly around the Mediterranean blackspots. The CMS Energy Task Force aims to minimise the impact on birds of energy infrastructure (such as wind turbines and power lines), bringing together energy and environment ministries and the energy sector.

Nicola's triumph in China

In leading attempts to tackle the threat to coastal waterbirds on behalf of BirdLife International and the international conservation community, a big career triumph lay ahead. Nicola said:

'It seemed to me that the unprecedented rate of coastal wetland land claim happening on the Yellow Sea coast of the Korean Peninsula and China was the biggest threat facing migratory waterbirds globally. Everyone said that it was impossible to fight. But I thought it was our duty to give it a go.'

The flagship for this work to conserve Asian tidal flats and associated habitats is the Critically Endangered Spoon-billed Sandpiper (*Calidris pygmaea*), of which fewer than 300 pairs remain. It was adopted by the RSPB and BirdLife, among others, as a priority species for global bird conservation. This iconic little wader has a bill which Nicola's young daughter observed looked like an ice cream spoon. With a limited breeding range in north-eastern Russia, it migrates down the western Pacific coast to its main wintering grounds in Bangladesh and Myanmar.

Like 50 million other migratory waterbirds, each spring and autumn it refuels on the wetlands of the Yellow Sea coast, which contains the world's largest continuous tidal flats. By 2016 its numbers had dropped 88% in ten years. Besides being trapped for food, the sandpiper's favourite stopover sites were being reclaimed for industry, infrastructure, agriculture and aquaculture. In particular, in 2006 Saemangeum, South Korea, the main staging site of Spoon-billed Sandpipers and many other waders, was destroyed by the world's largest coastal land claim project: the estuary was closed off from the sea by a 42km (26 mile) long wall.

Nicola first became aware of this at the 2008 IWSG conference. The catastrophic declines in waders reaching Australia following the loss of Saemangeum were discussed by Danny Rogers. This inspired her to use her expertise to fight to save the Yellow Sea coastal wetlands. There was symmetry in this: Danny revealed that the talk Nicola gave in Australia more than 20 years earlier had inspired him to work on waders!

Luckily IUCN was to hold its World Conservation Congress (WCC) in 2012 on the edge of the Yellow Sea at Jeju, South Korea. This provided an opportunity for Nicola to lead an engagement with the authorities in the Yellow Sea. She was involved in commissioning an IUCN situation analysis of coastal wetlands along the East Asian-Australasian Flyway (EAAF). This led to governments at the WCC adopting a resolution that for the first time fully acknowledged the problem of coastal wetland loss in the Yellow Sea and beyond. They agreed to take steps to address this. In 2017 Nicola facilitated negotiations between the governments of China, North Korea and South Korea which resulted in the formation of an IUCN-led Working Group between the three nations for the conservation of Yellow Sea coastal wetlands.

In 2018 Nicola wrote:

'Progress in Yellow Sea conservation over the past decade has been a huge concerted effort at every level – with local birdwatching groups counting the birds, local NGOs raising awareness, action on site management, fantastic research by national and international scientists, and VIPs speaking to high-level decision makers. It is the positive energy for coastal conservation developed in the EAAF [East Asian –Australasian Flyway] that is catalysing a global movement for coastal wetland conservation' (Crockford, 2018).

Nicola feels that the work in the EAAF has exemplified the flyway conservation approach which is characterised by bringing together every tool in the 'conservation kit' from local to global, and from global to local, to achieve a common objective through international cooperation that also ensures ecological connectivity – not just between places and the birds and other wildlife that depend on them, but also between the people who care for them.

The Chinese coastal conservation movement received a major boost in July 2018 when China introduced a law banning all further coastal wetland reclamation, promoting restoration instead. A year later a large part of the Chinese Yellow Sea shorebird habitat, at Yancheng, Jiangsu, secured World Heritage listing – the highest level of protection in the world. It came with commitment from China to nominate another sixteen of its top Yellow Sea migratory shorebird sites by 2022. The Phase I site includes Tiaozini, the most important staging site in the world for the Spoon-billed Sandpiper. Only a few years earlier this area had all the permissions to be converted into agricultural land and a port. This would have been an even bigger land claim project than that at Saemangeum, on the opposite side of the Yellow Sea.

In January 2020 Nicola received the Jiangsu Friendship award in China, granted to foreign nationals who have made 'outstanding contributions to the country's economic and social progress'. The award recognised her support for the Chinese authorities, especially Yancheng City, in their bid to secure inscription and then appropriate management of the World Heritage Site.

Nicola's is renowned for her internationally important flyway conservation work. She is also involved in caring for nature in East Anglia. Lockdown in 2020 gave Nicola the best work/life balance she has ever had. Without her hectic travel schedule she had more time to explore the surrounding countryside on the border of Breckland and the Fens. Missing her favourite activity of snorkelling on coral reefs and other warm waters (such as on her honeymoon in Vanuatu), Nicola took to snorkelling the local rivers to photograph the fish and other river life. Through posting these pictures on Twitter she became aware that these rivers were among the UK's 224 chalk streams amounting to more than 85% of the global total; 77% fail to meet good quality status. She now give talks on her snorkelling experiences to river conservation groups.

During the 2020 lockdown Nicola also discovered the fascination of fungi. She said: 'This has been a revelation, opening a whole new dimension and source of excitement on local walks. I found a very rare bracket fungus on an ancient oak on Cavenham Heath National Nature Reserve, ten minutes' walk from my house. It is so rare that a sample for identification was sent to Kew Gardens by the county recorder.'

In Britain we can be very proud that the work of the RSBP and BirdLife International has resulted in saving the habitat and populations of millions of waders in the Far East. For this difficult achievement, the spotlight must fall on Nicola Crockford. She has made a highly significant contribution internationally to the survival of shorebirds and other birds and to drawing attention to their plight.

Reference

Crockford, N., 2018, Perspective, Wader Study, 125 (3): 158–161. http://doi.org/10.18194/ws.00128

24. Elisabeth Schlumpf
Switzerland 1966-
Wild Bird Rescue and Education

Elisabeth Schlumpf was born on May 20 1966 in Switzerland. She grew up in Kilchberg, very close to Zürich, with a sister and a brother. Her parents were nature-lovers so she often had the opportunity to observe birds in the wild. Elisabeth loved animals; as a child she kept a Budgerigar, various small animals and a dog and a cat. Her mother was a librarian and the house was full of books.

Elisabeth became an apprentice in *haute couture* tailoring but did not follow this profession; instead her passion for painting led her to become a graphic designer for a music magazine.

Her sister was a keeper at Zürich Zoo and later started to work at Voliere Mythenquai in Zürich, the bird rescue centre. It was run by an association which was founded in 1897 (long before Zürich Zoo opened in 1929). In 1903 the first aviary was built with 63 birds from Switzerland and 60 from overseas. The current building was constructed in 1937 and has since been modernised. In 1957 two steel cages were built into the exterior wall in which members of the public could deposit birds that needed care or were no longer wanted.

I was amazed by this concept. It seems the idea stemmed from a hospital in Zürich where unwanted babies could be put into a chute, knowing that they would then be cared for.

Elisabeth went to Voliere Mythenquai to help her sister and she finally took over her work in January 2000. She very quickly learned how to care for birds, which had always fascinated her. She had observed them in the family's garden, observed them in the sky, sometimes hovering, sometimes playing; then again, arrow-fast when hunting, they claimed the airspace for themselves. But in the aviary she could get very close to them, to observe each one in detail, such as a trio of young sparrows.

'Each of the little ones had his own character. One of them stood boldly in front of the others while feeding, and opened his still small wings so that supposedly only he had access to the food. The second tried to silently squeeze through under the first one, while the third sat quite shyly in the corner and waited patiently. From then on I wanted to

Exterior cage for depositing rescued or unwanted birds.
Photograph: author.

get to know every single bird in our care. First and foremost it was observation! And reading, reading, listening and learning.'

'I could hold a bird in my hand for the first time, I could be bitten by a toucan, ring young Bali Starlings (an endangered species), hand a grasshopper to a Red-headed Trogon (*Harpactes erythrocephalus*), trim the nails of the Victoria Crowned Pigeon and get many bruises from its wing beats!'

To Elisabeth, the sounds of lories and parrots was simply wonderful. 'The bird world had me! The birds seemed so refreshingly honest!' Elisabeth is highly successful in rearing because of her knowledge of the species, its breeding behaviour, its origin and the climate and even the geographical altitude. With this information she tries to provide the most suitable foods and aviary environment. 'Birds are very special, beautiful, demanding, intelligent creatures that can easily live for 20 or more years', she says. 'And I must know my birds and this means I must closely observe them! Then I can recognise if they are not in good health.'

In 2013 I was staying with Lars Lepperhoff in Bern. We made our way by train and tram to an arboretum set on the shores of the lake in the centre of Zürich. Nearby a plain white building was modestly decorated with the word VOLIERE (aviary) with a painting of a toucan. Its appearance gave no clue as to the extraordinary nature of the place we were to visit.

Lars knocked on the door and called 'Elisabeth!' A tall, slim, attractive, dark-haired lady appeared and greeted us warmly. 'Come in!' She took us into a small room which was crammed from floor to ceiling with chicks of wild birds. They responded with loud food soliciting calls and widely gaping mouths. My first thought was: 'How can she cope with all these chicks?'

Yes, it was May, the height of the lost and abandoned baby bird season. She tended a box full of young Rooks, pushing tweezerfuls of food from a plastic container into their pink gapes. Moving on to a small cage containing feathered thrushes, Blackbirds and Starlings, she said that the number of wild birds brought in was increasing by 20% each year, due to such problems as lack of insects and loss of habitat.

I was overwhelmed by the sheer numbers, especially tiny chicks like Blue Tits. Imagine how much work it is for one person (sometimes two) to prepare and deliver their food! In May she works 12-13 hours daily, and at other times of the year not much less. Sometimes she has a helper; that day not.

Elisabeth's work schedule is almost impossibly demanding. In spring the alarm clock rings at 5am and work starts at 6.30am. The young birds which were delivered during the night in the 'baby hatch' take priority. Then the special foods for different species are prepared. This must be done quite fast, because the little ones are very hungry. Some rearing foods are administered with a syringe, other species need insects while some, such as the Goldfinch or Greenfinch, are given a special seedeater food. The Kingfisher needs fish and the woodpecker must have ants' eggs and larvae. And this is hourly! Then she must prepare the fruits and vegetables for the exotic species: toucans, parrots and fruit pigeons.

The freezer must be filled with a big variety of foods, because it is not possible to anticipate which species might be brought in. In 2019, for example, a rare bird, an Ortolan Bunting (*Emberiza hortulana*), was received, as well as a Cuckoo, Dipper, Bullfinch (becoming increasingly rare), Crossbill, Red-backed Shrike, Snipe, wagtail, tern, Kestrel and Treecreeper. Their dietary requirements are totally different, as are the manner in which they obtain and consume their food.

Elisabeth feeding young Rooks.
Photograph: author.

Female Heroes of Bird Conservation

Elisabeth with a young Crowned Hornbill.
Photograph: Lars Lepperhoff.

It is not only the chicks that are demanding. The telephone rings incessantly from 7am, when there are already people at the door, bringing in birds. At 10am, when the visitors' hall is opened, everything must be ready and clean.

This truly remarkable lady often works in the evenings, rearing birds that need a lot of attention, including night feeds. Writing articles about rearing the rarer species, such as the Crowned Hornbill (*Tockus alboterminatus*) who was her companion for three months in 2019, provides valuable information for other aviculturists.

Elisabeth has the four volumes of Oskar and Magdalena Heinroth's classic *Vögel Mitteleuropas* (Chapter 7). She refers to it if she has to hand-rear unusual European birds. Until the end of 2019 she raised 1,850 young or injured birds from House Sparrows to unusual species like the Wryneck (*Jynx torquilla*) and the Water Rail (*Rallus aquaticus*). The Heinroths wrote that it is impossible to hand-rear the Red-necked Grebe (*Podiceps grisegena*) – but Elisabeth was successful! In the first nine months of 2019, 1,365 wild birds were taken in, about 40 pet birds and 35 ornamental birds. There were 100 birds of 37 species in the Aviary. Breeding of the rarer ones was encouraged.

On the day of my visit she was interrupted by a man from the animal ambulance service delivering two plastic carriers. One of them contained 18 ducklings; the female parent was in the other. They were unable to escape from a drain, he said. Fortunately, the ducklings and duck could be passed on almost immediately to another outlet but the other chicks remained in Elisabeth's care until they were independent. 'What happens to them then?', I asked. She replied that they go to a release site in the country.

The animal ambulance man might arrive three or four times a day with more birds needing care. I was incredulous at the scale of Elisabeth's devotion. Anyone who has fed just a handful of insectivorous birds knows the frequent frequency of feeds and the demanding nature of the job. But this was only part of it! She took us into a large room that was packed with cages. There were several cockatoos, a Scarlet Macaw and dozens of smaller birds. All unwanted and dumped by their owners… So Elisabeth also has the difficult task of finding new homes for these arrivals.

Colour mutations of the smaller parrots are extremely popular with breeders, who hand-rear them for the pet market. Elisabeth explained:

'We do not keep, let alone breed, any colour mutations! The rapid over-exploitation of Nature by man is happening faster and faster, thus the habitats for animals and plants are getting smaller, so each one of us is obliged to do something, so we try to breed from the rarer birds. And through our constant educational campaigns, also via the media, we are obliged to ensure that young people have direct contact with the animal and plant world, so that they are encouraged to protect and preserve it. Zoological gardens, and here I include the Aviary, can open a small window to Nature. We can also reach the public with our educational work. More and more people inquire about birds, become curious, observe joyfully, and then pass on the newly acquired knowledge.'

Lars asked her what should be done to better protect the birds in Switzerland. Her reply?

'Education – on a grand scale! Cities, cantons and the federal government must act! It cannot be right that small associations working alone have to take over such tasks.

However, I would like to be able to create a visitor centre in the middle of Zürich. There, visitors should use monitors to get to know the natural ecosystems and habitats of exotic and native birds. This digital platform would draw attention to the worldwide protection of species and its urgency. It could introduce children and young people to our beautiful Earth and inform them about the miserable over-exploitation in which mankind is engaged.'

Many people work for the survival of birds, individuals and species, but few can truthfully say that they have devoted their entire lives to them. Elisabeth was married and she has a son – but I know that it is not easy to sustain a relationship when you work with such intensity with birds, including hand-feeding around the clock. To continue this work for 22 years – at the time of writing – is an enormous commitment and perhaps even a unique one considering that she is working alone much of the time. My admiration for her is unbounded.

Reference

Schardt, T., 2021, So arbeiten die Profis, *Wellensittich & Papageien Magazin*, Mai & Juni, 14-16.

25. Gláucia Seixas
Brazil 1966-
Intensely dedicated to the Blue-fronted Amazon Parrot

In Brazil the name of Gláucia Seixas is irrevocably linked with one popular species of parrot – alas, too popular. Few parrots worldwide have suffered such high losses of every year's hatched young as the Blue-fronted (*Amazona aestiva*). Also known as the Turquoise-fronted Parrot, illegal thefts of chicks from nests of this perceived common species hardly raised an eyebrow – until Gláucia became their champion.

Gláucia was born on November 8 1966 and raised in a very urban environment, in Rio de Janeiro. She always loved animals and spent many hours looking after stray cats in the neighbourhood. Her first contact with nature was at a camping site, with her family. Every other year she would also visit her grandparents in Rio Grande do Sul during school holidays. She recalled:

'My grandparents had a farm with chickens, sheep, cattle, dogs and other animals. I would often choose to be with the animals rather than to play with other children! I got my first kitten when I was seven years old, and it lived with me for 18 years. When I first saw it I was so happy and excited, and at that moment I realised I wanted to help animals. I didn't know where to begin, so when I finished high school, I decided to go to university and do a course that would allow me to help animals, while not necessarily looking after their health. I started a course on zoology and in my second year I found my biggest passion – animal conservation in their natural habitat.'

Gláucia graduated in Animal Science (Universidade Federal de Santa Maria, Rio Grande do Sul) in 1988. She obtained her Master's degree in 2000 and her PhD in 2009, both of them in Ecology and Conservation (Universidade Federal de Mato Grosso do Sul, MS). She commenced an externship in the Pantanal of Mato Grosso do Sul in 1988. In 1992 she started to work for the government environmental department there, in Campo Grande, at a wildlife rehabilitation centre, IMASUL (Instituto de Meio Ambiente de Mato Grosso do Sul). She was employed as an environmental manager for 11 years – as a wildlife rehabilitation co-ordinator for seven years and a biodiversity conservation manager for four years. Gláucia was at the front line of preparing and coordinating important governmental programmes and projects.

Dreadful scale of the illegal trade

She soon discovered that the Blue-fronted Parrots needed help. Little was known about their wild populations in Brazil but every year hundreds and hundreds of nestlings arrived at rehabilitation centres, victims of the illegal trade As an unexceptional example, in September 2008, 225 Blue-fronted chicks were taken to the CRAS animal rehabilitation centre in Campo Grande. Fifty-three died soon after – what a cruel waste of life and needless loss for grieving parent parrots – and yes, they do grieve. The chicks had been hidden in boxes of vegetables from Ivinhema, about 300km (186 miles) from Campo Grande. The centre then had a total of 400 confiscated chicks from that season's nests.

Something needed to be done! Despite the large home-range of this parrot, which includes inland areas of Bolivia, Paraguay and Argentina, in Mato Grosso do Sul the situation is very worrying due to the intense illegal animal trade and habitat loss. In fact, the Blue-fronted Parrot is heavily traded throughout its range, resulting in it being listed (belatedly) by IUCN as Near Threatened since 2019.

So in 1997 Gláucia initiated the Blue-fronted Amazon Project. She had the financial support of Parque das Aves and, later, funding from Parrots International. Her aim was to generate information about the biology and ecology of this bird, assisting in making decisions for its conservation and that of its environments, and to speak out against the illegal animal trade. She advocates the protection of their habitats, in the Pantanal, Cerrado, Atlantic forest and anywhere else where they occur.

A seminal moment with the Blue-fronted Parrots was not a happy memory, but it was very important to reinforce Gláucia's message that these parrots need help. On a field trip, she found that one of the nests she had been monitoring for several months had been destroyed by smugglers. She knew that two helpless nestlings were taken. Both parents were right next to the destroyed nest, desperately calling and looking for their nestlings, which were never going to be found.

She said: 'All I could think was "When is this going to stop?" It made me more determined to stay on the path, which I initiated in 1997, with the certainty that I am doing my best for them. And with every step I take, I hope to touch the heart of people who would join me in this fight.'

Prof. Dr Luís Fábio Silveira assists NGOs and the police in rescuing seized parrots. The Curator of Birds and Scientific Director at the Zoological Museum of the University of São Paulo, conservation and reintroduction to the wild of captive-bred or birds of threatened species are his special interest.

He explained: 'Between August and December thousands of chicks are confiscated, mainly in the states of São Paulo, Minas Gerais and Rio de Janeiro. This traffic has continued for decades along established routes by well-known and repeat offenders. Chicks are taken to sales events, mistreated, crammed into boxes, suffer heat and stress and sold at low prices.'

Gláucia married architect João Augusto in 1990. They have two children, Luca Seixas, born in 1993, and Rafael Seixas, born in 2005. Her boys have been on field trips with them since they were little and, alongside her husband, they help her whenever they can.

Field studies

In 1993 the Neotropical Foundation of Brazil (Fundação Neotrópica do Brasil – FNB) was formed to develop and implement environmental initiatives on a state level. The first years were dedicated to the conservation of the Parque Nacional da Serra da Bodoquena in Bonito (MS), created in 2000. In 2003 Gláucia left IMASUL to work with FNB, as a project coordinator until 2010, and then as Executive Superintendent until 2016. Besides representing the FNB, she coordinated the technical, financial and administrative staff, and all the financial resources for the execution of the policy management (habitat conservation, environmental education, etc). For almost two decades, she has conducted all the actions of the project. Since 2005 the Blue-fronted Amazon Project included in its scope the other small psittacine species in the South Pantanal of the Serra da Bodoquena, including Yellow-faced Parrots (*Alipiopsitta xanthops*) and Nanday Parakeets (*Aratinga nenday*). Gláucia's project includes taking children and community members into the field and educating them against catching parrots. Play activities, research with universities, parrot genetics and diet are included.

The population of the Blue-front is in a fairly good condition in the Pantanal. It includes confiscated chicks which are successfully reared and prepared for release, which can take many months. A number of ranches in the Pantanal take part in the release efforts. Some fazendas

Blue-fronted Amazon nestlings confiscated in Mato Grosso do Sul, Brazil.
Photograph: Nara Pontes, CRAS.

(very large private ranches where extensive cattle production may be combined with wildlife tours) allow free access to Gláucia and her team from FNB.

Gláucia studied roosting behaviour and found that most roosting sites are located in groups of trees with dense foliage surrounded by open areas, which may help in predator detection. Adult Blue-fronted Parrots sleep in roosts even when they have grown chicks in the nest, and only one parent stays at night in the nest during the first 20 days of the chicks' lives. Other psittacine species, such as Peach-fronted Parakeets (*Eupsittula aurea*), Scaly-headed Parrots (*Pionus maximilliani*), Orange-winged Parrots (*Amazona amazonica*) and Yellow-chevroned Parakeets (*Brotogeris chiriri*), may use these roosts in smaller numbers.

Gláucia's knowledge of the breeding behaviour of the Blue-front is literally second to none. Usually four eggs are laid, three chicks hatch and only two young leave the nest. For the first 20 days after the eggs hatch, both parents are very active around the nest, although only one (probably the female) stays all the time with the chicks. Rainy years are associated with better reproductive performance. Gláucia has also compared the growth of captive and wild chicks. Those studied in the wild (1997 to 1999, at Refúgio Ecológico Caiman) grew a bit faster; captive ones gain weight for a longer period. In wild-hatched chicks, the maximum weight gain per day is 10-20g, and occurs when they weigh 200-300g; this weight gain

Gláucia and Ana monitoring nests destroyed by poachers.
Photograph: Michel Lopes, IBAMA, MS.

stops (or even declines) when chicks are about 400g (at about 64 days of age). At the end of the growth phase, males are 20-40g heavier than females (Seixas and Guilherme, 2003).

Gláucia stopped the project's activities for the first four months of 2020, due to the Covid lockdown. She resumed activities in the reproductive season, from August 2020 to January 2021, as discontinuation of data would have been detrimental to the project. She collected data on reproduction, illegal trade of nestlings (and eggs) and the destructions of nests by smugglers, in the *Cerrado* and in the Atlantic Forest.

In Vale do Rio Ivinhema, in Mato Grosso do Sul (MS), the reoccupation of agricultural space by the sugarcane sector since the early 21st century has changed the mixed landscape. This region used to be dominated by sparse trees associated with livestock, but it now has carpets of monocultures, eliminating the *capoeiras* (vegetation in initial regeneration) and the few palm trees in the landscape. Up to 2018, Gláucia had identified and catalogued 252 nests; 95% of then were in two species of palms (*Acrocomia aculeata* and *Syagrus romanzoffiana*). Shockingly, 85% of the nests had been destroyed or the trees overturned for the extraction of the nestlings.

In 2020 Gláucia began a new project activity: the installation of artificial nests. In May 2021 she told me:

'I installed 57 nests and quickly fourteen (26%) were occupied. For 2021, my aim is to install another 200 nests. I am seeking financial support to make it possible. The PVC nest was donated by Parque das Aves and the Projeto Papagaio-de-cara-roxa, by SPVS. To monitor it, I counted on the collaboration of the park rangers of the Várzeas do Rio Ivinhema State Park (PEVRI), where it is installed. For the year 2021, I want to install wooden nests (not PVC), in the same region. I found an important partner (Nutrópica) but I need new funding partners to achieve this goal by the end of 2021.'

Nest-boxes are quickly occupied by Blue-fronted Amazons whose nests have been destroyed. Photograph: Blue-fronted Amazon Project.

Unfortunately all the 2020 education and outreaching activities of the project were cancelled due to Covid. These actions require close contact with local communities, in schools and events, for children and adults. This could resume only when the vaccination campaign was completed.

Gláucia is a rare and committed individual, like Jane Goodall of chimpanzee fame, or Neiva Guedes with the Hyacinth Macaw, who has devoted her entire working life with a great passion to one species. However, the Blue-fronted Parrot is not an icon, known throughout the world, as a special and endangered species. It was Gláucia who raised its profile. I would say to the thousands of people who keep this species as a beloved companion in the home, give something back! Donate to the project! Help a wonderful woman to save a wonderful parrot!

For more information access: The Blue-fronted Amazon Project www.papagaioverdadeiro.org.br, www.facebook.com/projetopapagaioverdadeiro, www.papagaioverdadeiro.wordpress.com and www.fundacaoneotropica.org.br.

Reference

Seixas, G. H. F. and M. Guilherme, 2003, Growth of nestlings of the Blue-fronted Amazon (*Amazona aestiva*) raised in the wild or in captivity, *Ornitologia Neotropical,* 14: 295-305.

26. Caroline Blanvillain
France/Polynesia 1966-
Saving Critically Endangered Polynesian Species

Caroline Blanvillain was born in Paris on December 10 1966. She was brought up by her father after her mother left home when she was 14 years old. Her father was born in 1900 and died in 1989 when she had almost completed her studies to be a veterinarian. He was Jean-Marie Blanvillain, a poet, singer and songwriter. His stage name was Jamblan. Curious to know more of his history, I discovered that he had written one of the most beautiful songs I know: *All of a sudden my heart sings*. To be linked to this song through my work was an amazing revelation to me! To discover Caroline's story was even more inspiring!

Caroline told me: 'I was 23 when my father died, living in suburban Paris and dreaming of the forests and feeling guilty about animal extinctions. He instilled in me a love of nature. I inherited his poetic vision of life. Our Paris apartment was filled with my animals, from rabbits, rats and snakes to rescued sparrows and Blackbirds – even though he was not an animal lover!'

After the death of her father, Caroline worked as a nurse. At the age of 23 she qualified as a veterinarian, and this was the first step of reaching her dream. She went out to Burkina Faso in Africa for a PhD thesis. The premature birth of her son forced her to return to France. After a difficult period she resumed her research at the National Museum of Natural History. For her veterinary thesis, she studied the potential of inter-specific embryo transfer to save species from extinction, but in addition initiated a study on the reproductive biology of the pudu from Chile (one of the smallest deer in the world) and of the bhoral (Himalayan goat). In 1998 she completed her thesis on the Arabian oryx, which became extinct in the wild, and was saved with captive breeding. Caroline practiced as a vet in the zoo of the Jardin des Plantes of the Paris Natural History Museum. She was then invited by Professor Jalbaer in London to complete her training in *in vitro* fertilisation and endoscopic insemination. The plan was to go to Vietnam to train Vietnamese researchers in these methods, but the appointment of her husband in a position on Tahiti island, in the middle of the Pacific, changed her fate.

In 1995, when she was only 29 years old, she was awarded the Fondation

Marcel Bleustein-Blanchet Prize for her vocation to save endangered species from extinction. She had followed her husband, Denis Saulnier, relocating between France and Polynesia on several occasions. French Polynesia is an overseas territory attached to France, located in the South Pacific. To move to this area, which is between Australia and California and covers 4 million square km (1.54 million square miles) of ocean, is a huge undertaking with a young child. The family later repeated this with three children, born in 1993, 1998 and 2002.

As the career of her husband progressed, in 1996 and in 2002, and again in 2010, she left her own career behind. Because of her insecure funding position, she was obliged to return to France with her husband in 2003. She had to re-enter the veterinary field and forget her conservation dreams.

Caroline – the intrepid field worker. Photograph: S. Ricatte.

Working in French Polynesia

Caroline had begun her conservation career at the NGO Société d'Ornithologie de Polynésie (SOP), founded in 1990. Between 1998 and 2002 she was a volunteer. As a post-doctoral student, she did not receive a real salary and had to raise funds and to spend her vocation prize money. When she started to receive a salary it was very low in respect of her level of education (scientific PhD in reproduction and veterinary PhD). At first it was a desperate campaign for money, and then a tremendous undertaking to do the field work. Caroline wrote many valuable scientific reports. She emphasises that in her work, she was not alone. 'Alone you cannot do anything. I had the help of family, colleagues, volunteers and donors.'

At the start, no money at all was given to SOP by the local government. Caroline successfully raised a total of US$150,000 in five years and initiated four recovery programmes for Critically Endangered bird species in order to prevent their extinction.

The one hundred plus islands in the South Pacific stretch for more than 2,000km (1,240 miles). They are renowned for their beauty, with coral-fringed lagoons, sparkling blue seas, rugged mountains and towering waterfalls. Divided into the Austral, Gamb-

Female Heroes of Bird Conservation

ier, Marquesas, Society and Tuamotu archipelagos, their ecosystems are fragile. The avifauna has suffered many extinctions, mainly due to invasive alien species, such as the black rat. Of the 35 land bird species that breed in French Polynesia, 30 are endemic and 20 of those endemic birds (67%) are threatened with extinction. More than 50 are already extinct.

Caroline's involvement in working with some of the most threatened species started in 1998. From that year until 2002 she worked with the Tahiti Monarch (see below) from the Society Islands. From 1999 to 2002 she was with the Tutururu project (Tuamotu-Gambier Archipelago) to find and protect the last population of the Critically Endangered Polynesian Ground Dove (*Alopecoenas erythropterus*). By 2021 it had a population of about 200 individuals and had three flourishing populations, all on restored islands. The dove had re-established a secure presence for the first time in hundreds of years. In 2000 and 2003 Caroline conducted the reintroduction of the then IUCN Critically Endangered Marquesan Imperial-pigeon (*Ducula galeata*) on Ua Huka. In 2008 it was down-listed to Endangered and in 2021 it had an increasing population of about 250 individuals.

The exquisite little (15cm long) Blue Lorikeet (*Vini peruviana*), also known as the Tahiti Blue Lory, is extinct on Tahiti. According to Manu's poster it is present on only five islands in the Tuamotus (Rangiroa, Arutua, Apataki, Kaukura and Tikehau), on three of the Society Islands and on Aitutaki in the Cook Islands.

In 2002 Caroline participated at the start of the Fatu Hiva Monarch recovery programme (Marquesas Archipelago). Since the first observation of black rats on the island in 2000, when it received the IUCN status of Critically Endangered, this flycatcher has declined extremely rapidly. In 2021 the population was estimated at 22 birds and only four breeding pairs.

In 2010 Caroline's husband was sent again to French Polynesia by his company. When she returned to Polynesia, after eight years in France, the situa-

*Poster of the Blue Lorikeet (*Vini peruviana*) prepared by Manu and BirdLife International.*
Photograph: Jean-Paul Mutz.

tions of the two monarchs were very disappointing (see below). Their numbers had deteriorated despite regular funds given by the local government since 2004. Caroline remembered:

'I had previously counted 47 Tahiti Monarchs but in 2010 I found only 36 remaining; I had counted about 200 Fatu Hiva Monarchs and they numbered fewer than 50. I then relaunched the campaign for funds. That was difficult: I was considered a "has-been". I wrote more than 20 applications in 2011 of which eight were successful and I raised more than US$440,000 for my association, writing 40 plus funding demands, of which 12 were accepted. Thanks to this money, in 2012 I again became an SOP employee, and we started to reinforce the actions to recover the French Polynesian avifauna. Acquiring enough funds to perform all the more urgent actions necessary to save our birds has been a continuous preoccupation for me. My salary cost less than 3,000 Euros to SOP each month, and I calculated that I raised 7.5 times my salary a year for five years in the name of my association or sister associations in Rimatara, Ua Huka and Rapa.'

Tahiti Monarch (*Pomarea nigra*)

The Tahiti Monarch, a flycatcher, was one of the most threatened birds in the world in 1998, when Caroline initiated its recovery programme with the help of Philippe Raust (SOP founding member). She explained:

'The Tahiti Monarch faces ten invasive species classified in the one hundred worst, and has a very low breeding potential. It was previously common all around the island of Tahiti but, in August 1998, only 12 monarchs were identified by SOP, in two valleys located on the west coast of the Tahiti islands. With the help of Peter Gaze, from the New Zealand Department of Conservation, we found two more sub-populations. One was in Tiapa Valley and one in Maruapo Valley – a total of 21 birds.'

Nest building occurred between June and March and peaked in October. A total of 159 nests were found; 49% of nests protected against rodents produced fledglings, against 10% of unprotected nest. Only 50% of nests were incubated. Of 80 incubated nests, 83% were successful and produced a total of 66 fledglings. Only about 50 of them survived longer than one month. Breeding success of pairs increased to nearly 90-100% from 2009, with regular control of introduced birds (Blanvillain and Ghestemme, 2013).

By 2016 BirdLife International had partnered with SOP Manu to support the project. In February heavy rains prevented fieldwork on Tahiti, ending with the tail of Cyclone Winston. Papehue Valley was one of three valleys where the Tahiti Monarch was found. Caroline, at the time SOP Manu's Conservation Projects Manager, feared the worst for three young monarchs she had seen fly just before the cyclone struck. With beating heart, she went to the valley to the three monarch territories – Faifai, Camps and Post Banian. She found over 100 fallen trees, far worse damage than in 1999, when the last real cyclone hit. She did not see the young monarch in Faifai, which was decimated, with none of the neighbouring trees still standing.

The Tahiti Monarch came close to extinction. Photograph: Caroline Blanvillain.

After a struggle of over an hour, Caroline reached the Camps area (usually 20 minutes from the valley entrance). To her joy, the youngest monarch was there, identified by his little black head, small black tail and orange body, perched at 9m (30ft) in a lonely African tulip tree (*Spathodea campanulata*). In the territory of the Post Banian pair, where one side of the habitat was intact, another fledgling was also alive. Caroline returned to Faifai. At that moment the little bird came out and started to follow her. Since there was almost no undergrowth, he was hunting on the ground. He was so cute and she was so relieved to see them all! (BirdLife International Pacific blog, March 11 2016.)

Almost one third of the fledglings survived in the 2015/2016 breeding year. 'With climate change upon us', said Caroline, 'any small isolated population of a Critically Endangered species is in real danger of extinction. If another strong cyclone hits Tahiti, its monarch may be no more.' The 2021 census was very positive; it revealed 103 adult birds, plus 17 fledglings.

An important part of Caroline's work has been to include local people in this recovery programme. She used them in the war against invasive birds, and to reduce the threats represented by invasive plant pests. From 2012 to 2021 more than 1,100 gardeners were involved and 5,000 children participated in its recovery through conferences, painting competitions and school education. The landowners were involved in a cultural exchange with landowners of the Takitimu Conservation Program (in the Cook Islands) in order to learn the benefits of saving a bird species. Caroline published many articles on the Tahiti Monarch. She also wrote seven episodes of a *'monarquo-novelas'* (telenovelas are very popular on Tahiti) on Monarch love stories. Some pairs remain all their lives together, but some males prefer young females, and some females change their mate each year.

Fatu Hiva Monarch (*Pomarea witneyi*)

When Caroline re-launched the recovery programme fewer than 50 survived. Cat control had been undertaken since 2010 and when a new trapping method and increased efforts resulted in more cats culled, the post-fledging survival of Fatu Hiva Monarchs in 2016 and 2017 increased. For the first time no mortality was seen for chicks, fledged juveniles or immature birds. If this trend continued, Caroline suggested that not only will extinction be averted, but there could be enough birds to translocate some to a rat- and cat-free island. Unfortunately, money is not yet available to extend the protected areas.

Ultramarine Lorikeet (*Vini ultramarina*)

The exquisite little blue and white Ultramarine Lorikeet, found only on the island of Ua Huka, was uplisted to IUCN Critically Endangered status in 2017. One of the few people to have first-hand experience of its crisis was Caroline. Before the decision regarding its status was made she pointed out that it had already disappeared from five previous locations: Nuku Hiva, Hiva Oa, Tahuata in 1915, Ua Pou in 1980 and Fatu Hiva in 2002. She wondered why (as indeed did I) it had been listed in the lower risk category of Endangered for so long. She asked: 'When do we start to consider a species as Critically Endangered? When is game over?'

We need passionate and informed people like Caroline to advocate strongly for correct IUCN status assessments. Get it wrong, and the likelihood of extinction increases greatly. She thought previous surveys had overestimated the population; the species is much less common in the uninhabited part of the island (Blanvillain *et al.,* 2012). Caroline reported that from August 9 to September 13 2018, in 20 transects established in eight habitat types, 286 birds were seen and the total estimate was about 2,647 individuals (Blanvillain, Annika Scheme and Olivia Grant, 2018, in prep.).

Caroline took the first biosecurity dog to Ua Huka to protect the island from the black rat. She was behind the creation of the Vaiku'a association, which took charge of the biosecurity dog. Before the census Caroline said: 'Even if the island is free from black rats there are other problems: some valleys are full of crazy ants (causing blindness in young pigs and goats) and the cats are proliferating. Habitat quality is decreasing. A lot of pandanus has been burnt in Vaikivi valley for crops and much understory vegetation is destroyed by cattle, horses and goats, many of which are free ranging all over the island.'

The Indianapolis Prize

This prestigious prize was an initiative of the Indianapolis Zoological Society. It aims to 'combine significant financial support with a programme that builds emotional and intellectual support' in conservation. It raises money to award $250,000 every two years to someone who has achieved something extraordinary. In 2020 Caroline was nominated for the prize; nomination is an honour in itself which she richly deserved. She was the prime mover in saving several Critically Endangered species.

Total commitment

A woman working in conservation on a low income, and with children to care for, might have to sacrifice her own career. Caroline explained: 'In 2016 we were supposed to return to France because my husband was not permitted to work for more than six years in French Polynesia with his company. But I told him: "No! I'm staying in French Polynesia!" Fortunately, he found a solution to stay here – so we are still together and I will stay until my end in this country to save its birds.'

Caroline is a truly inspirational woman. Under any circumstances her story would be remarkable but with her location dictated by her husband's career, and with three growing children, she achieved extraordinary successes.

Please visit www.manu.pf, the website of La Société d'Ornithologie de Polynésie Manu. Help to save these Critically Endangered species with a donation!

References

Blanvillain, C., H. Sulpice, D. Saulnier and G. Sulpice, 2012, Rapport sur la deuxième mission de Biosécurisation de Ua Huka (2-9 novembre 2012), SOP-MANU, Tahiti.

Blanvillain, C. and T. Ghestemme, 2013, Breeding biology and impact of introduced birds and predation on reproductive success of the Tahiti monarch (*Pomarea nigra*), Société d'Ornithologie de Polynésie, SOP Manu BP, Tahiti.

In preparation:

Blanvillain, C. (Eds Haere Po), Papeete, *Guide des oiseaux de Polynésie française*.

27. Andrea Angel
Chile 1968-
Albatross Specialist

Chilean by nationality, Andrea was born in Santiago on May 13 1968. When she was four and her sister was three years old, they had a unique and unforgettable experience. Her father was a union leader during Salvador Allende's presidency. While working in a bank he created the first ever on-site crèche to facilitate work for all the women employees. This idea was so novel, an exemplary initiative, that in 1972 it was visited by Valentina Tereshkova. She was the very first woman in space! Andrea recalled: 'I retain a childhood memory of my sister and I having the honour of handing flowers to her on her visit to the bank. So in a way I never really questioned whether I could or could not pursue a career based on my gender, with those examples and parents.'

Andrea's family became political exiles after the military coup in September 1973. They left to live in Norway for six years (1974-1980), and then moved to Mozambique for another six years (1980-1986). Aged 18, she returned on her own to Norway for three years. Her next move was to Chile to study biology as an undergraduate and to work as a university research assistant in marine systems (1989-2000). In 2001 she went to Cape Town, South Africa, to do her Master's degree in Conservation Biology. Based there since then, the exceptions were when travelling and working from 2002-2004. She met her husband in 2001 and they married in 2003, just before leaving for remote Gough Island in the Tristan da Cunha group (a British Protectorate). Her son was born in 2006 but she divorced in 2018.

Andrea's desire to save seabirds came after spending three years on various remote islands conducting research. She witnessed first-hand the effects of the various threats to albatross and petrel species. After that she took every opportunity to work towards preventing further declines and to improve the seabird conservation status. She is totally enamoured of the magnificent albatrosses. 'The bond that they have with their chicks is unbelievable. When they come together with their mate, spending 15 minutes just grooming each other, it is breath-taking.'

This cosmopolitan conservationist manages the Albatross Task Force programme in South Africa. Its primary

Female Heroes of Bird Conservation

Andrea Angel – passionate about seabirds.
Photograph: Andrea Angel.

objective is to address population threats to seabirds from fisheries and invasive mammals on islands. An advocate for improved compliance and legislation, she engages with the fishing industry and with the government to reduce seabird by-catch across fishing fleets. She also works with conservation organisations and institutions with the aim of implementing an ecosystems approach to fisheries management, through training and raising awareness.

Protecting the albatrosses

Since 2004 BirdLife International and the RSPB have been working with fishing communities and governments worldwide to save seabirds in the BirdLife International Marine Programme. Long-line fishing especially had a catastrophic mortality on populations. There have been some inspiring success stories resulting from the work of the Albatross Task Force. For example, in 2014 a 90% reduction in seabird bycatch was celebrated in the deep-sea hake fishery. In a single Namibian fishery 22,000 seabirds are being saved annually by the fishing industry collaborating with the Albatross Task Force. But still, albatrosses are dying, including the Tristan Albatross drowned by tuna vessels. (Readers: please do not eat tuna!)

In May 2019 the Agreement on the Conservation of Albatrosses and Petrels (ACAP) had declared a continuing crisis, as thousands of albatrosses, petrels and shearwaters were dying each year from fishing activities. The first ever World Albatross Day was held on June 19 2020. It raises awareness of the threats that continue to drive these birds towards extinction, and to say thank you to those who dedicate their lives to saving them.

I asked Andrea about experiences that had made a big impression on her. She told me of two events that have lived with her ever since and which, in many ways, cemented her career as a conservation biologist, and particularly her work for the protection of albatrosses. They both relate to the Critically Endangered Tristan Albatross (*Diomedea dabbenena*) when she lived for one year on Gough Island. One of the Tristan da

Andrea Angel

Photograph: Michelle Risi.

Cunha group, it lies 200km (124 miles) from any other island, and is inhabited by Northern Rockhopper Penguins (*Eudyptes moseleyi*), fur seals and the endemic Gough Moorhen (*Gallinula comeri*). Gough Island is considered to be the least disturbed, major, cool-temperate island ecosystem in the South Atlantic Ocean and hosts one of the most important seabird colonies in the world, containing 54 bird species and 22 breeding species.

'After being dropped off on the island we had no other contact with anyone else, except through email and occasional telephone communications. After six months you are either in love with the place or counting the days for the ship to return. I was in love with the place. As one of only two biologists we spent most of our time out in the field working among the albatrosses.

'It was on one of those days that I found myself alone on a hill taking a break. It was probably the first time, with my senses having become heightened, that I could really take it all in. I absorbed the complete silence and the feeling of isolation – we were a speck in the middle of the Atlantic Ocean – but most importantly I could really see and feel the albatrosses. It was in that moment of contemplation that I heard a *whoosh!* and saw the almost 3.5m (11ft) wingspan as a huge male flew over me so close I could almost touch him. I saw the feathers ruffle in the wind. He was so majestic and so completely in his element as he flew past, oblivious to my presence, leaving me utterly humbled and in awe, a feeling that remains with me to this day.'

'In contrast, a few days later we came across the horrifying sight of a chick, about two months old and still in down feathers, lying almost lifeless in its ground nest. It is normal for the parents to leave a chick alone at this age, while they fly off to sea in search of food, returning to feed it every three days or so. We watched as life slowly ebbed from it, having succumbed to the wounds created by invasive mice nibbling at them mercilessly for what would have been several nights, until the infection and fatigue from lack of sleep slowly killed it.'

'The parents seldom coincide when feeding a chick and never remain for more than a few minutes, except on this day. We saw the female arrive and head straight to the nest, with her side-to-side waddle (albatrosses are majestic in flight but not when walking). Realising something was not right she began making futile attempts to rouse the chick with her beak, walking round the nest over and over, and nudging the chick for several minutes. It was then that the male arrived and, when he landed a few metres away, the female approached him. They exchanged greetings – touching bills and making muted sounds before he too headed for the nest to feed the chick. We watched for almost half an hour at what remains for me the most moving and sad event of animal behaviour I ever witnessed. The male nudged the dead chick, attempting to raise it with his beak, and circling the nest as the female had done before him. She joined him as they repeated their attempts at rousing the chick, while also touching bills with each other and making cooing noises. They seemed unable to reconcile the loss of this chick which they had committed to raising and nurturing for 13 months.'

'At the smell of death however it does not take long before the carrion eaters – the Giant Petrels and Skuas – begin circling and edging closer. The male, however, in defence and extending his massive wings as he made loud bill-clapping and rasping calls, kept chasing them away. Finally, the female moved away and seemed to call for the male to join her, which he eventually did, apparently reluctantly. They then began to groom each other, touching bills and cooing and we, in tears, left them to their mourning.'

Andrea described her year on Gough Island as one of the best of her life. Of the other six team members, three were weather analysts who ran the weather station on Gough. South Africa was responsible for the maintenance of the base and until the mid-2000s also put together annual relief teams of weather people and biologists. There was some involvement with the Royal Society for the Protection of Birds. After 2004 the RSPB became more heavily vested in the seabird programme and took it over entirely. Andrea had been documenting the impact of giant mice predation on seabirds. She and her husband were the first to provide irrefutable video evidence of mouse predation, of which she is very proud: www.youtube.com/watch?v=wT14Q7pZJzo and www.goughisland.com.

'Not only was it a conservation biologist's dream to do this work but the eight of us made an amazing group. This is not often the case, as expeditions become larger with team members who do not grasp what being on a remote island entails. We, on the other hand, spared no opportunity to go out as a team. Settling into a completely stress-free life, with no outside pressure or need for decisions we are bombarded with on an everyday basis, is the way we are meant to live. To be in touch with your surroundings and not constantly distracted by outside influences is an elating experience. We learned to engage in meaningful and lengthy conversations and to trust each other implicitly. Being the only woman and in a relationship had its advantages and was crucial to us holding things together. Something which I learned was that the more quality time you spend with other people the more tolerant you become of seemingly irreconcilable differences.'

Overcoming difficulties

Andrea described difficulties that can arise when working in the field in a group. For three months she was the ornithological advisor on a tiny island off Mexico run by the military. She was with a team of hunters trapping and shooting invasive rabbits that were wreaking havoc with the environment. She had the advantage of language and culture, but was up against the most hardened macho males imaginable. While she never feared for her safety, gaining respect was difficult. She said:

'Here the tactic to employ was a different one – either you are the hapless female or the hardened "give me the heaviest sack to carry" kind, with only the latter providing the oppor-

Female Heroes of Bird Conservation

tunity to earn any respect. There must be no overt feminine behaviour and you must always be thinking how not to been seen as a sexual object, but at the same time not shying away from interactions. Innuendo must be brushed away without displaying outrage or offence as that only widens the perception that you are different and that you will react. Being Latin-American has helped. I can see through advances and deflect them. I feel women in general are more emotionally intelligent and can navigate these situations better. All the best field women I have met have this quality. Of course now, at 52, I am no longer quite such a target and can just get on with things – so age does help.'

Andrea described her experience in having the freedom to mother everyone without there being any expectations or sexual tension – which has been the case in similar teams. In her view these aspects and related ones are among the biggest hurdles that mixed gender teams have to deal with. Having been a field biologist for years before that, and also very much in male-only company, she knew how to be assertive while still retaining her femininity. In some areas she would need help but elsewhere she could be of help to others. Often the men in the team would approach her to

Andrea with Tristan Albatross chick, Gough Island 2007.
Photograph: Brian C. Bowie.

unburden and talk in a way they could not do with the other 'guys'.

For Andrea, 'working to conserve and protect our biodiversity has become one of the most important things to which I can dedicate my life. This is not only because our own survival depends on it but because without it, the world will be but a shadow of the amazing place it can be for my son and children like him.'

Andrea explained: 'My son Alén, now 15, has been immersed in the work that my ex-husband and I do since he was born. He is not a self-proclaimed birder but he has absorbed a lot. He prefers looking at things on the ground. With a great interest in rocks, at some point he wanted to be a geologist, perhaps influenced by David Attenborough's documentaries, but more recently he is leaning towards biology. He has a keen interest in nature and conservation issues. Today it is hard for kids not to be aware of climate change and all that is being lost, so they are reacting to the world today as activists, distrusting and defiant of institutions.'

Andrea is one of those rare people who found her niche in the world – a world so remote and beautiful that only Nature has any value. Only a few people will ever experience this.

Sad footnote:

In April 2021 the first documented death of a breeding female Tristan Albatross caused by house mice occurred. She sat injured on the nest with a chick beneath her. Later she was found dead. She had been ringed on Gough as a chick in 1986. The RSPB will launch a mission to eradicate every mouse on the island. You might like to donate to this important work.

28. Silvana Davino
Brazil 1968-
Wild Bird Rescue and Environmental Education

Silvana Davino was born in São Paulo on May 15 1968. As a child, she always had pets: dogs and cats, and wild species, such as capuchin monkeys, tortoises and parakeets. Her parents taught her to respect nature: her father was a geologist, with an environmentalist vision beyond his time, and her mother was a geographer who loved plants. Silvana dreamed of studying veterinary medicine, but ended up studying fashion; even so, her final course work was inspired by the Atlantic Forest of south-eastern Brazil, with its textures and colours of nature.

In 1992, when she was teaching silk painting classes, she met Pablo Melero, who worked in IT. They were married in 1994. Until 2003 they lived an unremarkable life in the city of São Paulo. After visiting São Sebastião, the island of Ilhabela, in the Atlantic Forest, they were captivated and decided to move to this picturesque haven. They bought the property known as Sitio Rodamonte. Not long after, a young Plain Parakeet (*Brotogeris tirica*), a small all-green species, with a broken wing, was found near the entrance. Silvana called him Pepa and hand-fed him. This was a new experience for her and an event that was to completely change her focus in life.

Local people learned about her dedication to Pepa and in 2012 they started to bring more parrots; one Maroon-bellied Parakeet (*Pyrrhura frontalis*) and four Mealy Parrots (*Amazona farinosa*) arrived. This was the start of a stream of injured or confiscated birds, and chicks removed from nests in the roofs of houses. Pablo and Silvana, with the help of biologist Patrick Pina, registered the property as a rehabilitation centre in 2014, in line with local legislation. The centre was officially named, ASM Cambaquara; it could receive, rehabilitate and release the parrot species found on the island, also the Green-billed Toucan (*Ramphastos dicolorus*).

At the Parrots International Convention in Campo Grande, Brazil, in 2015, I picked up one of Patrick's leaflets entitled 'Parakeets in the ceiling'. The behaviour of the Maroon-bellied Parakeet is very different to that of most members of the genus which are hard to observe and shun human habitation. The leaflets contained the words: 'They nest in natural cavities and have a predilection for forested habitats; however,

Silvana Davino with young Maroon-bellied Parakeets.
Photograph: Cambaquara ASM.

recent observations have pointed to a trend, similar to that seen in the White-eyed Parakeet, of making nests in roofs and becoming an urban problem.' The parakeets damage wooden structures and electrical wires and vocalise during the night. This nesting habit is not popular with local people. Often nests are destroyed or the chicks are illegally removed for pets. They can then be confiscated by the local authorities. Since 2014 chicks have been taken to Cambaquara to be hand-reared and released.

Rehabilitation

In 2016 I visited the tranquil island of Ilhabela. When I disembarked from the ferry I took a taxi to the property of Silvana and Pablo, who greeted me warmly. I met Patrick and his wife Elizabeth, who were feeding their baby. This was not a human one but a small insectivorous bird, a tanager, which had fallen from its nest. The month was November – spring – and already parakeet chicks were being reared. It was a joy to watch the gentle and caring way in which Silvana handled them. She obviously had a gift for interacting with birds. I enjoyed so much watching a flock of Maroon-bellied Parakeets at the feeders near the release aviaries. These were the lucky ones who had survived disastrous early days, to be lovingly reared, then given their freedom under caring supervision.

Silvana's small team started to work with veterinarians, biologists and environmental institutions, mainly funding their work themselves, plus some donations. The number of birds received increased every year. In November 2018, Silvana reported: 'This month we have taken care of more than 25 parakeet chicks. Some were attacked by dogs, cats or skunks and others collided with windows. For three years our volunteer Sandra has cared for some of the chicks in her house until they start to eat on their own. Then they come back here to learn to fly well and, eventually, to be released.'

The largest parrot species cared for at Cambaquara is the Southern Mealy Amazon (*Amazona farinosa*) which is 38cm (15in) in length and weighs about 600g. Their release aviary measures 12m (40ft) long, 4m (13ft) wide and the same height. All the young are

Released Maroon-bellied Parakeets at Cambaquara. Photograph: author.

ringed, thus they can be identified in later months. Patrick showed me a tree close by where a pair of released Mealy Parrots had nested. There was nothing more rewarding for Silvana when, in January 2018, for the second time, a released pair returned with a young one hatched in the wild. 'This makes us very proud', said Silvana. 'Four of them still come back to feed on external feeders. From here, late on some afternoons, I can see flocks of 35 individuals flying over and about eight perching on the property's trees, making a lot of noise.'

Silvana told me: 'In January 2019 we released ten more Mealy Amazons and a young toucan. Some had been here for four years! The toucan has been staying in the area feeding itself well from native fruits in the trees. We collect and freeze many fruits, so we can offer them year-round and the birds know what to look for when they are free.' By the end of 2019, 360 birds had been received

Pair of Mealy Parrots with, left, their wild-hatched young one. The pair were released at Cambaquara. Photograph: ASM Cambaquara.

and there had been 30 releases. There are two release sites – their property and one in a more remote forested area.

The population of Mealy Parrots on Ilhabela is isolated by hundreds of miles from other populations of this species. Patrick and Elizabeth have carried out studies and censuses there. They took me into this beautiful forest and showed me the wild parrots. The Atlantic Forest is one of the most heavily deforested regions on earth (Chapter 18); however, about 80% of this 33,600ha (84,000 acre) island is under tree cover, two thirds of which are well preserved forest.

In September 2020 Cambaquara was caring for 38 Mealy Parrots, 20 Maroon-bellied, six Plain and four White-eyed Parakeets. Some had been received after colliding with obstacles; others had been shot. Volunteer Sandra Tellefsen had been invaluable since 2015 in rearing many of the chicks in her own home.

Silvana felt a responsibility to learn as much as she could and graduated in biology from the University of Taubaté in September 2016. She took the position of technical manager of Cambaquara, formerly occupied by Patrick Pina for five years as a volunteer. In 2020 a new food preparation kitchen was built and the nursery constructed in 2012 was renovated.

Children enjoying painting Mealy Parrots.
Photograph: ASM Cambaquara.

Environmental education

Silvana's small team attends schools and local events. They display attractive banners that explain their work and address the theme of parakeets nesting in roofs. Many environmental education activities were carried out at Ilhabela State Park with children aged from five to 14 years. Silvana gave lectures on birds and the environment in nine schools, to about 600 students. Topics included ending the culture of keeping wild animals in cages, and respect for all forms of life.

'We bought pairs of binoculars for environmental education work with children. The idea is to teach them to observe the birds, admire them for their beauty and to gain more knowledge of our wildlife. The children will one day be the guardians of our forests and will learn to respect and conserve nature, instead of killing the birds with slingshot (very common in traditional native local communities) or imprisoning them in cages.'

Silvana gave lectures to boy scouts from other cities and talks to university veterinary students. In 2020, due to the pandemic, it was not possible to continue the educational work. The team produced videos for students to watch at home during social isolation, with themes about the Atlantic forest, its birds and trees. They are making a tremendous difference to parrot conservation and welfare on the island of Ilhabela – and further away. It is not only endangered fauna that needs protection. Worldwide, urbanisation has had a negative impact on countless species. Organisations such as Cambaquara set an example that all birds and other animals should be valued. Such initiatives are so important in changing attitudes of people who formerly gave little thought to the welfare of wildlife.

Sitio Rodamonte is a beautiful location for release of the parrots in which so much time and care has been invested. Surrounded by mature trees, it is right on the edge of the ocean. One morning I sat quietly, watching the sea break dramatically on the huge rocks that dotted the shoreline. I reflected on how two individuals and a tiny parrot chick which could so easily have gone unnoticed, or snatched up by a predator, had been the start of a project which had reached so many people and saved so many green-feathered lives. Silvana and her small team are dedicated, passionate people whose rich reward is to see the parrots and parakeets flying free where they belong.

Phoenix Landing, USA

Throughout Europe and the USA there are many parrot rescue centres. Nearly all are founded and operated by women. Without a strong team of volunteers they are likely to fail. One of the most successful, Phoenix Landing Foundation, in the USA, combines re-homing with parrot welfare and education. It was founded by Ann Brooks in the year 2000. She is a certified animal behaviour consultant.

Phoenix, her Green-winged (also called Red-and-green) Macaw, is the inspiration behind Phoenix Landing. Many birds need a succession of good homes, through no fault of their own. She realised that Phoenix should outlive her, and wanted to make sure there

Ann and Phoenix.
Photograph: Ann Brooks, Phoenix Landing.

was a reliable adoption option in place to ensure that Phoenix had a place to 'land.' So she retired from her important senior federal position to volunteer full-time with Phoenix Landing.

By 2020 it had rehomed almost 3,100 birds. Adoption is often inevitable because people's lives change and life-long care for individual birds must be organised. Some owners are prepared to wait one year or more for Phoenix Landing to find a suitable home for a parrot. Adoption procedures are strict. At the time of my visit in 2016 there were over 30 parrots in its facility in North Carolina and 113 elsewhere waiting for foster homes.

Spring was blooming. The streets of clapboard houses with long verandahs, gables and balconies, were lined with flowering cherry and almond trees. I had been invited to speak at their superbly organised symposium which takes place at the University of North Carolina-Asheville every second year. Over the two days there were four simultaneous lectures, each one lasting one and a half hours. It was a great pleasure to attend this meeting because every one of the 165 participants was so committed to parrot welfare. One of the aims of Phoenix Landing is to help veterinary students interested in avian medicine. Four of the ten speakers were avian veterinarians and two more were in general practice, and their lectures were eagerly attended. Elsewhere the educational activities for that year consisted of 20 events (lectures and workshops) in North Carolina, 19 in Virginia and eleven in Maryland.

Ann has set the gold-standard for parrot rescue and re-homing. Her educational initiatives and organisational skills are remarkable. Her love for parrots always shines through.
www.phoenixlanding.org.

29. Kilma Manso
Brazil 1971-
Fights Illegal Wildlife Trade; Lear's Macaw Conservation

In the world of conservation the name of Kilma Manso Raimundo da Rocha is known far outside of Brazil. It is associated with one species of macaw and its protection. Who or what inspired her to work in parrot conservation? This story is less well known – and should be told by Kilma in her own words.

'We are taught to love nature in schools and universities but this love is infinitely greater when we learn by example. My first and most inspiring example of love for animals was my mother – Jandira. Her wise and kind words and attitudes always taught me and my siblings to take care of animals. We lived in a region in the *caatinga* biome, where periods of drought are constant. Many animals are at risk, especially malnourished young mammals abandoned by their mothers who could not produce milk. We learned, from a very early age, the true sense of empathy for animal lives. Mama told us that we should not spend our free time only playing since there were so many animals that really needed care, and even birds that fell from their nests.'

'This led me to face the biggest dilemma of my life: how could I not choose to be a veterinarian? However, because I have so much empathy for animals, I knew that I would not be emotionally competent to act in any situation in which an animal was suffering. So, I chose to study agronomist engineering. My roots are in the countryside, and I knew that working on farms would keep me close to nature and to animals.'

A remarkable parrot

Shortly before entering university Kilma received what would become the most valuable gift of her life, a Blue-fronted Parrot (*Amazona aestiva*) who she named Porcina. She had been acquired at an illegal wildlife market, and she was young and aggressive. Dedication and care were needed to win her trust and affection. The parrot lived free, usually perched on the trees in her garden, and often climbing or flying to the office on the first floor where she would play with the pens, notebooks and equipment. She loved to be part of Kilma's activities – and this parrot played an influential role in her life. She reminisced:

'Among all the wildlife conservation activities in which I participated, the one that marked me most was caring for 517 confiscated parrot chicks. They were apprehended in the *Caatinga* region of Pernambuco State. Late one night I received a call from IBAMA that the chicks were on their way to its facilities in Recife. I immediately sent messages to our partner institutions, Brazilian and foreign, requesting support for the purchase of food. Very early the next day, I went to IBAMA and found that the number of employees caring for animals in IBAMA's facilities was less than a dozen.'

This near-catastrophic event, salvaged by Kilma's rapid response, knowledge and compassion, was notable for the high number of parrot chicks and the lack of structure (physical, personal and financial resources) and facilities of the Brazilian environmental agency IBAMA. She related:

'The Head of the Fauna Sector gave me permission to run campaigns for carers. We managed to enlist almost three hundred volunteers! However, most had no experience with birds. We started to train them daily. Parrots International (USA) sent funds and arranged with Hagen Bird Food (Canada) to donate almost 500kg (1,100lbs) of parrot food.'

'I dedicated myself exclusively to this for three months. One chick got hurt. It was probably only 20 days old and would not have survived unless separated. I requested authorisation to take him home. As the days went by, this young Orange-winged Amazon (*Amazona amazonica*), who I called Chris, started to walk around the garden. On one of those walks my Blue-fronted Amazon, Porcina, at that time, 28 years old, flew down close to him, curious. Chris pushed his beak into Porcina's beak and started to shake his head very fast, in a food soliciting movement, probably imagining she was his mother. To my delight, Porcina – who had never laid eggs or fed chicks – then regurgitated food to him. Immediately, she went to eat again, and then she went back to feed Chris! From that moment on, she fed him whenever he looked for her!'

If she had hatched the egg, the instinct to feed the chick would have been strong. But she did not. Porcina's actions were therefore remarkable. When he was independent he had to be returned to IBAMA. All the confiscated young were the subject of legal action against the traffickers. Porcina and Kilma missed him terribly.

'For 29 years she played such a special role and my immense love for her awakened in me the need to be even more empathetic with the other beings. She was and always will be the greatest stimulus to maintain my determination to fight for animals and the conservation of wildlife. This applies especially to parrots that, like her, were and continue to be victimised by wildlife trafficking and deforestation in Brazil and in the world.'

The illegal wildlife trade

Kilma started to specialise in agroecology and reforestation of the *caatinga* as an agricultural model that does not impact the environment and allows coexistence with wildlife. Despite her academic background being related to agrarian sciences, her inclination towards the environment prevailed and she dedicated her career, and directed her Master's degree, to the Forest Sciences area.

In her fieldwork she witnessed the illegal wildlife trade which, in Brazil, is responsible for the annual capture of millions of wild animals. The death rate is very high due to the terrible conditions in which they are kept until their sale. Kilma said: 'The very strong feeling of indignation in seeing so many animals being sold and kept in such precarious conditions led me to take another decision that changed my life. I joined the Federal Police Department (DPF) because of its renowned performance in the repression of crimes against wildlife.'

Soon Kilma specialised in combating wildlife trafficking throughout Brazil, with special emphasis on the illegal trade in parrots. In a short time significant work was carried out at the police station where she was employed, in Recife. As a result she was invited to work at the Coordination for Repression of Environmental Crimes, in Brasília, at the DPF Headquarters. 'We had the opportunity to lead numerous investigations of great impact throughout Brazil, especially those related to wild parrots.'

Lear's Macaw protection

In 2005 she was invited to be the Head of the Ecological Station of the remote Raso da Catarina, in Bahia state – a conservation unit specifically created to protect the only remaining Lear's Macaw (*Anodorhynchus leari*) population. Their location was not was discovered by scientists until 1979. One of eight eco-regions of the *caatinga,* the altitude varies from 380m (1,250ft) to about 800m (2,630ft). Extending over 30,800km² (11,900 square miles), it is a beautiful area of red and yellowish sandstone canyons, and cliffs used by the macaws for roosting and breeding. *Caatinga* is tropical semi-arid vegetation adapted to extreme periods of drought (usually nine months of the year), exclusive to

The roosting area of Lear's Macaw. Photograph: author.

Brazil. It comprises many deciduous and thorny species, also succulents. When Kilma became involved, the population of the macaw was close to 200 birds, and its greatest risk of extinction was from smuggling. Kilma accepted the invitation and moved to Paulo Afonso city. As a native of the region, her knowledge and ability to cooperate with local people, and above all, to earn their respect, was crucial to the recovery programme.

She recorded:

'Working with *in situ* conservation activities deepened my knowledge of the environment, and led me to a broader and more humanitarian view of the local populations that live in rural areas. Unlike working as a police officer, acting as a conservation unit manager allowed me to interact deeply with the inhabitants, to know their living conditions and their relationship with the environment and to carry out environmental education with farmers and their families. Above all, we act to protect macaws and other parrots that feed on corn, and to prevent hostile retaliation against birds. It is a very challenging and enriching job, in knowledge and in experiences, and that contributed to my choice to continue working for conservation. Hence, my siblings, friends and I created ECO, an NGO specifically dedicated to environmental conservation work, and animal protection.'

Kilma is a professor of courses related to environmental and engineering fields at the State University of Bahia. 'Teaching is a magnificent job', she says. 'More than just preparing our students for a profession, it allows us to make them better people – who understand their responsibilities.

Corn replacement project by ECO

The importance of Kilma's work was highlighted in BBC News Brazil in an article by Evanildo da Silveira on December 28 2020. She was quoted at length about Lear's Macaw population increase of from 60 to 1,694 during more than three decades, due to the involvement of different institutions. The work included protection from poaching; preservation of the species' habitat; research on the macaw and its environment and environmental education. But with the population increase came conflicts with farmers – corn growers, who use corn to feed people, cattle and chickens. Kilma explained that the damage is usually quite severe, resulting in the loss of practically the entire cultivated area. A large flock of Lear's Macaws is capable of destroying one hectare of crops (about 1.5 football fields) in a day or two. In defence of their plantations, growers use stones, sticks and even firearms.

The macaws feed on corn because of the significant increase in deforested areas, with the destruction of native vegetation, including the fruits (like tiny coconuts) of the licuri palm, which was their principal food. The increasingly prolonged droughts have also had a negative impact, reducing the supply of natural food in the *caatinga*. Kilma is the executive director of ECO (Ecological Conservation Organization). Since its corn replacement project was started, and up to the end of 2020, approximately 8,300 60kg sacks of corn had been distributed. This benefitted about one thousand small farmers whose crops had been attacked. To deliver the corn and to assess macaw damage to crops, Kilma and her small team cover an immense area of more than 5,000km² (1,930 square miles).

Kilma works voluntarily for ECO. She leads the unique corn reimbursement project which was conceived by Linda and William (Bill) Wittkoff, founding directors of the Lymington Foundation. Linda was a legendary environmentalist. Kilma described the opportunity to know her as destiny; they shared so many common goals. 'It is impossible to think about this project without making reference to the Wittkoffs, since they were the ones who first financed it, together with Parrots International.' Throughout the project's 16 years of existence up to 2021, the Lymington Foundation has made great efforts to raise funds for the project's needs, including buying the corn sacks.

Kilma with farmer José Bonfim who protects the Lear's Macaws on his land.
Photograph: Alan Jones.

Bill Wittkoff recalled:

'My late wife Linda and I first knew Kilma when we were part of a group interested in Spix's and Lear's Macaws. The Brazilian Environment Ministry (IBAMA) invited us to visit the sites of these birds in the north-east, in the municipalities around Curaçá and Jeremoabo in Bahia state. In the initial meeting, in November 2005, Kilma was introduced as our logistics and security authority. She was a federal police officer and a life resident of the region with total knowledge of the culture, characteristics and geography. Little did we know just how capable she would prove to be.'

'Kilma orchestrated much of this trip for about 15 persons. On the first stop in Jeremoabo, she gave us a fascinating personal demonstration of perpetrator arrest, martial arts and weapons expertise. She explained to us the problems for Lear's Macaws of illegal trade and food shortages. It was there that Linda, together with Mark Stafford of Parrots International, proposed the idea of the Corn Replacement Project.'

'Kilma is not only an engineer, a master of business administration, a federal government authorised land surveyor and a professor on three university faculties, she is passionately devoted to conservation and to parrots in particular. Well versed in the nuances of this peculiar Brazilian north-east culture, she operates in all its aspects with an astounding fluidity, but with personal authority and "the right touch" for any occasion. In our 60 years of knowing the "Brazil scene", Kilma is the most talented and effective lady we have met and one of proven honesty and integrity. It has been an honour and a gift to know her.'

As founder of ECO, Kilma has played a significant part in the growth and protection of the Lear's Macaw's population. She is an inspiring example of a woman who found her true place in the world and used her integrity, versatility, initiative and compassion to make a significant contribution to bird conservation. She is a truly inspirational woman! However, let Kilma have the last word:

'In my opinion, gender is something very small when compared to what has been done in conservation. What really matters are the efforts to reach a goal and how they can touch other's hearts. Inspiration, more than being related to race, gender, religion or citizenship, comes from example. There are wonderful examples of women and men who have dedicated their career and their lives to conservation purposes. Their efforts have contributed to change lives and to make our planet a better place for all beings.'

Érica Pacifico Brazil 1981- Fieldwork to save Lear's Macaw

Another Brazilian woman who has been inspired by the charismatic Lear's Macaw to devote most of her working life to its recovery is Érica Pacifico. She is a researcher affiliated to the Museum of Zoology of the University of São Paulo, as a collaborator. Prof. Luis Fabio Silveira, the Museum's Scientific Director, told me: 'Erica has a huge energy in the field. I have no doubt she's one of my best students, and a true inspiration for biologists. I always invite her to give some classes in my courses and the students love her.'

Specialising in Wildlife Management, Érica has a Master's Degree in Zoology, a PhD in Conservation Biology (Lear's Macaw population demography, genetics and ecology) and a MSc. in zoology and ornithology (Lear's Macaw breeding biology). Her PhD research was on the dynamics of the remaining population, using a multidisciplinary approach with molecular tools, ecological modelling, stable isotope analysis and indices of breeding success. She has co-ordinated the Lear´s Macaw Breeding Biology Monitoring Project, without interruption since 2008. Every breeding season she can be found dangling precariously from a rope and wriggling into macaw nesting tunnels. You can watch the intrepid Érica at work here: www.youtube.com/watch?v=oi7iGDiznuc.

In 2016 Érica and her team of five researchers, three local guides and six volunteers, mounted a 45-day expedition and travelled 1,500km (937 miles). They observed 35 nests at four breeding sites and banded (ringed) 47 chicks in 31 nests. Faecal and blood samples were collected to check for disease and more faecal samples for a seed dispersal scheme in collaboration with the Museum of Natural Sciences in Madrid.

The researchers discovered and catalogued 24 new food items and collected 300 feathers for DNA testing, to genetically identity individual birds. This is essential for long-term monitoring of nests. A highlight was discovering nests in the Baixa do Chico, an Indian reserve in a dry area of sandy soil, where agriculture cannot be practised.

Érica Pacifico.
Photograph: Érica Pacifico.

The population there consists of about 60 birds. Three roosting sites (usually crevices near the top of sandstone ravines) were discovered between 2014 and 2017. Disturbance from farmers and their machines is a problem, also honey gathering in forests and cliffs. Nest invasion by Africanised bees is being addressed with trap boxes to capture swarms and with crossbow bolts loaded with repellent. Invasive species removal to increase breeding attempts is a vital part of the strategy.

In February 2021 Érica was finishing fieldwork, at Boqueirão da Onça, the site where the population was functionally extinct. The population there was decimated in the 1980s by illegal capture and hunting, leaving only two birds, non-breeders. Érica had the important job of managing the exciting release project to augment the population. She was very well qualified to monitor the macaws before and after release, having worked in zoos, specialist bird breeding conservation centres and as a consultant on environmental impact studies based on avifauna. The released birds were captive-bred at Loro Parque Fundacíon in Tenerife, in the Canary Islands, plus two recently captured in the wild and rescued from the illegal pet trade. Before release the biologists developed a training programme. Snakes, birds of prey and even humans needed to be recognised as a threat. The 'soft release' had been managed with great care, thus the outcome was totally successful. This was to be Erica's last field work for a while. Her daughter was born in May 2021!

By the end of 2020 forty Lear's Macaws had been hatched by Loro Parque. Seventeen had been returned to Brazil and eight had been released into the wild. Successful releases of captive-bred birds in special conservation programmes, such as that for Lear's Macaw, gives much hope for the future survival of many endangered bird species. The work of dedicated specialists, such as Kilma and Érica, played a big part in the IUCN status of this macaw being downlisted from Critically Endangered in 2008 to Endangered today.

A new threat emerges

However, there is never room for complacency. In 2021 French energy company Voltalia was preparing to construct a wind energy facility 26 km (16 miles) from the main breeding site – a distance a macaw can cover in un-

Lear's Macaw bred at Loro Parque, Tenerife.
Photograph: author.

der 30 minutes – but other areas used by the macaws are closer to the proposed project. The area is recognised as being globally important for conservation, a site of Alliance for Zero Extinction and a Key Biodiversity Ara.

On July 22 2021 the Public Ministry of Bahia confirmed that Brazilian environmental law was violated and that the project should be suspended or cancelled completely until appropriate steps are taken to assess potential environmental impacts. International conservation organisations have united against the threat, with a plea that Voltalia relocate and restore habitat. More than 78,000 people signed a Change.org petition to stop it. The project provides for the initial installation of 28 wind turbines and a further 53 in a second phase. It would include a 50-km energy transmission network through the municipality of Jeremoabo.

Alarmed about the supression of licuri palm fruits during wind farm installation and potential macaw turbine collision during operation, since 2014 Érica has encouraged wind companies to apply compensatory measures that would benefit macaw feeding areas and locations of potential population expansion, that were neglected by conservation actions in the past 40 years. Érica and her field team dedicate field efforts to study Lear's Macaw movements and flight behaviour, with the support of experienced scientists in this field, focused in the areas speculated by wind companies. If the project goes ahead they aim to suggest areas of wind farm exclusion and to suggest turbine operation criteria, to avoid macaw collisions.

Lear's Macaw does not need further threats to its survival. Erica told me: 'Most of its habitat is still not protected and no measures have been taken to manage overgrazing by cattle and goats, further compromising Lear's Macaw habitat quality and food resources.'

30. Sarah Otterstrom
USA/Central America 1972-
Working to support Wildlife and Impoverished People

One aspect of parrot symposiums that is very satisfying is the opportunity to meet people who previously were just names connected to research and conservation. At the IX International Parrot Congress in Tenerife in September 2018 I met an inspirational conservationist whose work I had followed through the website of Paso Pacifico (www.pasopacifico.org).

Sarah was born in the USA on February 3 1972. She grew up in the Pacific North-west and spent her childhood exploring the forested ridgeline behind her home. When her father moved to Costa Rica during her teenage years, she travelled to visit him. She was captivated by the Central American forests and studied biology and conservation at university in Costa Rica. Leading natural history tours in the rainforest was her next step. A deep appreciation for the region's biodiversity motivated her to pursue her doctorate in Ecology at the University of California, Davis.

Sarah directed her research location to Chococente in Nicaragua. It was declared a Wildlife Refuge in 1983, in order to protect sea turtles and the dry forest which contains Yellow-naped Parrots (see also Chapter 20). In Nicaragua, Central America's largest country, this parrot remains in only a few small areas. It survives in a narrow strip of land between Lake Nicaragua and the Pacific coast where forest fragments are surrounded by agriculture and ranching and, along the coast, by tourism developments. In the 20-year period from 1990 to 2010, Nicaragua and Honduras lost more than 30% of their forests.

The Yellow-naped Parrot (also called Amazon) was hit very hard. Undoubtedly one of the most handsome and loquacious of *Amazona* species, its mimicry abilities are legendary. She told me: 'I was involved in ethnographic research focused on subsistence for local, indigenous people of the dry tropical forests of Nicaragua. During that time, I came to know the cultural importance of the Yellow-naped in rural communities where families keep these birds as uncaged pets. When I started Paso Pacifico I knew immediately that this species would need to be one of our conservation flagships'.

This handsome parrot, overflowing with personality, can sing, whistle and imitate human speech perhaps more accurately than any other parrot, except the Grey. This ability has made it a bigger target for poachers than any other in Central America, apart from the Scarlet Macaw. Combined with serious habitat loss, this has led to a catastrophic decline in numbers, suggested as about 50% between 1980 and 2000. As a result, in 2017 the IUCN threat category of the Yellow-naped Parrot was uplisted from Vulnerable to Endangered. However, the recent catastrophic crash in its numbers has resulted in the suggestion that it might be uplisted to Critically Endangered. It is found in Mexico and Central America, occurring along the Pacific slope of the isthmus in southern Mexico (Oaxaca and Chiapas), Guatemala, Salvador, Nicaragua and north-western Costa Rica, the Bay Islands of Honduras and the Caribbean slope in eastern Honduras and north-eastern Nicaragua.

Sarah at the Loro Parque Parrot Congress in 2018. Photograph: author.

Sarah founded Paso Pacifico in 2004, since when she has been the Executive Director. Her work is extremely important for the survival of this parrot. She told me: 'Making it one of our flagship species was a wise strategy. It has been relatively easy for us to engage communities on this conservation topic, including explaining the species' decline and persuading people to protect the wild birds. After years of working on its conservation, we at Paso Pacifico have become very attached to the species. Our field team is convinced that the wild birds know and recognise them, we have watched the roost size continue to grow, and with each new year comes a number of fledglings that bring us hope.'

Sarah felt frustrated by the lack of commitment of international conservation NGOs to the communities around the reserve and to the ecological landscape. There are dozens of farming families living within the boundary of the protected area; it includes remnants of tropical dry forests, and a beach that is a major sea turtle nesting site. While working there, Sarah saw New Yorkers buy up large portions of the area, and she personally worked to convince them to abandon plans for a golf course.

When Sarah started Paso Pacifico she contacted everyone she knew, explaining her project and asking for donations. Now it is supported by Loro Parque Fundación and the International Institute of Tropical Forestry, United States Forest Service. The small projects she started had big effects. She lent 15 farmers $200 each so they could build silos to store their beans and sell them when the market was high. By maximising their profits, they were less inclined to farm deeper into the forest, where they were more likely to cut down trees.

Sarah emphasises the importance of the Yellow-naped Parrot as a disperser of seeds in the fragmented forests. Her aim is that eventually a substantial area of forest will be preserved as a corridor, allowing animals to migrate to larger forested regions. Habitat improvement continues, with 34,000 trees planted as future parrot food sources, to add to the 35,000 planted in 2013 and 2014. Sarah's research has focused on the ecological impact of fire in tropical forests.

Nest protection in Nicaragua

Since 2008 Paso Pacifico has monitored Yellow-naped Parrot nest sites in the Rivas Isthmus in Nicaragua's southwest corner. In 2012 it launched a pilot project, placing PVC nest-boxes near recently lost nests, with assistance from Tom White (US Department of Fish and Wildlife). Since 2014 it has also used artificial nests made of cement. In 2015, 22 nests were monitored – in tree cavities and in artificial nests. Six young Yellow-naped Parrots were radio-collared to provide information on their ecology.

Local people, including former poachers, are paid to protect a nest on their own properties, with a high cash reward for successful fledgings – more than double that of the black market price. Twenty-four Yellow-naped Parrots fledged in 2018 – a record number! Three quarters of these were saved through the incentive scheme. The news was even better in 2020, with 39 young fledging. These successes earned ten poor rural families US$2,600 for protecting the nests.

Sarah's initiatives to involve local people deserve to be replicated worldwide! By 2016 more than 200 Junior Rangers co-operated with the environmental education coordinator of Paso Pacifico to monitor the parrots in Nicaragua, helping to ensure that the next generation will understand the importance of this work. A sling-shot for binocular exchange was part of the educational scheme. By 2021 more than 400 Rangers had graduated. Many of them remain with the programme and help to mentor younger children. In 2021, its turtle rangers travelled to the nesting area of the rare Scarlet Macaw (fewer than 20 left in Nicaragua) to watch over a nest. A young macaw fledged – the first in the country in four years!

Volunteers and Rangers are encouraged to become active birders. In 2021, forty-one birders visited forests, farms and lakes across six departments in

Female Heroes of Bird Conservation

Young team from Paso Pacifico recording the bird species counted. Photograph: Paso Pacifico.

Nicaragua as part of the Global Big Day birding challenge. The birders recorded each sightings on eBird and, for the third event in a row, the Paso Pacifico team had the highest Global Big Day species count in Nicaragua, with 211 species. This team helped to propel Nicaragua to the 4th place in species observed in Central America.

The marine conservation programme of Paso Pacifico has had a huge impact in saving sea turtles, such as the highly endangered hawksbill, green, Olive Ridley and leatherback. Until the important nesting beaches were protected by Paso Pacifico volunteers, poachers were taking turtle eggs; then they were persuaded to take incentive payments, instead of selling the eggs. This organisation rebuilt two turtle hatcheries. Female rangers saved 3,700 eggs, incubating and hatching them, during the 18 months up to 2021. Junior rangers helped the baby turtles back into the sea. False eggs made with a 3D printer, containing electrical tracking devices, will be deployed to track stolen eggs in the future.

Osmar Sandino, their Marine Science Coordinator, attended a Paso Pacifico-led field course as an undergraduate student in 2011, and then started as a volunteer in Nicaragua. He praised their work, not only for the conservation initiatives, but for giving him the opportunity to become a marine biologist and for helping people in need in the area. In Pochote, women were assisted with their oyster farms, which provide an important source of protein.

I asked Sarah for an outstanding memory from the field. She told me that in early 2019 she made a one-day visit to northern El Salvador. Biologists and locals all reported that the parrots were nearly extinct and could not be found. 'We walked into the field and in the first ten minutes, a pair of Yellow-naped flew overhead. We could not believe it! We were able to follow them to the nesting area and set up protection for that nest for the year, yielding three healthy young. This was the first nest recorded and protected in that region. After two years of searching for more parrots and pairs, we believe that this was possibly one of the only active pairs. It was like finding a needle in a haystack.'

Sarah is an Ashoka Fellow – among the world's leading social entrepreneurs. They are recognised for transforming society's systems, providing benefits for everyone and improving the lives of millions of people. She was the recipient of a Spirit of Entrepreneurship award. Paso Pacifico is an inspiring example of the achievements of one woman, starting with nothing more than enthusiasm. It can not only save locally endangered species, but motivate the people to join in the long-term, when they are given help.

I admire Sarah very much for her initiative and determination. This would be creditable anywhere – but Nicaragua is one of the most difficult and dangerous countries in which a conservation scientist can work. She concluded: 'I need to be honest in saying that I never expected parrots to captivate me in the way that they have. I have come to realise how important their populations are for the future of our forests. I feel so privileged to work on Yellow-naped Parrot conservation.'

Sarah is truly a remarkable and compassionate person, dedicated not only to wildlife but also to the people of the region, many of whom also face an intense struggle to survive.

Please visit Paso Pacifico's website and donate to one of their projects.

31. Jennifer Smart
UK 1972-
RSPB Scientist and Wading Bird Specialist

Jen, as she likes to be known, was born in Glasgow, Scotland. She was not a child who grew up with binoculars in her hands. She admits that she did not discover her interest in birds until she was in her early twenties. Just before she started college her mother persuaded her to go on a boat trip to Bass Rock on the Firth of Forth, home to a huge seabird colony. A leaving party the night before meant that she was a little the worse for wear but: 'I was blown away by the Gannets and the Puffins, so my interest in ornithology *really* began that very day.'

She said: 'I started out in practical conservation in the early 1990s, working in country parks and nature reserves, getting dirty, and engaging with lots of people, especially children, through environmental education work. I became more and more involved in monitoring birds through volunteer surveys and as a bird ringer, so I then returned to education to get a degree in Ecology, followed by a PhD at the University of East Anglia.'

Jennifer Smart is particularly interested in coastal and freshwater wetlands, farmlands and grass heaths. An expert at finding wader nests, and monitoring chicks and adults, her other field skills include bird ringing and tagging. Her special interest is in waders or shorebirds, as they are known internationally, such as Lapwings, Redshanks and godwits. They breed in wetlands, an important area of study because many species have undergone dramatic declines across Europe during the past 50 years. This is mainly due to the reduction in the size and quality of their breeding habitats. More recently shorebirds have been unable to stabilise their populations, due to high levels of nest and chick predation. Jennifer concentrates on avian population ecology and identifying strategies to improve bird conservation status.

She has been a scientist with the Royal Society for the Protection of Birds (RSPB) since 2006, working up through the ranks to a Principal Conservation Scientist. In October 2015 she was presented with the RSPB award for an outstanding contribution to conservation science and in 2020 she gained the Marsh Award for Ornithology. Both prizes recognised her contribution to the conservation of waders. They also

Jennifer with godwit in 2020. Photograph: Mark Smart.

report and website were so successful. Her integrity and professionalism gave this Centre real credibility among our peers, partners and supporters. On top of this, she still managed to run a team, bringing in funding and students, and to publish papers'. The Centre has been essential in providing a coordinated and central voice for the RSPB's scientific research.

One of the things that really motivates Jen is to be able to do science that has real world impact. Much of her research has focused on identifying and testing conservation solutions and this has been influencing today's management of some of the largest breeding wader populations in lowland areas of the UK.

acknowledged her wider science communication work and her role as a model and mentor for the next generation of conservation scientists, especially women. Jen is immensely proud to have received these awards. Dr Sam Franks, who nominated her for the Marsh award, said: 'She shares her expertise and leadership with humour, compassion, enthusiasm and openness, and is an exemplary and inspirational role model to many.'

Dr David Gibbons, Head of the RSPB Centre for Conservation Science, had high praise for her work. 'Jen has demonstrated real leadership, determination, energy and enthusiasm in ensuring that the launch of the RSPB Centre for Conservation Science, its associated

Monitoring Black-tailed Godwits

Two species of godwits occur in the UK as migrants. The Bar-tailed (*Limosa lapponica*) is the more common. One hit the headlines in 2021 when it set a record for the longest non-stop bird flight ever recorded. It made the 11-day journey from Alaska to New Zealand, flying the 12,000km (7,500 miles) across the open Pacific Ocean apparently without landing. Possibly this route provides wind-assisted passage. It was one of four birds that had been feeding on the Alaskan mudflats on clams and worms for two months.

Much rarer in the UK is the Black-tailed Godwit (*Limosa limosa*). Jen led

Female Heroes of Bird Conservation

Jen led the research team that monitored the Black-tailed Godwit.
Photograph: Jonathan Taylor.

a research team in England to try to understand the cause of the decline in the breeding population. This wader became extinct as a breeding bird in the UK from the mid-1900s until 1952, when it was again seen in The Fens. The population grew to a peak of 64 breeding pairs there in the mid-1970s but declined to about 40 pairs due to flooding and predation. Project Godwit is now ensuring it survives as a breeding species in Britain. This partnership between the RSPB and the Wildfowl and Wetlands Trust (WWT) benefits from funding from the EU LIFE programme. It aims to improve breeding success in the wild and it rears Black-tailed Godwit chicks in captivity where they are protected from predation. The young are released at fledging age in sites with breeus, keeping us alive!'ing habitats that have been created and restored for this species. Early signs of success include many of the captive-reared young returning to breed. The UK population is increasing.

In 2020 funds were desperately needed for godwit conservation and for the International Wader Study Group (IWSG). Jen and her husband Mark hatched a plan. They would cycle to all the reserves visited by godwits that had been reared and released. During one

The route to raise funds.
Photograph: Fiona Jones; graphic Jen Smart.

week in August 2020 they raised £5,380 for godwits and more than £2,200 for the IWSG by cycling the 960km (600 miles) from Somerset to East Anglia. A remarkable effort by this couple who are so passionate about waders!

In 2021 Jen took on a new position, as the RSPB's Head of Conservation Science for Scotland and Northern Ireland. She manages 15 to 20 scientists. She said: 'I have a brilliant team of staff and of post-graduate students. Inspiring the scientists of the future is important to me and I get a real buzz from seeing staff and students develop through my training and leadership.'

Jen has had a long involvement in the work of the British Ornithologists' Union (BOU), where she was associate editor of its journal *Ibis* (2012 to 2016), and chaired their Engagement Committee (2014-2016), before chairing their *Ibis* Management committee (2016-2021). She is now chair of the International Wader Study Group. This organisation unites the global community of scientists, citizen scientists and conservation practitioners.

Jen has some sound advice for aspiring scientists. 'Know where you want to go and how you might get there. It won't be easy and you will probably have to deviate occasionally, but having a plan will help you to make the right life decisions. Treat others the way you would like to be treated. Don't be afraid to get involved in other things and organisations because that's how you will meet new people and make connections that will last a lifetime.'

32. Sara Inés Lara
Colombia 1973-
Founder of Women for Conservation

Sara Inés Lara was born on March 8 1973 and grew up in a small village in Popayan, in the department of Cauca, in the Colombian Andes. Throughout her childhood, Sara's inspiration was her mother, who was highly respected in the local communities for her involvement with marginalised women. She taught them to support themselves with crafts such as knitting and sewing. Their main means of survival had been exploiting natural resources, for food and also for the wildlife trade.

Tragically, Sara's mother died at the age of 42 from brain cancer. Sara's life then took a terrible turn. She was subjected to physical, sexual and psychological abuse by her father. She eventually graduated from the University of Cauca as an engineer. She enjoyed learning about civil engineering and this provided her with strong management skills that she was able to apply later. She worked on major infrastructure projects, including the UK Channel Tunnel Rail Link, where she was a member of the Geology Department and Tunnels.

Engineering was an unlikely career start (influenced by her father) for someone who, not many years later, would be recognised as an inspirational leader in conservation but who had no involvement with this sector in her early years. She had been deeply traumatised by the relationship with her father and when she had the opportunity to return to Colombia and Ecuador she was overwhelmed by the beauty of nature. It helped her to find peace with herself and to move on.

I first went to Colombia, a republic in north-western South America, in 1976, lured by its birdlife. It was then recognised as having more bird species than any other country worldwide. For the first time I encountered indigenous people, the Ticuna tribe. I was fascinated to observe their way of life. Today about 100 ethnic groups survive in Colombia, accounting for 3.5% of the national population. One of these groups is the Páez, also called Nasa. Unlike many indigenous tribes they resisted the onslaught made by the Spanish conquistadors in the 16th century. They retreated into the mountains. An interesting aspect of their culture was that they had male and female chiefs. They were survivors. Five centuries lat-

Sara Inés Lara.
Photograph: ProAves.

er I met a survivor of another kind with Páez ancestry.

ProAves and the American Bird Conservancy (ABC)

Sara's work with ProAves started during a year as a volunteer with project management. She was introduced to the team by Paul Salaman, who was leading the Yellow-eared Parrot (*Ognorhynchus icterotis*) project. Sara ensured that all goals were met promptly with excellent financial controls. In 2003, after one year, the board offered her the position of founding Executive Director. Sara said: 'We worked extremely well – such a dynamic team with extraordinarily talented people. We built the organisation and became very successful.'

Under her leadership, they established and managed 17 nature reserves to save endangered species. In 2005 I met Sara for the first time when her husband Paul Salaman invited me on a field trip to see some of Colombia's most endangered parrots, in order to write about this ground-breaking work. Visiting some of the reserves, and especially watching the iconic Yellow-eared Parrot, was an experience that left a deep and lasting impression on me. I was moved by the dedication and knowledge of the ProAves personnel, mostly young, with whom I was fortunate to spend time.

Staying for a short while at the home of Paul and Sara, I was enchanted by the warmth of Sara's personality, her friendliness and her lovely smile. I saw her in the role of mother to her beautiful, confident young daughter and her very young son but I discovered little about her work. I felt she was someone very special but I was yet to learn in what respect.

Sara's influence in ProAves

Working with ProAves as the first Executive Director until 2009, she oversaw the transformation of this NGO from a small group of bird conservationists to an effective professional conservation organisation. It grew to employ more than 50 full-time staff, and made a huge impact (and still does) on the protection of birds and their habitats across Colombia. From four projects when Sara started, ProAves expanded under her management to over 150 projects, in 22 of Colombia's 31 departments, with 70 plus donors and partners. By 2021 ProAves had 28 reserves, covering 36,400ha (90,000 acres).

One of their success stories is the El Paujíl ProAves Reserve where direct conservation and environmental education has saved the Critically Endangered turkey-sized Blue-billed Curassow (*Crax alberti*) by banning hunting. The population density of the curassow has increased from 3.1 individuals per square km in 2004 to over 8.4 individuals in 2020. This significant increase shows clearly the importance of the protected areas and of working with the community.

One of Sara's proudest achievements is her involvement with the recovery of the Yellow-eared Parrot from only approximately 80 individuals to about 2,800. 'This', said Sara, 'is proof that at a time when the crisis of biodiversity and extinction are threatening our planet, we can prevent extinction with quick actions.' *It became the world's most successful parrot conservation programme.*

Sara has two younger siblings. She describes them as 'both amazing people'. Her brother Miguel Angel helped to set up the famous ProAves Parrot Bus, which toured Andean villages with conservation messages. His ideas and

Murals of the Yellow-eared Parrot decorate buildings in the small town of Roncesvalle. Photograph: author.

creativity made it a great success. Elizabeth helped Sara with the women involved in craft-making. She was the key person in selling and finding outlets for their jewellery in the UK. She hosted and sold products at fairs, always talking about conservation and the role of women, showcasing how economic empowerment benefited conservation and protection of endangered species. Elizabeth also spent a year in El Dorado helping to train women on hospitality services for ecotourism; she gave English classes and facilitated workshops for women involved in the project. After six years of direct involvement she moved to Australia.

In 2009, Sara joined the American Bird Conservancy to become the Vice President of International Programs. She worked closely with an international team to lead efforts to restore habitats of endangered species, to ensure that conservation goals were met and to help countries to develop sustainable finances for conservation programmes.

After leaving the American Bird Conservancy, she worked for Permian Global, an organisation that tackles climate change through the protection of tropical forests. Then she worked for the Rainforest Trust and Alex Antram, an employee, said:

'Conservation truly is Sara's life, running through her family and across the networks she's fostered over the years. She's exceptionally hard working, open and earnest in protecting wildlife and helping people in need.

Sara with the author in San Diego, 2010.
Photograph: author.

She sometimes puts herself at risk to bring help to where it is needed most. She will never stop fighting for what she feels is right in terms of conservation and human rights.'

In February 2020 Sara was back at ProAves in the capacity of temporary part-time Executive Director, to help to reorganise and restructure the organisation. The board quickly appointed her permanently to this role.

Women for Conservation

Sara's principal interests include preventing species extinction, safeguarding tropical habitats, and alleviating poverty. In 2004 she took a remarkable step to combine her love of nature with her drive to empower women. She

Female Heroes of Bird Conservation

established Women for Conservation (www.womenforconservation.org). This initiative quickly spread to communities neighbouring ProAves' nature reserves, where local women learned about the importance of safeguarding their natural environments. With this knowledge, they were motivated to develop projects that reduced deforestation, including producing eco-friendly artisan products and reducing their usage of wood-fuelled stoves.

A very important aspect of the work of Women for Conservation is providing access to workshops on family planning and sex education. Unintended pregnancies, especially among teenagers, interfere with their education and create instability in rural households.

Along with emergency campaigns such as ending deforestation in El Pangán, Women for Conservation organises longer-term projects. In 2020 fund-raising commenced for an ambitious programme that will start the conservation careers of 90 women. A three-month specialised training programme will prepare them for work as forest guards, naturalists and rangers. This will be a transformative experience for them, especially given the lack of opportunities and sometimes violence in their communities.

Sara works closely in the field with her daughter Isabella. Both are inspired by the Andean indigenous concept of Pachamama/Mother Earth. Their methods are based on building trust and nurturing relationships, protecting threatened species, and helping the people and places that need the most care, people and places that are sometimes ignored, abused, and exploited.

Isabella: in her mother's footsteps

In May 2021 Sara told me:

'Isabella has been working since the beginning of the pandemic coordinating and managing the El Dorado reserve and addressing many issues that needed attention. She is in charge of the rangers and supervises land protection. As you can imagine, this has become a hard job. Isabella is an amazing conservationist; her passion is incredible. She combines her love for art with conservation, using art to connect with children

Isabella with Gonzalo Cardona Molina. Gonzalo, guardian of the Yellow-eared Parrot and a most valued ProAves field biologist, was murdered in January 2021.
Photograph: ProAves.

and young people. She has painted several murals with the communities, runs the training programme for women, and of course teaches about family planning. She is a true example to other young women. Isabella has volunteered since she was a little girl, always helping me when I was attending events and selling the products made by the Women for Conservation groups. Even when she was small she participated. She was a volunteer at the Bird Fair at Rutland Water in the UK when ProAves promoted bird tourism in Colombia. Isabella caught everyone's attention, wearing traditional dress at the stand. She welcomed all the visitors and talked to them about our Women for Conservation initiatives at seven years old, and for several years more!'

The beautiful Gorgeted Puffleg (*Eriocnemis isabellae*) was named after her, making her the youngest person ever to be celebrated in the name of a hummingbird. Endemic to Colombia, and known from a single location in the cloud forests of Serrania del Pinche, the hummingbird was discovered in 2005 and was confirmed as a species new to science in 2007. Loss of habitat has given it the IUCN status of Critically Endangered.

One of 100 Great Latin American Women

A great and well-deserved honour was bestowed on Sara by *Billiken*, the oldest children's magazine in Latin America. A publication entitled *100 Grandes Mujeres Latinoamericanas* featured inspiring female leaders and role models from the fourth century to the present. They included leaders, politicians, educators, artists, scientists and athletes from Latin American countries. Great recognition is given to Sara as a conservationist and her quest to protect endangered species and their habitats. She is teaching girls that there is an opportunity to work in conservation and that their involvement can help to protect the natural world on which we all depend. Many other organisations are recognising what she has to teach us, especially about empowering women in conservation. For this reason, in 2021 she was invited to present a paper at the important Women in Science meeting to be held in Paris in October that year.

Sara's passion, compassion and initiatives make her one of the most remarkable women I ever met. It is a privilege to know her.

33. Alicia Manolas
Australia 1982-
Biomonitor Assistance Animal Trainer

Tiberius is an amazing Blue and Yellow Macaw (*Ara ararauna*) and Alicia is a remarkable woman. She was born in the Australian bush on November 1 1982. Her mission is to make life better for parrots in general and to show how these highly intelligent birds can change the lives of people with life-threatening health problems.

Alicia grew up some hours out of Perth, right in the flight path of a flock of Red-tailed Black Cockatoos (*Calyptorhynchus banksii*). How fortunate to be familiar with such a spectacular bird at an early age! Her home was on a small bush block backing onto a big nature reserve with little human access. The area had been logged a hundred years ago by the early settlers, and turned into farms. When she was small, in the 1980s, it was being subdivided into hobby farms. The little remaining bush within was destroyed and turned into motocross tracks or heavily humanised in other ways. Despite this, Alicia spent a lot of her childhood bird-watching.

Local farmers would log their properties and often bring down trees with parrot nestlings inside. At three years old she received her first parrot chick, a pink and grey Galah Cockatoo (*Eolophus roseicapillus*). Local farmers took more birds to her, victims of road accidents and logging. Sometimes she went to her primary school with a tiny featherless bird in a flour bag around her neck and a tub of mashed Weetabix breakfast cereal and vitamin powder, together with a bent teaspoon. She described this as a home-made baby bird kit!

She received a lot of newspaper and TV coverage for being a top young bantam breeder. Her father taught her to make the best genetic matches to create her own poultry line to show. No one was interested in her parrot work, or her re-education experiences with horses.

Alicia lived in Bunbury, in coastal Australia, 175km (109 miles) south of Perth. It is known for the bottlenose dolphins that swim close to the beach at Koombara Bay and for the parkland fringed with mangroves and rich in birdlife. However, officials of the city council did not welcome flocks of parrots to which they offered poisoned wheat. When zoning regulations made it difficult to keep poultry, resulting in birds dumped at roadsides, Alicia set up Parrot & Pet Poultry Rescue & Sanctuary. After a while the council forced her to close, denying its need. It is a different situation today with more people taking in rescued birds outside the city limits, thus avoiding zoning registration issues and complaints with the City of Bunbury.

Unfortunately, when Alicia was in her early twenties she became disabled with seizures and multiple pain diseases. This is where Tiberius came in. She trained this macaw to be her primary biomonitor assistance animal. In this category we usually think of dogs, assisting visually impaired people or alerting someone to an imminent seizure or diabetic risk. Few people are aware that parrots are so sensitive that they are just as good or even better than dogs in some of these roles.

She told me: 'Tiberius has been keeping me alive the past 15 years. He warns approximately two minutes before a heart attack or stroke, or as soon as he senses the strain on my internal organs. He also gives a much shorter 20 second warning of a severe costochondritis [inflammation of the cartilage in the rib cage] attack, trigeminal neuralgia attack, and seizures. All these drop me on the floor out of my wheelchair.'

I confess that I was unaware that parrots were used as medical assistance animals until Alicia contacted me. I think she made an excellent choice in a Blue and Yellow Macaw – in my opinion one of the most sentient and intelligent of all parrots. Alicia has trained other assistance parrots. She told me that Greys can also be used for this purpose but they are not permitted to be kept in Western Australia.

My first question to her was: 'How do you train a biomonitor bird to recognise an impending attack or pain episode?' She replied:

Alicia and Tiberius.
Photograph: Owen Wylde/Ferretfoto@ferretofoz.

'It starts with the bird bonding very closely with the human – really living in each other's pockets, always beside each other and forming an impenetrable trust bond. For months! Next comes what I call "bomb-proofing" – getting them used to everything. After six months, and if happy, the bird will usually naturally start to give an alarm before episodes. It senses the strain on the internal organs, and the change in the breathing.'

During the training period the patient hits the alert noise of choice. Alicia uses a small innocuous sounding electric alarm clock that makes a *beh-beh, beh-beh* noise, close to what a macaw can already do, but, she says, 'different enough for folk to take notice. The bird then connects the noise to the episode. Finally, the person who is suffering alerts specialist medical aid, if possible.'

Alicia explained: 'The bird will already have a natural alarm call and can be trained to make this call more quietly. With a smart enough bird, you change them over to the alert/alarm noise of your choosing. Some will never fully grasp that mimic factor, and so you must always be prepared to work with what the bird is capable of.'

After 15 years of working with Tiberius, his pitch now denotes type of collapse, his volume denotes severity, and the intensity/speed of the *beh-beh* noises indicate how soon the attack is coming. This is a remarkable achievement.

'A happy, healthy relationship sees a bird excited to learn and eager to please. It eats when you eat; it sleeps where and when you sleep or close by, showers with you or watches you. That togetherness, love and care is the true bonding secret.'

In 2020 Alicia needed to retire Tiberius. He had previously suffered a wing injury after being assaulted by a cruel security guard. He was kicked in the left wing, shattering the primary feathers which never grew again. She started the search for a suitable young macaw and found a hybrid male, a so-called Catalina (a hybrid between a Blue and Yellow and a Scarlet Macaw). Then this bird also suffered at the hands of an unsympathetic person. During the vital first bonding week someone came into the house and deliberately and cruelly terrorised the young macaw. The trauma it suffered meant that it could never work as a biomonitor bird; in fact, it developed behavioural issues and needed remedial work. To part with him was soul-wrenching, said Alicia, but after that experience, she had no choice.

'Any person who intends to train a medical biomonitor assistance bird must realise that it needs to be happy and confident', said Alicia. 'It takes time and patience. It is advisable to start with a 4-6 month old fully weaned parrot, rather than a rehabilitated rescue. It should be a "blank slate", ready for its new life, and knowing no fear. Cockatoos and the Scarlet Macaw are usually too mercurial, despite generally having sufficient intelligence, though there are always exceptions to the rule. You choose the parrot for intelligence as best you can, for outgoing temperament, steady and gentle, and utterly full of itself. It had better be a climber or talker rather than a flyer, the three main types in the bigger birds, as they best suit the lifestyle of going everywhere with a human.

'I don't know how to train a bird to pick up a dollar in a bird show, or to ride bird roller skates, or how to fly figures of eight on command; however, I do my utmost to teach them to survive in our very human environments while working with us, keeping us alive!'

Much of Alicia's knowledge of bird behaviour comes from watching birds in the wild – in Australia, Canada, the UK, and also in Eire and in France. She told me: 'I would love to see macaws in their natural habitat one day!'

Alicia describes herself as an avian behaviourist and Assistance Animal Trainer who has been re-educating humans, and the parrots who are biters/pluckers/screamers, to give them better lives. She no longer has a team of volunteers or a bird property, but one day she hopes to own a small place with space for aviaries. She wants to work again in rescue, rehabilitation and re-homing and to train other people in this work.

She has been enlisted to help educate staff in a range of assistance animals. Alicia explains how looking a working dog in the eye could distract it from its job, and cost someone their life, but ignoring a working parrot is completely the opposite situation, as it is 'a jolly sight smarter' and the human interaction is part of its reward for working.

To promote ideal-care minimum standards for pet parrots is the aim of this courageous and determined lady. Currently she is promoting parrot-keeping education via lectures at schools and presentations at fetes or anywhere she is invited. 'It's not a proper 'degree' in bird-related subjects, but it's a lifetime of blood, sweat and tears!'

In Australia Non-Canine, Medical BioMonitoring Assistance Animals have had rights for only ten years under the Disability Discrimination Act. Animals in the other category, Emotional Support Animals, have no rights at all.

34. Sarah Comer
Western Australia
Fieldwork with Critically Endangered Species

Sarah Comer was born in Perth, Western Australia, in the mid-1960s. Its huge biodiversity makes Western Australia an area of immense importance. In fact, Australia's only biodiversity hot-spot occurs in the south-west of the state. Biodiversity hotspots are defined as regions 'where exceptional concentrations of endemic species are undergoing an exceptional loss of habitat'. Globally only 36 areas are designated in this way. Separated by harsh deserts and arid lands from the rest of the country, 100 vertebrate species and more than 4,000 endemic plants have evolved in south-western Western Australia. Unfortunately, clearing for agriculture resulted in the loss of more than half of native habitats between 1945 and 1982.

Sarah grew up appreciating its uniqueness. She recorded:

'My father was a physicist with his eyes on the stars, yet he and my mother inspired in me an awareness of the colours, sounds and uniqueness of the Australian flora and fauna. Our treasured times in the bush, when we were camping and travelling around the Australian landscape, represented places of wonder, peace and fascination. After travelling the world as a young adult and realising how unique home was and how much I felt I belonged in the wildness of Western Australia, I took the opportunity to study and look for a career in conservation. I wanted to help to protect, conserve and share my passion for all things wild.'

Sarah had a particular fascination with birds, plants and pollination but found that work opportunities lay mainly in Landcare movement. This proved to be a great insight into working with communities and custodians of the country. Then, in 1999, she was offered an ecologist's job with CALM (now DBCA – the Department of Biodiversity, Conservation and Attractions), Western Australia's state conservation agency, working on the south coast of Western Australia. She made the move from Cowaramup to Albany with her family. By the year 2000, approximately 90% of the hot-spot's 310,000 square km (120,000 square miles) of primary vegetation had been cleared. By 2009, only about 7% of native vegetation had

The beautiful and endangered Western Ground Parrot.
Photograph: Alan Danks, DBCA.

survived in Western Australia. The once extensive areas of eucalyptus woodland had been reduced to a patchwork of fragments. The great diversity of fauna and flora was threatened, along with its designation as a biodiversity hot-spot.

One of the responsibilities of Sarah's new job was managing the Noisy Scrub-bird (*Atrichornis clamosus*) recovery programme. This was already a success due to the many years of collaborative efforts between scientists and managers, following the rediscovery of the species in 1961. And this dream job, based in the heart of the biodiversity hotspot, came with opportunities to work on numerous other threatened species recovery projects, including the Western Ground Parrot (*Pezoporus flaviventris*). In addition, the job presented an opportunity to be one of a growing number of women directly involved in landscape scale management of reserves, which included a role in bushfire management.

Probably no more than 150 individuals survive. They inhabit areas of heath and sedges. Closely related to the Night Parrot (*Pezoporus occidentalis*), they are elusive but diurnal – not nocturnal. In 2003, DBCA established the Western Ground Parrot Recovery Project, monitoring, recording and tracking this cryptic bird. Sarah recalled: 'In my first year in Albany the enigmatic Ground Parrots could still be heard in the floristically rich heath habitat less than one hour's drive east of Albany, but only five years later they had disappeared from this site and declined dramatically in the Fitzgerald River National Park.'

Determined not to let the species slip into extinction on their watch, DBCA undertook a massive project to try to halt the decline, especially as it related to the control of invasive cats. Given the remoteness of Cape Arid, the last known population of the parrot, Sarah was spending many weeks and months camping with a small group of staff and volunteers. 'Many of these were also women', said Sarah. 'They continue to inspire and motivate the weary workers to get the job done, while continuing to learn, investigate and adapt as we gain insights into the ecology and biology of this unique bird and how best to manage feral cats.'

In 2003, the species was known from Cape Arid and Fitzgerald River National Parks, both on the south coast. It also inhabited the Waychinicup-Manypeaks area (near Albany); however, the last definite record was in 2004, and the last from Fitzgerald River National Park in 2012. Tragically, on December 20 2019 lightning sparked blazes that razed nearly 40,000ha (100,000 acres) in Cape Arid National Park and the nearby Nuytsland Nature Reserve, including crucial Ground Parrot habitat. This was an additional devastating blow, as in October and November 2015 bushfires had impacted an estimated 90% of the occupied habitat. In 2016 scientists heard the parrots calling in the reserve – for the first time since 2006. They were elated. However, late next afternoon elation turned to fear when they spotted smoke on the horizon in Cape Arid National Park. They plotted the location and immediately called the Parks and Wildlife fire management staff. But: '… the new fire could burn through this area where we had only just rediscovered the birds. What an emotional ecological roller coaster' (Comer *et al.,* 2016). Those who work with critically endangered species have their hearts in their mouths; and the vulnerability of the Ground Parrot meant another serious fire could spell its extinction.

The project team started to tackle the invasive felines in the mid-2000s and by 2015 they were starting to see some positive results. The last remaining population of this appealing little bird was not showing the same rate of decline as those to the west. The extensive bushfires in 2015 left very little of the protective dense heath habitat unscathed. The recovery team initiated a workshop in collaboration with the IUCN's Species Survival Commission and other conservation professionals from around Australia to identify priorities for conservation of the ground parrot (www.dpaw.wa.gov.au/images/documents/plants-animals/animals/creating_a_future_for_the_western_ground_parrot_workshop_report.pdf).

Sarah at work fitting a VHF transmitter to a Western Ground Parrot.
Photograph: Alan Danks (DBCA).

The second major priority (the first being securing the wild population) was to reestablish the Ground Parrot in an area from which it had recently disappeared. The Department of Biodiversity, Conservation and Attractions' staff, community group Friends of the Western Ground Parrot, Birdlife WA and other volunteers completed the first translocation of seven parrots to an area east of Albany in May 2021. Five years of intensive monitoring and preparation went into the protection and selection of the site, including climate modelling.

In August 2021 Sarah told me: 'There is something quite magical about working with a parrot that can be heard only as the sun rises and sets. We have been delighted by the persistence of the birds in their new home. They are moving about exploring their new habitat, and we've managed to keep tabs on most of them, although we've had to do a lot of the telemetry work from the air because of the large distances. And with two of the females settling well into the release area we are quietly optimistic that this first step in reestablishing a population may be successful.'

The birds were monitored using radio transmitters for about 12 weeks before switching to acoustic monitoring. There is scope to release more birds. Locating 'future-proofed' sites is giving hope for the long term persistence of this enigmatic species, and the myriad other unusual species that occur in the biodiversity hotspot of south-western Australia.

Sarah paid tribute to her colleagues.

'While many of the team I work with are wonderful men, many inspirational women play a major role in the work we do. Abby Berryman worked tirelessly on preparing documentation for the translocation, and Abby Thomas and Helena Stokes worked on logistics, pre- and post-capture monitoring and on feral cat control. Many other women, with passion, commitment and critical thinking ability, made the capture work a pleasure in spite of the many logistical challenges. Women provide so much to teams working at the coalface of conservation and, in the case of our work on the south coast and with Ground Parrots, this team is demonstrating the capacity to bridge the gap between delivering conservation science and management.'

Taxonomic note

The Western Ground Parrot (*Pezoporus flaviventris*) is classified by IUCN as Least Concern but by BirdLife Australia as Critically Endangered. IUCN/Birdlife International does not recognise two species and therefore lists the Western Ground Parrot as a subspecies of the Ground Parrot (*Pezoporus wallicus*) in the Least Concern category. This approach ignores genetic evidence.

Reference

Comer, S., A. H. Burbidge, D. Algar, L. Clausen, A. Berryman, J. Pinder, S. Cowen, A. Danks, J. Pridham and S. Butler, From the ashes. Creating a future for Western Ground Parrots, *Landscope,* 31 (4), 11-15, 2016.

35. Memorable Moments

Good, bad, uplifting or sad, there will always be memorable moments for those who get to know individual birds or local populations. These moments can be highly emotional and imprinted on the memory for ever more. This is especially the case for those field scientists working with threatened species. They create memories which are joyful, also those of deep concern through the urgency to act fast.

Saving hawks in Colombia

In Colombia, Esther Vallejo works to stop the slaughter of raptors. Every year more than five million migrate from North America to Central America and Colombia. They are killed to eat, because many farmers believe that their fat has curative powers. An important roosting site for Swainson's Hawks (*Buteo swainsoni*) and Broad-winged Hawks (*Buteo platypterus*) is located in Tolima, central Colombia, where thousands of hawks are shot annually. As a result, this location is critical for conservation, education and monitoring.

In spring 2020 the Rufford Foundation, which helps to fund the project, along with Hawk Mountain Sanctuary and the US Fish and Wildlife Service, started a new raptor conservation initiative in the key corridor for migrating raptors. They established the 'Tolima Raptor Count', the only one currently active in the region and included officially in the hawk watch sites network of the Hawk Migration Association of North America (HMANA) (HawkCount.org). The first official count occurred in 2020, in Tolima, and revealed the unexpectedly high total of 402,562 individuals. Of these, 252,516 were Broad-winged Hawks. The establishment of the count site was coupled with education outreach and the training of local conservationists, roosting and shooting sites identification and dissemination of information promoting raptor conservation awareness through social media, interviews, and other communication outlets.

Two successful spring seasons in Tolima revealed more than 400,000 and 600,000 raptors (2020 and 2021 respectively) of ten species in the Tolima region, and one autumn exploration in

Female Heroes of Bird Conservation

Esther Vallejo.
Photograph: Alfredo Beltran Santos.

Antioquia. Esther told me about her memorable moments in censusing raptors in Tolima. In spring 2021, with the hawk counters, she witnessed at sunset the arrival of about 1,000 Broad-winged and Swainson's Hawks.

'Near to the counting site, I observed how raptors, looking for a good spot to overnight, landed in trees that quickly housed dozens of individuals. It was a beautiful scenario, with a valley covered with "hawk trees" and in the background the Andes bathed by a colourful sunset. The next morning the local community knew through social media that this could be a day of great raptor activity. And so it was! By March 19, more than 200,000 raptors were recorded daily. This surpassed the number of the previous year, where the peak day was 65,000 individuals. The new monitoring site has surprised us and arouses more questions about the migration of raptors in Colombia. We hope to continue this effort in order to have a better understanding of migration routes in South America, and to contribute to conservation of migratory raptors, promoting hawk-watching rather than shooting, and appreciation rather than persecution, through education and training the local community.'

In Costa Rica, the Macaw Recovery Network (MRN) was founded in 2019, led by Sam Williams from the UK, a very experienced conservation scientist. It takes a holistic approach to conservation, balancing *in situ* and *ex-situ* efforts with community integration and habitat conservation. Much of the work concerns the Scarlet Macaw, whose nests are monitored where possible on the Nicoya Peninsula. This population originates from about 50 Scarlet Macaws, mostly captive-bred, that were released on Punta Islita (www.macawrecoverynetwork.org).

The head bird manager is Brittany Decker. She will never forget what happened one day in May 2019 following a turbulent night of strong winds and heavy rain. A Scarlet Macaw nest in a dead palm tree was at great risk of flooding. Sometimes such nests collapse before the young can fledge. One particular nest was examined after a storm, using a camera attached to a long pole, because of the danger of climbing such an unstable tree. The camera revealed that the two chicks, only just starting to feather, were sitting in water. Their parents were close by, but refusing to enter the nest.

Brittany watched as strategically placed ladders and ropes were placed to give extra support to the tree. It was climbed by the lightest and most experienced member of the MRN, who risked life and limb to scoop the two chicks out of the water. They were taken to the clinic at the Captive Breeding Centre, placed in a brooder and fed. The team's next action produced remarkable results. They erected a nestbox next to the dead palm. When the chicks recovered they took another risk and placed them in the nest-box. After a few hours the parent macaws entered and fed their young. Sadly one did not survive but the other fledged in July. The most heart-warming and unforgettable moment for Brittany came when the young macaw was seen feeding alongside her parents (Decker, 2019).

Another lady devoted to saving parrots is Nathalie Lycke. She started a rescue centre for parrots in Belgium. What was her never-to-be forgotten moment? After months of work she, and her many volunteers on the day,

The courtship dance of the male Andean Cock-of-the-Rock is unforgettable.
Photograph: author.

were ready to open to the public. But at the appointed hour the place was empty. 'Nobody is coming!', she cried! She had invited the mayor – and suddenly he walked in – followed by 1,500 local people! 'I was euphoric!' she said.

Nathalie is involved in an exciting project in Panama. She knew that eight of her confiscated Red-and-green Macaws (*Ara chloropterus*) originated from Panama. Nathalie had been there in May, a time when about one hundred illegally captured parrots, especially Amazons, are offered at roadsides for about US$10 each. Some are confiscated by officials. They are taken to her Belgian colleague, Joyce, who rehabilitates them. After two or three months they are feeding on fruits and seeds native to the area, grown in hotel grounds. They have minimum human contact and are then released. At first they return to the aviary for food but after a while they are integrated into wild flocks. Nathalie applied for CITES permits and returned her macaws to Panama in the early part of 2020. Their young will ultimately be released.

For me, euphoria came in the experience of watching Scarlet Cocks-of-the-Rock (*Rupicola peruvianus*) at a communal display ground. It was their sheer beauty and the energy and vibrancy of the display that was such an emotional experience it brought tears to my eyes.

This iconic species, Peru's national bird, is found in cloud forest on the eastern slopes of Andean mountains. I was in Ecuador, at 2,000m (6,000ft). As males jump, often on to a vertical perch, and flap their velvety black wings, the intensity of their scarlet plumage is almost overwhelming. The harsh, almost hysterical call, and the pale, alert eyes seem to accentuate their beauty. To see a dozen or so dancing simultaneously, waiting for a brown female to appear, was spell-binding.

Memories of local birds

Len Howard (Chapter 9) had a very close relationship with the Great Tits that visited her cottage. A female that she called Twist was unusual in that she seemed to understand some words. As a full-grown fledgling she would take naps perched on Len's knee or preen her feathers while perched on her hand. Len could raise her hand close to her face and gently rub down the tit's back. For a wild bird to tolerate that action, which would normally relate to a predatory attack, shows the degree of trust that existed between them. One day she was astonished when Twist responded to 'Give me a kiss' by touching Len's nose with her beak. She thought this was chance – but next day she responded to the words in the same way and continued to do so for the rest of her life. If Len asked her a second time she would look at Len with a puzzled expression, not responding, and if she tried to coax her, she glanced at Len very crossly. After an hour or two she was again responsive.

When Twist was hungry and Len had cheese for her, Twist would give three hurried kisses in succession, but even when tempted with cheese, she would not comply if asked twice running. She never offered a kiss without being asked and other words did not produce one. Such precious observations!

In Canada Louise de Kiriline Lawrence (Chapter 10) lived near the shore of Pimisi Bay. She lived in Green Woods, a lofty hall of aspens and birches. Her house 'grew out of the rock, log joined to log taken from the forest'. When her husband left for the long years at war, she started to observe the birds and to write about them. 'The great horned owl was one of the first birds to appear on my written pages' she recorded.

'Gravely you turned on us your facial disk. The rusty brown coloring margined by black of each cheek and the fringe of fluffy white feathers around your hooked beak appeared very distinctly and beautifully drawn as you sat against a backdrop of shaded rock and evergreens. At deliberate intervals gray membranes worked across your yellow orbs, shutting their light off and on as you observed our stealthy approach to get a closer look at you. There was, we thought immense dignity and aloofness in your pose and in your slow motions, as if you alone belonged to this wild and enchanting scenery – and we did not. Presently your softly feathered wings lifted and spread, hooked talons disengaged themselves from the perch, and as a speckled shadow, borne on a breath of wind, vanished among the trees' (Lawrence, 1968).

References

Decker, B., 2019, Chica's Bumpy Road to Survival, *PsittaScene*, Autumn: 14-17.

Lawrence, L. de, 1968, *The Lovely and the Wild*, McGraw-Hill Ryerson.

Turner, E. L., 1924, *Broadland Birds*, Country Life, Ltd, London.

36. The Future for Women in Conservation

On Women in Science Day in February 2021, BirdLife International admitted that 'entrenched biases and gender stereotypes are steering women and girls away from scientific fields. But given the current challenges of climate change, nature loss and COVID-19, it's more important than ever to harness *all* the talent and innovation we have at our disposal… the BirdLife partnership is full of amazing women of all ages and stages in their career… Here at BirdLife, we strive to lead by example and inspire the next generation of female conservationists.' (BirdLife International, blog February 21 2021).

The opportunities are there and, increasingly, they are being taken by women. BirdLife International has a female executive officer. Patricia Zurita is also the first woman from a developing country to lead an international conservation organisation. This appointment makes it clear that the only obstacles in the way for many woman are lack of confidence in their own abilities. They must aim high!

Asuncion Ruiz did! She is the CEO of SEO BirdLife, BirdLife's Spanish partner. She has advice for women pursuing a science career:

'I would tell them that nothing and no one should ever cut their wings and that, in times of difficulty, they should join forces and flock together. All of us are needed for science to fly high and live up to its potential. It is completely inconceivable that in the 21st century society we think that we can progress without girls and women having access to equal participation and progress. A society can only advance if all people have the same opportunities' (BirdLife International blog, February 21 2021).

I asked Neiva Guedes (Chapter 21):

'How important is the role of women in science today?' She replied that women are very important because they are persistent, courageous and hard-working. She said: 'Unfortunately, this is not widely recognised or valued financially. But in science, women can go wherever they want. I always tell young women: "Enjoy what you do, do it well and be persistent!" They are capable of doing many tasks at the same time.'

Working in Brazil, Ana Navarro is a PhD student. Her project involves the use of stable isotopes in museum specimens and birds captured in the field, to compare the use of habitat and diet between historic and modern birds. She will employ future projections, to provide information for species conservation actions in Brazil.

She told me: 'My daily sources of inspiration are the works developed by women in ecology and wildlife conservation. It motivates me to see women occupying important job positions in areas previously occupied only by men, although I know to reach such positions is much more difficult for women. Still, seeing such inspiring women playing a key role in bird conservation inspires me to persist, and leads me to think that one day I can make a difference too.'

A new career in your forties

To utilise all the talents which women possess, and which increase as they mature, I emphasise that it is not too late for women to start a career in science or conservation when they are in their late thirties or forties. Age must not be a barrier and this must be recognised by decision-makers in senior positions. Professor Jane Clarke is an English biochemist and academic. The advice that she offers is: 'If you don't like what you are doing, stop it! Life's too short…'

Jane Clarke was a teacher in a secondary school. Then in 1986 her husband took a job in the USA. She accompanied him and decided to do a part-time Master's degree. She became involved in research. She said: 'I didn't fit the pre-defined norm of an academic from the outset. I fell for research. It was so exciting – the not knowing, problem solving and following your nose when you've got an idea. It's the best job in the world being a research scientist. But when I first approached the Biochemistry Department at Cambridge about continuing my research, they said "You're forty years old, you've got two children, you're joking. Go away!"'

Since October 2017, Jane Clarke has served as President of Wolfson College, Cambridge. She is also Professor of Molecular Biophysics, a Wellcome Trust Senior Research Fellow in the Department of Chemistry at the University of Cambridge. She is an inspiring example of what determination can achieve. To research scientists she says: 'Be curious. Don't be frightened of being wrong.' Jane Clarke proved that mature women, with a family, can start a new career in science.

In this book I have related the stories of several remarkable women who changed their career course in their forties. In 1895 Althea Sherman was 42 when she started to observe birds. She became a trial-blazer in American ornithology – an extremely important scientist. Len Howard was 48 before she could start to study birds and Louise de Kiriline Lawrence was 45, after an important nursing career.

Female Heroes of Bird Conservation

Initiatives in Africa

In some countries getting a foothold in conservation can be very difficult for a woman, especially if a university education is not available. They must look for a different route. In Africa wildlife conservation was until recently a profession in which few women were to be found. In the broader sense, including game reserves and wildlife tourism, men had almost total domination. In the 21st century, and in the African continent, this is changing rapidly. In the early years a handful of women took on these roles but by 2020 there were hundreds. Several lodges now have an all-female team of safari guides. In Tanzania, Dunia Camp has a totally female staff, including the general manager.

The prevention of poaching and dealing with human-wildlife conflicts (animals attacking livestock) is an extremely dangerous occupation but even here women can excel. In Kenya, a team of Maasai women at the Olderkesi Community do this work. The head of the station there, Helen Mako, said: 'There is no job now that a woman can't do.'

In Uganda Judith Mirembe's passion was birding. She enrolled in a University in Kampala in 2012, for a degree in environmental science, but she worried about career prospects. She approached Herbert Byaruhanga, the managing director of Bird Uganda Safaris. She trained part time with him as a bird guide to build her skills while juggling her schoolwork. In Byaruhanga's 20

Judith Mirembe in Shoebill habitat (Shoebill in background). Photograph: Zoological Society of London.

years in the business, he had encountered an estimated 120 male guides and only 30 females. 'Birdwatching has become popular in Uganda, but the woman's place is still seen as the kitchen', Judith says. With Byaruhanga's encouragement, she formed a group dedicated to empowering jobless female college graduates to break through the male ranks of the industry. She recruited 10 ladies and launched the Uganda Women Birders' club in 2013. She has travelled to birding events in Europe and North America as a representative for Ugandan Ecotourism.

Over the years, dozens of employed members of the group have helped to teach new guides and connect them with tour companies. The costs of training and gear are largely covered by scholarships and donations. In 2015 the club received $30,000 from the United Nations Development Programme. In addition, they received funds from

The Future for Women in Conservation

friends, international and local fairs, and the Uganda Wildlife Authority.

Judith is also involved in research – on one of the most iconic bird species in the entire continent. The Shoebill (*Balaeniceps rex*) is an intriguing giant stork-like bird. Her work on it started in 2017, as part of the EDGE (Evolutionary Distinct and Globally Endangered Fellowship) sponsored by the Zoological Society of London. The objectives were to measure abundance of the Shoebill in two wetlands (Mabamba and Makanaga) on the shores of Lake Victoria. She also monitored the threats faced by the Shoebill. She told me: 'The Fellowship ended in 2019 and has unfortunately stalled since I have no funds. However, I would like to carry on and to make a long-term project with the surrounding communities at Mabamba wetland. I trained some community members on monitoring Shoebill populations, as a citizen science initiative. I will continue applying for funding to carry this on.'

Judith is a woman of the future of bird conservation in Africa. How regrettable that she was held back by lack of funds!

The female influence must increase

So often birding leads to a focussed interest in conservation; in fact, most of the incredible women featured in this book started as birders, and some of them had no mentors. They were led by their passion.

There are countless other women, worldwide, overcoming difficulties and prejudices in conservation fieldwork. They deserve our respect and gratitude. Their numbers are increasing and will continue to increase and they need to be encouraged and assisted in every possible way. As we have seen with Judith, funding can be a key aspect.

We can of course be very grateful for the men in these professions – but they seldom have similar obstacles to overcome.

The influence of women, even when still in their teens, was never demon-

The extraordinary Shoebill.
Photograph: author.

strated more powerfully than by Greta Thunberg. At only 15 years old she made front page news in *The Times* and in *The Guardian*. On April 24 2019 *The Guardian*'s headline quoted Greta: 'The message to MPS: you lied over climate.' This Swedish icon for change inspired thousands of young people in Europe, the USA and Canada to stage school strikes to make adults listen to her message to save the planet. She has continued to make news and to be quoted internationally ever since, as proof that there is no limit to what a woman can achieve, regardless of her age.

Index, People

Illustrations in **bold** type.

Abiadh, Awatef 10-11
Angel, Andrea **113**, 191-197 **192**, **196**
Antram, Alex 225
Armando 97-99
Astor, Lady 39
Ataide, Roseno **155**
Bailey, Florence Merriam 105-107, **106**
Bailey, Vernon 106-107
Baltzer, Fritz 17
Barber, Theodor Xenophon 70
Barclay-Smith, Phyllis **24**, 82-87, **83**
Baret, Jeanne 3, 4
Barnes, Tony, PC 6
Bauer, Edgar 99
Baxter, Evelyn 108-109
Bedford, Duchess of 47
Benchley, Belle 12
Berger, Roberto 99
Blanvillain, Caroline 184-190, **185**
Bond, Judy 46
Bonfim, Jose **208**
Boulenger, George 15, 16
Boyd, Hugh 166, 167
Bradley, Guy 37
Brewster, William 36
Brightsmith, Donald 145
Broley, Charles 91
Brooks, Ann 202-203, **202**
Brown, Morgan 96-97
Bujaroska, Aleksandra 9

Burger, Joanna 111-112, **111**
Byaruhanga, Herbert 244
Campos, Zilca 8
Cardona, Ganzalo **226**
Carson, Rachel 4, **24**, 83, 87, 88-94, **89**, 105
Cheeseman, Lucy Evelyn 2, 14-15, **14**, **24**, 108
Clarke, Jane 243
Comer, Sarah 232-235, **235**
Commerson, Philibert 3
Coudreau, Henri 52-53
Crockford, Nicola **113**, 165-172, **168**
Croukamp, Anna 129-136, **133**
Croukamp, Carmel 130, **133**, 133, 136
Croukamp, Dennis 130, 131
Davino, Silvana 198-202, **199**
Decker, Brittany 238-239
Delacour, Jean 65, 82-83, 84
DeLord, Delphine 120
DeLord, Francoise 118, 119-121, **119**
DeLord, Jacques 118
DeLord, Rodolphe 120
Descartes, Rene 105, 111
DeWolfe, Barbara Blanchard 4
Diamond, Alan 46
Donaldson, Robert Preston 82
Downs, Colleen **113**, 159-164, **162**
Durham, Bishop of 34
Durrell, Gerald 13

247

Edge, Rosalie Barrow 30
Edinburgh, Duke of **158**
Emilio (Don) 97
Ferreira, Luciana **155**
Fontoura, Fernanda **155**
Franks, Sam 219
Freeman, Dorothy 93
Fuertes, Luis Agassiz 26
Gardiner, Linda 39, 82
Gardner, Laura 13, 22
Gibbons, David 219
Goeldi, Emil 52, 54
Gondim, Maria Fernanda 5-6, **5**
Goring, Hermann 20
Gould, Elizabeth 3
Gould, John 3, 85
Gregson, Jo 13, 22
Griscom, Ludlow 67
Grondahl, Paul 100, 102
Guedes, Neiva 8-9, 105, **113**, 151-158, **155**, **158**, 183, 242
Habben, Mark 22-23
Hagmann, Gottfried 52
Hall, Minna 36
Heck, Lutz 20, 21
Hediger, Heini 17
Heinroth, Katharina 18-21, **18**
Heinroth, Magdalena 18, 24, 57-61, **58**
Heinroth, Oskar 18-20, 21 57-58, 59-61
Hemenway, Harriet Lawrence 31, 34, 35-36, **36**
Herwig, Doris 103
Hornaday, William 35
Howard, 'Len' 2, 4, 70-74, **72**, 78, 107-108, 109, 240, 243
Howard, Hildegarde 3
Huber, Jacques 54
Hudson, W. H. 33
Huxley, Julian 74

Johns, Linda 110
Joyner, LoraKim 105, 142-149, **147**
Kaplan, Gisela 46, 111
Kear, Janet 13
Kearton, Richard 40
Keaveney, John 138
King, Cathy 22
Kipps, Clare 109
Kiriline de, Gleb 75-76, **76**, 77
Koldeway, Heather 23
LaBastille, Anne 11, 95-103, 110
Lara, Isabella Cortes 226-7, **226**
Lara, Sarah Ines 113, 222-227, **223**, **225**
Lawrence, Harriet – see Hemenway
Lawrence, Leonard 77, 79
Lawrence, Louise de Kiriline 66, 75-78, **76**, 240, 243
Lehmann, Lilli 32
Lemon, Etta (Margaretta) **24**, 31-35, **34**, 37, 38, 39-40, 82, 106
Lemon, Frank 33, **34**, 37, 82
Lemon, William 32
Leopold, Aldo 68
Lepperhoff, Lars 174
Lindner, Lorin 137-141, **138**
Lloyd George, David 38
Lorenz, Konrad 59, 65, 68
Louise, Princess of Denmark 75
Luchetti, Natalia 4-5, 115, 116
Lycke, Nathalie 239-240
Mako, Helen 244
Manolas, Alicia 228-231, **229**
Manso, Kilma 204-209, **208**, 211
Manzanares, Tomas 146
Massingham, Harold 39
Mayr, Ernst 68
Melero, Pablo 198
Mencke, Bruno 57
Meyer, Gilbert Victor 17
Meyer-Holzapfel, Monika 17, **17**

Minton, Clive 167
Mirembe, Judith **113**, 244-245, **244**
Morais, Raimundo de 53, 55
Morrison, Guy 166
Munn, Charles 152
Navarro, Ana 6, 243
Newton, Alfred 34
Nice, Leonard Blaine 63, 64, 65, 68
Nice, Margaret Morse 2, 62-69, 107
Nicholson, Edward Max 85
Nudd, Alfred 42, 43
Nudd, Cubit 43
Nuechterlein, Gary 99
O'Brien, Stacey 111
Olivar, Julio 55-56
Oliveira, Leticia Soares Marques de 6-7, **7**
Otterstrom, Sarah 213-217, **214**
Ouhiba, Thoraya 11
Pacifico, Erica 210-212, **210**
Peat, Louise 22
Perrin, Mike 161-162, **162**
Phillips, Eliza 34, 35
Pina, Patrick 198, 201
Pittman, Tony 153
Plair, Bernadette 113, 122-128, **124**
Procter, Joan 15-16, **16**, **24**
Radke, Otto 21
Ray, Gabrielle 38
Reichenow, Anton 51
Rintoul, Leonora 108-109
Rocha, Patricia Rendall 9
Roosevelt, Theodore (President) 36
Ruiz, Asuncion 9-10, 242
Salaman, Paul 223
Sandino, Osmar 216
Sargent, John Singer 36
Sargent, Sir Malcolm 70
Schlumpf, Elisabeth 173-177, **175**, **176**
Schroder, Werner 20, 21

Scott, Sir Peter 13, 98
Seale, Bill, **139**
Seixas, Glaucia 178-183, **181**
Seth-Smith, David 84
Sherman, Althea 25, **26**, 63-66, 243
Sick, Helmut 52, 53, 54
Silveira, Luis Fabio dedication, 5, 56, 179-180, 210
Simmons, Matt 139-141
Smart, Jennifer 218-221, **219**, **220**
Snethlage, Emilie dedication, 2, 50-56, **51**, **53**
Solly, Beatrice 82
Somenzari, Marina 7-8, **8**
Speirs, Doris H., 68
Stafford, Mark and Marie 153, 209
Stresemann, Ernst, 53
Symes, Craig 161-162, **162**
Taverner, Percy 78
Taylor, Mrs H. J. 29
Tellefsen, Sandra 199, 201
Thoreau, Henry David 100
Thunberg, Greta 246
Tinbergen, Niko 68
Tomotani, Barbara 8, **9**, 116
Trautman, Milton 64, 67
Turner, Emma 2, 4, 11, **24**, 40-49, **42**, 107, 108
Vallejo, Esther 237-238, **238**
Veiga, Ana 117
Vincent, Jim 42
Wallace, Amy 79
Watts, George Frederic 34
Weinzettl, Marcia 14
White, Tom 215
Williams, Sam 238
Williamson, Emily 33, 40
Wirmimghaus, Olaf 161, 162
Wittkoff, Linda 208, 209
Wittkoff, William 208, 209

Wood, Sharon 29
Woolf, Virginia 39
Wright, Mabel Osgood 62
Yepez, Itala 117
Zurita, Patricia 116, 242

Index, Bird Species

Illustrations in **bold** type.

Albatross, Tristan 191-195, **193**, **196**
Antbirds 4
Auk, Little 33
Avocet 58
Bittern, Eurasian 43-45, **45**, 58
Blackbird, European 32, 42, 71, 72, 73, 174
   Red-winged 27
   Yellow-hooded 125
Bunting, Ortolan 175
   Snow 46-47
Bustard 58
Cardinal 64
Catbird 27
Chickadee, Black-capped 78-79
Chicken 110
Cockatoo, Galah 120, 228
   Moluccan 137, **138**, 138-139, 141
   Palm 120
   Philippine 120
   Red-tailed Black 228
   Sulphur-crested 120
   Umbrella **139**
Cock-of-the-Rock, Peruvian **239**, 240
Corncrake 168
Cuckoo, Eurasian 45, 169-170, 175
Curassow, Alagoas 134
   Blue-billed 224
Curlew, Slender-billed 168-170, **169**
   Stone 43, **44**

Diver, Red-throated 100
Dove, Mourning 29
   Polynesian Ground 186
Eagle, Bald **91**, 91, 138
   Crowned 159
   Harpy 120
   White-tailed 58
Egret, Snowy 35, 38, 95
   Great White 35
Flamingo 65, 96, 120
Flicker, Northern 27
Flycatcher, Scissor-tailed 64
Godwit, Bar-tailed 219, **219**
   Black-tailed 219-221, **220**
Goldfinch, American 26
Goosander 165
Goose, Barnacle 165
   Greylag 165
   Nene 13, 120
   Snow 167
Grebe, Atitlan (Giant) 11, 96-100
   Great-crested 33
   Junin 104
   Pied-billed 98
   Red-necked 176
Grouse, Black 58
   Sage 92
Hawk, Broad-winged 237
   Swainson's 237
Heron, Purple 58

Honeycreeper, Blue 33
   Red-legged **86**, 87
Hornbill, Crowned 176, **176**
   Ground 120
   Rhinoceros 120
Hummingbird, Gorgeted Puffleg 227
   Ruby-throated 28
Hummingbirds 28-29, 32, 33, 34
Ibis, Scarlet 96, 132
Jacana, Wattled 125
Jackdaw **59**
Kea 120
Kestrel 27, 46, 175
Kite, Red 40
Knot, Red 40
Leaftossers 6
Lories 120
Lorikeet, Blue 186, **186**
   Ultramarine 189
Macaw, Blue and Yellow 119, 122-127, **126**, 228-230, **229**
   Blue-throated 121
   Great Green 146
   Green-winged (Red-and-green) 127, 154, 202-203, 239
   Hyacinth 8, 36, 151-158, **153**
   Lear's 206-212, **211**
   Red-bellied 125
   Scarlet 119, 127, 146, **147**, 171
Merganser, Brazilian 5
   Hooded 102
Merlin 46, 166
Monarch, Fatu Hiva 186, 187, 189
   Tahiti 186, 187-189, **188**
Moorhen, Gough 193
Nightingale 109
Nightjar, European 59
Nuthatch 64, 165, **166**
Oilbird 96
Oriole, Golden 47

Osprey 58
Owl, Great Horned 240-241
   Screech 27
   Short-eared 43, 45-46
Oystercatcher 47
Paradise, Birds of 32, 33, 38
   Ribbon-tailed 38
Parakeet, Grey-breasted 134-135
   Maroon-bellied 198, **199**, 199, **200**
   Nanday 180
   Orange-chinned 148
   Orange-fronted 137, 148
   Pacific 143, 148
   Peach-fronted 181
   Plain 198, 201
   White-eyed 199, 201
   Yellow-chevroned 181
Parrot, *Amazona*, Blue-fronted 132, 134, 178-183, **180**, **182**, **183**, 204-206
   Festive 120
   Lilac-crowned 140
   Mealy 198, 199-201, 200, **200**
   Orange-winged 181
   Red-browed 134
   Red-lored 111-112, **111**, 146
   Red-spectacled 133-134
   Red-tailed 134
   Vinaceous-breasted 134, **134**
   Yellow-headed 140, 148
   Yellow-lored 148
   Yellow-naped 142, 143-145, **144**, 148, 213-214
   Cape 161-164, **161**
   Golden (Conure) 14, 120
   Grey 73, 130, 229
   Scaly-headed 181
   Western Ground 233-236, **233**
   Yellow-eared 223
   Yellow-faced 180

Penguin, Northern Rockhopper 193
Phoebe 27
Pigeon, Crowned 120, 178
    Marquesan Imperial 186
    Nicobar 120
    Papuan Mountain 120
Plover, Kentish 58
    Ringed 47
Quail, Bob-white 62-3, 88
Rail, Water 176
Redstart 57
Robin, American 27, 63
    European 42, 72
Rook 174, **175**
Ruff/Reeve 45, 58
Sanderling 89
Sandpiper, Spoon-billed 170-171
    White-rumped 166
Scrub-bird, Noisy 233
Shoebill 19, 245, **245**
Silverbill 118
Snipe 45, 165, 175
Sparrow, House 109, 173
    Song 62, 64, 65, **65**, 66, 67, 68
    White-crowned 4
Sparrowhawk 91
Spoonbill 58
Starling, Bali 174
Sugarbird, Blue 33
    Red-legged **86**, 86-87
Swift, Chimney 27-28, 30
Tanagers 33
Tern, Common 48
    Gull-billed 58
    Little 48
    Roseate 48
    Sandwich 48
Thrasher, Brown 26, 27
Tit, Blue 32, 42, 71, 174
    Great 71, **72**, **73**, 74, 79, 109, 240

Toucan, Green-billed 198
    Toco 132
Trogon, Red-headed 174
Tui 166
Vulture, Cape 159
Warbler, Barred 58
    Blackburnian 64
    Blackcap 57
    Black-throated Blue 64
    Magnolia 64
    Melodious 109
    Seychelles 83
    Wood 165
Wheatear, Pied 109
Woodpecker, Grey-headed 58
    Pileated 64
Wryneck 176

Index, Conservation and Rescue Organizations

American Bird Conservancy (ABC) 225
Audubon Society 30, 36, 37, 39, 65, 95
Beauval Research and Conservation Assoc. 120
BirdLife International 9, 84, 87 172, 186, 187, 192, 242
Cambaquara ASM 198, 199-202
Centre for Conservation of Birds of the Atlantic Rainforest 133
CRESTT – Centre for the Rescue of Endangered Species of Trinidad and Tobago 128
ECO (Brazil) 207, 208, 209
Fundação Neotropica do Brasil – FNB (Neotropical Foundation of Brazil) 180, 181
Hawk Migration Association of North America (HMANA) 237
ICBP 82, 84
Instituto Arara Azul 154, 155 158
Loro Parque Fundacion (LPF) 14, 211, 215
Lymington Foundation 208
Nature Conservancy Council (NCC) 167
One Earth Conservation 146, 149
Parrots International 208
Paso Pacifico 213, 214
Phoenix Landing 202-203

ProAves 223-224, 225, 226
Royal Society for the Protection of Birds (RSPB) 33, 34, 35, 37, 38, 39, 82, 87, 165, 167, 168, 169, 172, 195, 197, 218, 219, 221
Societe d'Ornithologie de Polynesie (SOP) 185, 187, 190
Wildfowl & Wetlands Trust (WWT) 220
Wildlife Conservation International (WCI) 152
Women for Conservation 226, 227
World Parrot Trust (WPT) 152, 153
World Wildlife Fund (WWF) 102, 152, 158
Zoological Society of London (ZSL) 13, 14, 23, 84, 245

also by Rosemary Low
PARROT CONSERVATION

432 pages 140mm x 200mm
70 colour photographs   paperback
ISBN 978 1 92554 646 0
Published in 2021 by Reed New Holland

Signed copies from the author
rosemaryhlow@gmail.com